CONAWAY

Charles Wm. Conaway

School of Information & Library Studies

SUNY at Buffalo

November 24, 1971.

Information Analysis and Retrieval

Information Sciences Series

Editors

ROBERT M. HAYES
Director of the Institute of Library Research
University of California at Los Angeles

JOSEPH BECKER
Vice President
Interuniversity Communications Council (EDUCOM)

Consultants

CHARLES P. BOURNE
Director, Advanced Information Systems Division
Programming Services, Inc.

HAROLD BORKO
University of California at Los Angeles

Joseph Becker and Robert M. Hayes:
INFORMATION STORAGE AND RETRIEVAL

Charles P. Bourne:
METHODS OF INFORMATION HANDLING

Harold Borko:
AUTOMATED LANGUAGE PROCESSING

Russell D. Archibald and Richard L. Villoria:
NETWORK-BASED MANAGEMENT SYSTEMS (PERT/CPM)

Charles T. Meadow:
THE ANALYSIS OF INFORMATION SYSTEMS, A PROGRAMMER'S
INTRODUCTION TO INFORMATION RETRIEVAL

Launor F. Carter:
NATIONAL DOCUMENT-HANDLING SYSTEMS FOR SCIENCE AND
TECHNOLOGY

George W. Brown, James G. Miller and Thomas A. Keenan:
EDUNET: REPORT OF THE SUMMER STUDY ON INFORMATION
NETWORKS CONDUCTED BY THE INTERUNIVERSITY COMMUNI-
CATIONS COUNCIL (EDUCOM)

Perry E. Rosove:
DEVELOPING COMPUTER-BASED INFORMATION SYSTEMS

F. W. Lancaster:
INFORMATION RETRIEVAL SYSTEMS

Ralph L. Bisco:
DATA BASES, COMPUTERS, AND THE SOCIAL SCIENCES

Gerald Jahoda:
INFORMATION STORAGE AND RETRIEVAL SYSTEMS FOR
INDIVIDUAL RESEARCHERS

Allen Kent:
INFORMATION ANALYSIS AND RETRIEVAL

Information Analysis and Retrieval

(Based on *Textbook on Mechanized Information Retrieval,* First and Second Editions, 1962 and 1966)

Allen Kent

DIRECTOR, OFFICE OF COMMUNICATIONS PROGRAMS
UNIVERSITY OF PITTSBURGH

A WILEY-BECKER-HAYES PUBLICATION

BECKER AND HAYES, INC.
a subsidiary of John Wiley & Sons, Inc.
New York · London · Sydney · Toronto · Bethesda

To my wife Rosalind,
and our family

Information Sciences Series

Information is the essential ingredient in decision making. The need for improved information systems in recent years has been made critical by the steady growth in size and complexity of organizations and data.

This series is designed to include books that are concerned with various aspects of communicating, utilizing, and storing digital and graphic information. It will embrace a broad spectrum of topics, such as information system theory and design, man-machine relationships, language data processing, artificial intelligence, mechanization of library processes, nonnumerical applications of digital computers, storage and retrieval, automatic publishing, command and control, information display, and so on.

Information science may someday be a profession in its own right. The aim of this series is to bring together the interdisciplinary core of knowledge that is apt to form its foundation. Through this consolidation, it is expected that the series will grow to become the focal point for professional education in this field.

Preface

Considerable change has taken place in the field of information retrieval since the publication of the first edition in 1962 and the second edition in 1966 of *Textbook on Mechanized Information Retrieval,* on which this book is based. The computer has become deeply entrenched as the major tool in the field. But, as shown by the considerable attention paid to evaluation and testing of systems, consideration of the computer has led to neglect of fundamentals.

Therefore the purpose of this book remains the same as that of *Textbook on Mechanized Information Retrieval*—to teach basics to those who have had no previous exposure either to the field or to computers, or both. Therefore, the action is slowed to the point where the logical principles of information retrieval systems are laid bare. Other books have been published that emphasize computer programming—this one does not.

It would be useful if I could use the term "basic information retrieval-system language" to describe my intent. The analogy is the use of "basic machine language" in programming, which ensures that the optimum program is written, given a certain problem and a certain computer.

My purpose is to reach bedrock in fundamentals, so that the student need take nothing for granted that a vendor of systems may wish to claim. As more and more systems are made available for purchase and lease, the more important it becomes to learn about the booby traps.

It has been my experience, in teaching the introductory course based on this book, to about 2000 students, that an unusually good synthesis of the course can be achieved by assigning each student the task of designing a retrieval system (see Chapter 10). The raw materials for this assignment are sets of marginal-hole punched cards and peek-a-boo cards. The synthesis is achieved through the process of designing the system; the cards are only the tools that permit this end to be achieved. Although these are not modern tools, they have a very great advantage in teaching and learning: the basic retrieval logic of the computer can be explained by the teacher with stark simplicity and can be understood by the student without ever having been exposed to a computer. This approach has been useful even with those who are computer sophisticates. They may have learned about computers in relation to the solution of numerical analysis problems; and their tendency is to think of information retrieval in terms of that experience. They too must be exposed to fundamentals before they can be returned, with confidence, to their environment.

ALLEN KENT

Mount Lebanon, Pennsylvania
January 1971

Acknowledgments

Primary thanks for this textbook must be given to approximately 2000 graduate students at the University of Pittsburgh who took the course on mechanized information retrieval and used the earlier editions of this textbook. This course has been offered thirty times over a period of eight years.

The experience gained through their comments, through their reactions of insight or despair, made possible a thorough reworking of the previous book.

Thanks also to my wife, who took time out from her own book to read galleys and page proof.

A. K.

Contents

Information Analysis and Retrieval

One

Introduction

I. WHY MECHANIZED INFORMATION ANALYSIS AND RETRIEVAL?

The field of information retrieval derives from the struggle of man to control his environment or at least to avoid being destroyed by external forces. The struggle articulates into requirements to make decisions continually. The quality of the decisions depends fundamentally on the problem-solving capability of the decision maker, but initially on the quality and relevance of information brought to bear on the problems. Here, then, is the fundamental rationale for man to accumulate and organize information relating to past accomplishments.

Emphasis on "information retrieval," particularly involving the use of computers, has grown in the past several decades because of four interrelated factors:

1. *Time scale changes.* The time scale of information gathering for decision making and control has been reduced drastically. This change corresponds to increases in the rates with which competitive activity, international aggressive action, and changes in public opinion can deteriorate economic, military, and political situations.

2. *Changes in quantity of available information.* There has been a dramatic increase in the amount of information that is freely available (that is, published in one form or other), resulting in the characterization of the situation as an information explosion. This situation has three dimensions of frustration:

    a. The impossibility of an individual reading and remembering all of the literature that has a reasonable probability of being of use later.

b. The economic impossibility of individuals or their organizations processing for later retrieval the majority of literature of possible pertinent interest.

c. The inadequacy of traditional library methods and tools in coping effectively with the detailed requirements of individuals in identifying information pertinent to a given problem.

3. *Changes in nature of information requirements.* The increasing complexity of the problems of society has led to a consequent requirement for information from an ever-widening diversity of fields. This has resulted in the need to achieve insight into otherwise obscure or uncertain situations through the use of large amounts of fragmentary information from widely scattered sources.

4. *Changes in importance of information sources.* The increasing internationalism of industrial, educational, and political organizations has been leading to increasing emphasis on information for decision making and control derived from many sources and geographic areas not formerly considered important. This trend has increased the need for communicating information quickly that previously could be transmitted on a more leisurely basis.

The four changes described above have resulted in various agencies undertaking information-processing and disseminating functions. These include governmental organizations, professional and trade associations, universities, and profit-making industries.

II. PROBLEMS–OLD AND NEW

As a result of these changes, new tools, new communication systems, new means of information organization, and new means of dissemination have been proposed and developed. Each in turn has helped both to alleviate old problems and to uncover new problems.

A. Influence of the Computer

The use of computers to search indexes to large files has led to the trend of increasingly precise and detailed indexing. This in turn has increased the cost of such analysis to the point where few organizations have the means to process for their own use the information that would be of possible use in the future. This has led to centralization of information-processing activities, e.g., by government agencies and professional societies, in attempts to amortize the cost over many users. But centralized services have been imperfect, and decentralized as well as specialized information centers have been developed in an attempt to overcome some of their limitations.

The speed with which computers can search large files carries with it a consequent high cost. In an attempt to amortize this cost over many users, there has been a trend to utilize the batch-processing capabilities of computers to handle as many questions as possible at one time. But the results of this trend is a decrease in effective speed of search, since time elapses while a sufficient quantity of search requests are accumulated. This has led to consideration of how time-sharing computers may be utilized to provide search results in real time.

The processing speed of computers has also led to consideration of how whole texts may be searched to advantage. But this consideration brings up the problem of whether algorithms can be developed that would permit programs to identify significant information as opposed to mere identification of words as they may appear in a given text.

B. Influence of Communication Systems

Modern communication technology offers the opportunity to transmit information in the form of data, voice, and images. Using this technology, the information resources of all organizations can be shared by permitting remote inquiry through an appropriate network system. The availability of time-sharing computer systems with their ability to tie into network systems makes it possible to contemplate an inquirer sitting at a remote console interacting with a multiplicity of information resources in real time. However, in considering how to translate theory into practice, it becomes obvious that fundamental knowledge is lacking with regard to questions such as the following.

1. How can the differing philosophies of indexing source materials be rationalized when several resources are to be exploited to satisfy a single inquiry?
2. What criteria would inquirers use in judging relevance of information provided interactively when networking systems employing modern communication technology are used?
3. What will the behavior of an inquirer be if he has the opportunity to conduct information searches personally through a console? What training problems will be involved? What programs need be written to provide an adequate conversational ability to permit effective interaction?

C. Influence of New Means of Information Organization

The pressures for greater and greater penetration into the subject matter of source materials have been evident as the quantity of published information has reached the point at which traditional classifying and indexing methods are not able to provide literature search results with the precision, relevance, and quantity limitations being demanded.

This has led to the requirement for precise specification of problems and questions of inquirers, which in turn demands corresponding means for precise specification of the subject matter of the source materials. This consideration has led to increased pressure for subject analysis expertise which approaches the expertise of the inquirer. On the other hand, the personnel requirements for processing the increasing quantity of source materials have not been matched by available skilled manpower. Consequently, alternative methods of processing have been considered, proceeding successively through the use of:

1. Generalists rather than specialists.

2. Automatic means for analysis of information, involving either portions or the entire text of the source materials.

A study of the results of application of both of these methods indicates that imprecision and inconsistency in analysis are not avoided, leading to uncertainty in the results of exploitation of large files. Accordingly, other means have been sought to overcome the consequences of this uncertainty. Explorations have resulted in the development of various vocabulary control and search strategy techniques. Testing and evaluation of these techniques have become a matter of increasing interest, leading to the identification of increasingly fundamental problems on:

1. The nature of information transfer from source materials to the inquirer.

2. The criteria for relevance judgments of inquirers, and their dependence on incremental learning.

3. The nature of concept formation.

4. Most basic: the learning and thinking processes.

D. Influence of New Means of Information Dissemination

It has been interesting to observe the development of means for information dissemination in such a manner as to correspond selectively to the "profile" of interests of inquirers, thus keeping them informed periodically of published materials in the precise areas of their professional work. However, the changing interests of many inquirers require that careful attention be paid to means for obtaining feedback in order to provide a dynamic response to indications or even saturation of changes of interests. The need for development of means for observing inquirer behavior without undue interference with normal work habits has led to a consideration of the methodology of the behavioral sciences. But this methodology must take into account the fact that the average information user can spend only minor fractions of his time relating to information services. Accordingly, the mass effects of new dissemination methods can be discerned only with large populations of users, leading to the need for the careful application of statistical methods to discern real effects and their significance.

III. MECHANIZATION IN LIBRARIES

The foregoing has stimulated reexamination of the traditional libraries and the very significant investment that has been made by society in their development and maintenance. Increasing demands for library service, even of a traditional nature, have led to investigations of how new tools and communication systems might streamline these functions, which, despite the growing importance of information storage and dissemination centers, still is the main instrument of society for providing democratic access to recorded knowledge. The result has been the application of computers and other data processing equipment to the control of circulation records, serial records, and even to the conversion of catalog information to machine-processible form.

Communications technology has been exploited in connection with interlibrary loan procedures (the traditional library response to resource-sharing requirements). The location of desired materials has been facilitated by the mechanism of almost real-time communication systems such as teletype. In addition, image-transmission systems are being considered for the provision of copies of materials without physical removal from existing collections.

But there are legal implications involved in the application of the new technology in the library. The convenience of providing copies of published materials and the continuing trend toward conservation of storage space through the use of microform brings up consideration of violation of copyright through promiscuous processing, copying, and transmission of such materials. This legal problem, and the related economic problems is causing concern to various elements of society: the publisher, the authors, and the user public.

Although machines have been used in the library for some time in order to make more efficient the job of running the library, mechanized information retrieval in the library has only recently become a factor in planning user services. But there is now a growing understanding of the need for access to recorded knowledge that must be satisfied by providing rapidly, conveniently, economically, and with precision, that portion of the current or previous literature that will be useful

- to a particular individual
- at a particular time
- for a particular problem or interest
- and in a form that is useful to him

regardless of

- where it was generated
- in what form or language
- or how it must be located and processed

The utopian dream is to have information available on the day of publication, neatly translated into one's mother tongue, and packaged in quanta that are of infinitely variable size and content.

But the services that are emerging and that will develop are much more costly in visible expenditures than traditional activities, and the question must be explored regarding how to market these services, either through filling overt requirements or through stimulating interest that did not exist before. This has not been a trivial problem, since the library function has been considered to be free to society ever since the principle was established by Andrew Carnegie toward the end of the 19th century.

IV. BRIEF HISTORY

It is not the purpose of this section to provide historical background in the sense that priorities may be established. Rather, a brief perspective is given, with only a few highlights that seem to illustrate the peaks and valleys of the information-retrieval field, with particular reference to the U.S. scene.

One of the early warnings relating to the literature explosion came from Joseph Henry, Secretary of the Smithsonian Institute, in 1851:

It is estimated that about twenty thousand volumes, including pamphlets, purporting to be additions to the sum of human knowledge, are published annually; and unless this mass be properly arranged, and the means furnished by which its contents may be ascertained, literature and science will be over-whelmed by their own unwieldy bulk. The pile will begin to totter under its own weight, and all the additions we may heap upon it will tend to add to the extension of the base, without increasing the elevation and dignity of the edifice.

One of the most important means of facilitating the use of libraries, particularly with reference to science, is well digested indexes of subjects, not merely referring to volumes or books, but to memoirs, papers, and parts of scientific transactions and systematic works. . . . Everyone who is desirous of enlarging the bounds of human knowledge should, in justice to himself, as well as to the public, be acquainted with what has previously been done in the same line, and this he will only be enabled to accomplish by the use of indexes of the kind above mentioned.

From the report of Joseph Henry, secretary of the Smithsonian Institute, to the Board of Regents, in its *Annual Report . . . to the Senate and House of Representatives for 1851*, p. 22.

The explicit warning issued by Secretary Henry went unheeded for over a century. Literature kept piling up, indexed and classified routinely by various conventional methods. Henry's statement was forgotten or ignored, as were similar warnings issued from time to time by those who saw the danger inherent in the accumulating bulk of literature.

The avalanche came in the decade following World War II. Recognition of the crisis came first from the scientific periodicals, which had traditionally provided a medium for recording and publishing the fruits of research.

Scientific periodicals felt the pressure first because of the postwar expansion in scientific and technological research. Increasing expenditures in time and money by industry and government had provided a stimulating climate, and as research facilities were developed by government agencies, industrial concerns, and universities, the result was a new flood of knowledge so great that existing methods for collecting and organizing the records could no longer be considered effective.

At the same time a realization was developing that the pace and effectiveness of research could be further stimulated in another way: by intelligent insight into what had gone before, or what had been reported in the literature.

In other words, the importance of the literature was fully realized at the exact moment that control of the literature seemed impossible.

It was finally acknowledged that traditional library tools were limited in their ability to cope with many of these new problems. This widespread realization motivated efforts to surmount such limitations by using more versatile devices and equipment.

Recognition of the postwar information problem in the United States is generally credited to Dr. Vannevar Bush, who, in 1944, was challenged by President Franklin D. Roosevelt, in a letter:

Dear Dr. Bush: The Office of Scientific Research and Development, of which you are the Director, represents a unique experiment of team-work and cooperation in coordinating scientific research and in applying existing scientific knowledge to the solution of the technical problems paramount in war. Its work has been conducted in the utmost secrecy and carried on without public recognition of any kind: but its tangible results can be found in the communiques coming in from battlefronts all over the world. Some day the full story of its achievements can be told.

There is, however, no reason why the lessons to be found in this experiment cannot be profitably employed in times of peace. The information, the techniques, and the research experience developed by the Office of Scientific Research and Development and by the thousands of scientists in the universities and in private industry, should be used in the days of peace ahead for the improvement of the national health, the creation of new enterprises bringing new jobs, and the betterment of the national standard of living.

It is with that objective in mind that I would like to have your recommendations on the following four major points:

First: What can be done, consistent with military security, and with the prior approval of the military authorities, to make known to the world as soon as possible the contributions which have been made during our war effort to scientific knowledge?

The diffusion of such knowledge should help us stimulate new enterprises, provide jobs for our returning servicemen and other workers, and make possible great strides for the improvement of the national well-being. . . .

Dr. Bush responded with a report,[1] which made clear:

While most of the war research has involved the application of existing scientific knowledge to the problems of war, rather than basic research, there has been accumulated a vast amount of information relating to the application of science to particular problems. Much of this can be used in industry. It is also needed for teaching in the colleges and universities here and in the Armed Forces Institutes overseas. Some of this information must remain secret, but most of it should be made public as soon as there is ground for belief that the enemy will not be able to turn it against us in this war. To select that portion which should be made public, to coordinate its release, and definitely to encourage its publication, a Board composed of Army, Navy, and civilian scientific members should be promptly established.

Later, in 1945, Bush published an article[2] (often quoted since then) which stated:

Science has provided the swiftest communication between individuals; it has provided a record of ideas and has enabled man to manipulate and to make extracts from that record so that knowledge evolves and endures throughout the life of a race rather than that of an individual.

There is a growing mountain of research. But there is increased evidence that we are being bogged down today as specialization extends. The investigator is staggered by the findings and conclusions of thousands of other workers— conclusions which he cannot find time to grasp, much less to remember, as they appear. Yet specialization becomes increasingly necessary for progress, and the effort to bridge between disciplines is correspondingly superficial.

Professionally our methods of transmitting and reviewing the results of research are generations old and by now are totally inadequate for their purpose. If the aggregate time spent in writing scholarly works and in reading them could be evaluated, the ratio between these amounts of time might well be startling. Those who conscientiously attempt to keep abreast of current thought, even in restricted fields, by close and continuous reading might well shy away from an

---

[1] V. Bush, *Science—The Endless Frontier*, Report to the President on a Program for Postwar Scientific Research, U.S. Government Printing Office, Washington, 1945.

[2] V. Bush, "As We May Think," *Atlantic Monthly,* **176,** 101-108 (July 1945).

examination calculated to show how much of the previous month's efforts could be produced on call. Mendel's concept of the laws of genetics was lost to the world for a generation because his publication did not reach the few who were capable of grasping and extending it; and this sort of catastrophe is undoubtedly being repeated all about us, as truly significant attainments become lost in the mass of the inconsequential.

The difficulty seems to be, not so much that we publish unduly in view of the extent and variety of present-day interests, but rather that publication has been extended far beyond our present ability to make real use of the record. The summation of human experience is being expanded at a prodigious rate, and the means we use for threading through the consequent maze to the momentarily important item is the same as was used in the days of square-rigged ships.

· · · · ·

The real heart of the matter of selection, however, goes deeper than a lag in the adoption of mechanisms by libraries, or a lack of development of devices for their use. Our ineptitude in getting at the record is largely caused by the artificiality of systems of indexing. When data of any sort are placed in storage, they are filed alphabetically or numerically, and information is found (when it is) by tracing it down from subclass to subclass. It can be in only one place, unless duplicates are used; one has to have rules as to which path will locate it, and the rules are cumbersome. Having found one item, moreover, one has to emerge from the system and re-enter on a new path.

The human mind does not work that way. It operates by association. With one item in its grasp, it snaps instantly to the next that is suggested by the association of thoughts, in accordance with some intricate web of trails carried by the cells of the brain. It has other characteristics, of course; trails that are not frequently followed are prone to fade, items are not fully permanent, memory is transitory. Yet the speed of action, the intricacy of trails, the detail of mental pictures, is awe-inspiring beyond all else in nature.

Man cannot hope fully to duplicate this mental process artificially, but he certainly ought to be able to learn from it. In minor ways he may even improve, for his records have relative permanency. The first idea, however, to be drawn from the analogy concerns selection. Selection by association, rather than by indexing, may yet be mechanized. One cannot hope thus to equal the speed and flexibility with which the mind follows an associative trail, but it should be possible to beat the mind decisively in regard to the permanence and clarity of the items resurrected from storage.

Consider a future device for individual use, which is a sort of mechanized private file and library. It needs a name, and, to coin one at random, "memex" will do. A memex is a device in which an individual stores all his books, records, and communications, and which is mechanized so that it may be consulted with exceeding speed and flexibility. It is an enlarged intimate supplement to his memory.

It consists of a desk, and while it can presumably be operated from a distance, it is primarily the piece of furniture at which he works. On the top are slanting translucent screens, on which material can be projected for convenient reading. There is a keyboard, and sets of buttons and levers. Otherwise it looks like an ordinary desk.

In one end is the stored material. The matter of bulk is well taken care of by improved microfilm. Only a small part of the interior of the memex is devoted to storage, the rest to mechanism. Yet if the user inserted 5000 pages of material a day it would take him hundreds of years to fill the repository, so he can be profligate and enter material freely.

Most of the memex contents are purchased on microfilm ready for insertion. Books of all sorts, pictures, current periodicals, newspapers, are thus obtained and dropped into place. Business correspondence takes the same path. And there is provision for direct entry. On the top of the memex is a transparent platen. On this are placed longhand notes, photographs, memoranda, all sorts of things. When one is in place, the depression of a lever causes it to be photographed onto the next blank space in a section of the memex film, dry photography being employed.

There is, of course, provision for consultation of the record by the usual scheme of indexing. If the user wishes to consult a certain book, he taps its code on the keyboard, and the title page of the book promptly appears before him, projected onto one of his viewing positions. Frequently-used codes are mnemonic, so that he seldom consults his code book; but when he does, a single tap of a key projects it for his use. Moreover, he has supplemental levers. On deflecting one of these levers to the right he runs through the book before him, each page in turn being projected at a speed which just allows a recognizing glance at each. If he deflects it further to the right, he steps through the book 10 pages at a time; still further at 100 pages at a time. Deflection to the left gives him the same control backwards.

A special button transfers him immediately to the first page of the index. Any given book of his library can thus be called up and consulted with far greater facility than if it were taken from a shelf. As he has several projection positions, he can leave one item in position while he calls up another. He can add marginal notes and comments, taking advantage of one possible type of dry photography, and it could even be arranged so that he can do this by a stylus scheme, such as is now employed in the telautograph seen in railroad waiting rooms, just as though he had the physical page before him.

. . . . .

The applications of science have built man a well-supplied house, and are teaching him to live healthily therein. They have enabled him to throw masses of people against one another with cruel weapons. They may yet allow him truly to encompass the great record and to grow in the wisdom of race experience. He may perish in conflict before he learns to wield that record for his true good.

Yet, in the application of science to the needs and desires of man, it would seem to be a singularly unfortunate stage at which to terminate the process, or to lose hope as to the outcome.

Then followed a period of approximately 10 years of development of small-scale information-retrieval systems, using easily available and relatively inexpensive tools such as the marginal-hole punched card and the electromechanical card sorter, among others.[3] And then came the first reports regarding the possible existence of centralized, automated information-processing activities in the U.S.S.R., which gained credence with some observers. One such report authored by V. P. Cherenin appeared in 1955, in a paper entitled "Certain Problems of Documentation and Mechanization of Information Search." An excerpt from the translation of this paper suggests that:

    ... The time is not far when a new revolution will occur in the storage and dissemination of data, similar to that which was produced by the invention of printing. It is difficult to guess how it will occur; nevertheless, by letting our imagination roam, it is possible to visualize the following information service of the future.

    ... All arriving and all existing data, after the necessary editorial processing and suitable exterior styling, are photographed at a considerably reduced scale on photographic film. Instead of large runs, only several copies of such microfilm are produced and are sent to one or several information centers. These centers transmit continuously over many waves all the data available in them at a tremendous sequence frequency of frames of microfilm, reaching, for example, a million per second. With such a transmission speed all data accumulated by humanity can be transmitted over many waves within a comparatively brief time interval—something like several minutes.

    ... Any frame of the microfilm can be received in any place on a special television screen equipped with a selecting device. All the instructions, classification schemes, table of contents of the microfilm with indication of the number of frames, and code designation required for the use of such a televisor are transmitted at the start of the microfilm, therefore eliminating the need for using any kind of printed information.

    ... It is difficult to overestimate the flexibility and effectiveness of such an imaginary method of storing and disseminating data. Undoubtedly such a method or something analogous to it will turn out to be cheaper than the existing methods, when the volume of data will reach a definite limit. It goes without saying that, just as after the appearance of printing, the handwritten form of recording still remained in use, the appearance of a similar information service will still find a part of the data stored as before and disseminated in the form presently in existence. *Let us remark that, in spite of the fact that the information service of the future described above is quite fantastic, all the*

---

[3] R. S. Casey, J. W. Perry, M. M. Berry, and A. Kent, *Punched Cards,* 2nd ed., Reinhold, 1958.

technical units required for its realization are in existence at the present time and being constantly improved.

The successful launching of the Russian satellite "Sputnik" caused speculation on the role of information-retrieval services in opening up an apparent gap between the United States and the U.S.S.R. in the sciences and technology. This led to many public discussions and congressional investigations. It was generally concluded that[4]

The wide dissemination of scientific and technical information is the cornerstone of scientific progress.

and

The great majority of business firms are at a disadvantage in securing the benefits of up-to-the-minute technological knowledge because they cannot, in view of their relatively limited size, employ or contract for the research personnel and activities necessary to channel to their uses the vast reservoir of present-day technology.

As a result of hearings chaired by the then Senator Hubert H. Humphrey, it was concluded that:

All agencies generally agreed that there was an urgent need for the development of improved systems of engineering and for the installation of mechanical, electronic retrieval equipment adaptable to specific programs in order to make certain that all available scientific information would be readily accessible to government agencies and to members of the scientific community.[5]

Then followed a period of somewhat generous federal support for the development of mechanized information storage and retrieval systems. The trend was toward centralization of activities, focussing on the professional society, if not the federal government. However the mood of the federal fund-granting agencies was not one of patience, and an atmosphere of "crash" developments ensued. But it became apparent that the newly developing systems needed to evolve and couldn't be forced into operation prematurely, primarily because those who were to be served by these new systems generally did not yet know how to exploit more sophisticated approaches to information retrieval.

For this reason, as well as technical developmental problems, and possibly for political reasons, a number of adverse reactions seemed to set in, one of which was articulated by Dr. James Killian, Science Adviser to President Eisenhower, in a report dated December 7, 1958:

---

[4] *Documentation, Indexing, and Retrieval of Scientific Information,* Senate Document No. 113, 86th Congress, 2nd Session, Committee on Government Operations, 1960 pp. 2-3.

[5] *Documentation, Indexing, and Retrieval of Scientific Information,* Senate Document No. 113, 86th Congress, 2nd Session, Committee on Government Operations, 1960, p. 7.

From a purely practical point of view, it must be remembered that much of the day-to-day work involved in the dissemination of scientific information— that is, the writing, editing, abstracting, translating, and so on—is done either by scientists or people with technical skills of a very high order. Many of these people perform such chores in addition to their regular scientific work and it is quite inconceivable that they could be induced to affiliate themselves on a fulltime basis with a centralized agency. Put the matter another way: The case for a Government-operated, highly centralized type of center can be no better defended for scientific information services than it could be for automobile agencies, delicatessens, or barber shops.

But the field continued to move along, bit by bit, with such programs as the National Library of Medicine Index Mechanization Project, the modest and realizable objective of which was to develop and demonstrate improved methods for the rapid and efficient publication of comprehensive indexes to the literature, making use of mechanical applications. This objective was a far cry from the earlier goal of the field, a mechanized information storage and retrieval center which would permit effective custom searches to be made. Nevertheless, this modest start was indeed the precursor of a much more sophisticated computer-based system at the National Library of Medicine, which even now is emerging in its second version.

Of course, Dr. James Killian's drastic statement of 1958 could hardly stand unmodified, and the next White House Science Adviser, Dr. Jerome B. Wiesner, Special Assistant to President John F. Kennedy for Science and Technology, participated in the issuance of a report through the President's Science Advisory Committee on the responsibilities of the technical community and the government in the transfer of information.[6]

This report, popularly called the "Weinberg[7] report," pointed out:

Since strong science and technology is a national necessity, and adequate communication is a prerequisite for strong science and technology, the health of the technical communication system must be a concern of Government. Moreover, since the internal agency information systems overlap with the non-Government systems, the Government must pay attention to the latter as well as to the former.

The Government must be concerned with our non-Government communications systems for another, less obvious reason. The technical literature with its long tradition of self-criticism helps, by its very existence, to maintain the standards, and hence the validity, of science, particularly of basic science. The Government, as the largest supporter of basic science, has a strong interest in

---

[6] *Science, Government, and Information,* The White House, January 10, 1963.

[7] Dr. Alvin M. Weinberg, Director of the Oak Ridge National Laboratory, served as Chairman of the Panel on Science Information, which was involved in preparing the report.

keeping viable this mechanism of critical review of the science it supports.

Several of the recommendations of the report are as follows:

We shall cope with the information explosion, in the long run, only if some scientists and engineers are prepared to commit themselves deeply to the job of sifting, reviewing, and synthesizing information, i.e., to handling information with sophistication and meaning, not merely mechanically. Such scientists must creaté new science, not just shuffle documents: Their activities of reviewing, writing books, criticizing, and synthesizing are as much a part of science as is traditional research. We urge the technical community to accord such individuals the esteem that matches the importance of their jobs and to reward them well for their efforts.

. . . The Panel sees the specialized information center as a major key to the rationalization of our information system. Ultimately we believe the specialized center will become the accepted retailer of information, switching, interpreting, and otherwise processing information from the large wholesale depositories and archive journals to the individual user. The Panel therefore urges that more and better specialized centers be established.

We believe the specialized information center should be primarily a technical institute rather than a technical library. It must be led by professional working scientists and engineers who maintain the closest contact with their technical professions and who, by being near the data, can make new syntheses that are denied those who do not have all the data at their fingertips. Information centers ought to be set up where science and technology flourish. We believe that the large, Government-supported laboratories could become congenial homes for groups of related specialized information centers.

. . . The Panel recognizes that mechanical equipment offers hope for easing the information problem. Commercially available equipment is not the remedy in every case; economics, size, frequency of use, growth rate, depth and sophistication of indexing must be examined in detail for each collection before a specific system is to be mechanized. There is a need for equipment specifically designed to retrieve documents from very large collections. The recent study under the auspices of the Council of Library Resources, recommending automation of the Library of Congress, should be evaluated with a view toward its implementation both as a means of improving the services offered by the Library and of advancing the art of automatic retrieval.

An attractive *technical* solution to the problem of the dissemination and retrieval of documents is the centralized depository. This would acquire documents in a field of its own responsibility; it would broadcast abstracts in a regular announcement bulletin; copies of the full texts would be available on order from the depository.

· · · · ·

The central depository has some advantages as a substitute for, or better, as a supplement to, conventional publication. It is extremely fast; it rationalizes the preprint; it compacts the circulating literature; it funnels the accumulation from a given field in one place for efficient retrieval. By relieving the conventional journals of their implicit obligation to process every contribution that might be conceivably useful to science, it can leave them with the more creative and manageable responsibility of selecting and encouraging the best contributions for wide distribution. Centralized facilities can also be the focal point for the development of automatic processing techniques that are uneconomical for widely scattered services.

The reactions to this report have been quite dramatic, with a number of institutions and agencies fostering the development of specialized information centers.

But, perhaps the specialized information center thrust, taken alone, was only a part of the solution to the burgeoning problem, and the strong centralization theme began recurring. Representative Roman C. Pucinski of Illinois was perhaps most vociferous in this regard, in proposing the establishment of a National Research Data Processing and Information Retrieval Center.[8]

In an attempt to treat the centralization theme definitively, Arthur D. Little Inc., Cambridge, Massachusetts, undertook a study financed by the National Science Foundation. The final report of the study,[9] listed as its first recommendation:

Do not support large-scale centralization of mechanized-document retrieval facilities at this time. A large centralized facility drawing upon current state of the art of document retrieval techniques could probably not achieve the main objective for which it was designed—provision of an effective, exhaustive, document retrieval capability to supplement efforts to prevent duplicate research or development investments. Responsibility for showing that a proposed centralized facility would be feasible and would satisfy this objective must be borne by the proponents of centralization, employing quantitative evaluation techniques such as those we have developed.

The underpinnings of this report have been seriously challenged by a group of invited commentators.[10]

So, although differences of opinion are evident with regard to how far to go in mechanization, centralization, or specialization, the field moves along, with some solid results, increasing acceptance, and increasing dependence on mechanical and electronic information retrieval evident in programs of the

---

[8] H.R. 1946, First Hearing held May 27, 1963.

[9] *Centralization and Documentation,* PB 181548, Office of Technical Services, July 1963, p. 3.

[10] A. E. Oettinger, R. C. Pucinski, A. Kent, M. Taube, M. Wooster, and G. Salton, "A Forum on Centralization and Documentation," *Communications of the ACM,* 8, 704-710 (November, 1965).

National Aeronautics and Space Agency, National Library of Medicine, Defense Documentation Center, the Chemical Abstracts Service, and others.

V. COMPUTERS AND DECISION MAKING

A. Purposes of Storing Knowledge

The first philosopher who is somehow installed in happy self-sufficiency aboard a satellite far above the earth will have an enviable privilege: He can view knowledge as an end in itself. On a more realistic level, human beings are accustomed to storing knowledge for various more mundane reasons. The individual cherishes, and saves, material that interests him. He may store it away uncritically, magpie-fashion, without thought. He may misjudge the probability that the material will continue to interest him over a period of time. His decision, to save material or to throw it away, is often difficult. Will he want to use this material before it is replaced by something newer and of greater value to him?

Today the question is no longer a philosophical one. Experience in technology, in industry, and in government proves that the availability of knowledge is essential to the maintenance of our civilization. The storage of knowledge in libraries and files has become an immediate and intensely practical problem.

These considerations bring us to our first definition. A *library*, or a *file*, for the purposes of this book, will designate any collection of documents or graphic records containing information of sufficiently high probable utility or importance to warrant its orderly arrangement and retention over a relatively long period of time.

B. Information and Needs for Rapid Decisions

The two quotations which follow are typical of many that might have been chosen, relating to the importance of information in decision making.

. . . Probably never in history has the office gone through a revolution as great as that of the past year. White collar tasks and management aims have changed drastically; the business machines seem, finally, to have found themselves; new equipment keeps pouring out, all of it more efficient than its predecessors.

Yet out of this wealth of tools and techniques has sprung a new problem for management; the very real question of how the flood of information today can best be controlled. For flood it has become, to the point where many experts predict that the executive lineup of the average corporation will soon include the title: "Vice President—Information."[11]

. . . . .

Advanced managements are realizing the need for a new way of thinking about information. This is the evolution from "management by exception" into "management by objectives," with its accent on decision-making rather than evaluation of operational results. This emphasis on intelligent decision-making is affecting the planning and installing of computing systems by focussing attention on what information is of real worth, and by centralizing and giving higher corporate status to the whole information responsibility. At present, the idea is so new that there is no agreement on where the information function should report in the organization chart. At International Latex Corporation, the group headed by Lionel Griffith which is setting up the information was told "to visualize the *totality* of the business, and then to formulate information handling for all decisions and control. This has resulted in . . . a three-dimensional model of rational information flow . . . a highly centralized data processing "hub." Under this system, a distinction is made between the "intellectual" content of work in any area of activity, and the "mechanical" methods of providing the information for the intellectual operation. Plans also call for a "war-room" where all intelligence is centralized, as well as a novel use of sound, wherein basic management data, continually up-dated, will be available on sound tracks. Executives, instead of requesting a report, may dial into the system and receive the latest intelligence over the phone.[12]

Systems engineering like that described at International Latex dramatizes the changing requirements for speed of access to information that decision makers can use in controlling their organizations. The related increase in the rate with which competitive activity, international tensions, and changes in public opinion affect economic, military, and political situations is essentially a function of the changes in modern communications. Information today must be immediately accessible in a thousand places, on ten thousand subjects.

Another source of urgency is the increase in the volume of literature itself—a wave that has become a flood. Recognition of this urgency has given rise to a cry for a new effectiveness of control, control based on the functions of modern electronic equipment. The decision-making process is becoming essentially a process of analysis, a series of successive approximations through constant refinements of purposes and through closer and closer discrimination of

---

[11] "The Office: The Great Information Revolution," *Dun's Review and Modern Industry,* September 1963, p. 95.
[12] Data Processing Digest, 6, 10 (June 1960).

facts. But the process must be an informed analysis, based on information selected and supplied with superhuman accuracy and speed. Again the answer seems to lie in modern electronics.

C. Computers in Our Modern World

Mechanized information retrieval is the subject if not the title of this book. We therefore plunge into this subject by first considering the computer, a notorious example of "the machine." This is a useful approach because some of the developments in the computer field are analogous to trends in mechanized information retrieval, and may give insight into the problems that are yet to be solved in the use of this new tool for effective research.

Mr. Ralph J. Cordiner, formerly chairman of the board of the General Electric Company, was quoted by *Business Week* as saying:

When the history of our age is written, I think it will record three profoundly important technological developments:

Nuclear energy, which tremendously increases the amount of *energy* available to do the world's work;

Automation, which greatly increases man's ability to use *tools*;

And computers, which multiply man's ability to do *mental* work.

Some of our engineers believe that of these three, the computer will bring the greatest benefit to man.

These words were written in 1958,[13] when the computer industry was already achieving the status of a young giant who did not know the use or the limits of his own strength. The computer revolution had hardly begun.

The vast potential of the computer in various types of organizations has not yet been realized. The history of the computer has been plagued by false starts and mistakes in use. Although its adoption has been carried out with an enthusiasm that is often emotional or almost religious in tone, the computer has too often remained the young giant, confronting a parent organization that is unsure of what to do with this new and powerful servant.

But there have also been dramatic examples of the successful use of computers. In addition, although initial, short-term results have been a disappointment to some organizations, one significant fact remains. Few computers have been returned, many more are on order, and various organizations are installing second, third, and fourth computers, and more. The computer revolution is indeed in full force.

It is obvious that a number of opposing forces are at work. Here, for example, are a few of them:

---

[13] *Business Week,* No. 1503, 68 ff. (June 21, 1958).

1. Administrative Costs. The administration and operation of a major organization has created a paper jungle. Estimates of the cost of processing all of the information required for decision making vary from half of the administrative costs to half of the sales price, that is, half of the selling price of the product or service produced. Thus, considerable enthusiasm greets any device, no matter how unlikely or remote, that shows promise of controlling administrative costs.

2. The "Human" Tradition. Manual, human operations are sanctified by a tradition far older than the structure of modern business practices. Because the business world recognizes this tradition, it resists the substitution of automatic routines. In order to overcome that resistance, the initial tendency was to exaggerate the mere ability of the computer to replace human effort. Such exaggeration led to a distorted interpretation of the computer's role, and handicapped a true estimate of its potential.

3. Structural Reorganization. Successful uses of computers have not been simple translations of existing clerical routines. Instead, they are new practices based on a reshaping of organizational structure. Such applications can exploit the potentiality of the computer to perform mountains of work in an expeditious way. Here the opposing force comes from supervisory and middle-management personnel whose positions are involved in the reshaping of organizational structure. These people naturally engage in last-ditch attempts to block a development that would eliminate their functions.

4. The Systems Engineer. The optimal performance of a computer demands independent analysis of organizational structure. This need is being met by the systems engineer, a combined administrator-logician-mathematician-electrical engineer-accountant. The systems engineer must function as a kind of referee in the intraorganizational power struggle. On one side stand those with modern theories of administration. On the other are the traditionalists, usually older men, often those involved in the establishment of the very system that they now see threatened by reorientation to "the machine."

In practice, the computer has created new jobs and new opportunities for people. It has demanded reeducation and retraining. But those people who are willing to adapt themselves to the new system are usually rewarded with higher status and higher pay. Instead of eliminating jobs, the new computer systems have enabled companies to absorb a new volume of operation undreamed of by either management or staff under precomputer conditions.

Another word about those who, worried about their jobs, have attempted to set up barricades against computer installations. They may slow the computer revolution, but they do not stop it. By expending so much energy on obstruction rather than on construction, they succeed only in surrendering to others the key positions in the newly structured organization that they themselves were otherwise best qualified to hold. The enemy, if one must be named, is the short-sighted individual himself, rather than the entirely neutral presence of the computer.

The computer revolution has been compared, in scope and significance, to the industrial revolution of the past century and a half. We have not heard the last of the one, nor will we soon hear the last of the other.

This sketch of the introduction of the computer has been presented to illuminate, by analogy, some of the factors involved in the development of mechanized information retrieval and its acceptance by the modern world. The library is experiencing a revolution within its own quiet walls. Nonconventional principles have been introduced, bringing with them machines and devices of formidable aspect. Information retrieval has met many opposing forces not unlike those described above. The nature of this conflict is part of the history of mechanized information retrieval, the subject of this book.

VI. DEFINITIONS

A. "Mechanized"

Although the word "mechanization" usually conjures up the picture of a computer, another definition is more suitable for this book: mechanization involves the organization of the powers of any complex body. This definition implies that a machine is to be considered as more than a single physical device; it is to be considered as a system that consists of interacting parts. Some of these interacting parts may be devices, some may be human beings, and some may be procedures.

Thus "mechanization," for the purposes of this book, may be ascribed to card manipulation techniques in an individual file or to an information center that utilizes various mechanical equipment to a large-scale digital computer that has been made part of a sophisticated system of information retrieval.

B. "Information"

"Information" is more than books, regardless of the early impressions we all gained as student-clients of the library. Information that is considered useful or worthy of retention over a period of time appears in many forms other than that of the traditional book. Information in this widened sense may, in certain contexts, include artifacts, inscriptions, and decorations which are the records of the anthropologist and the historian. Such records may vary in form from that of the Dead Sea Scrolls to the Rosetta Stone. In the field of information retrieval, the word "information" is usually restricted to designate *documents* (or other graphic records) *which record this information for later reference and use.*

Some examples of these modern graphic records include, in addition to books, pamphlets, periodicals, newspapers, reports, photographs, films, micro-film, recording on tape or other media, charts, maps, indexes, clippings, and letters. The physical form of these records varies considerably. There is a considerable variety also in the means by which the records may be read.

We may consider as information any recorded knowledge that may be useful to some decision maker. This recorded knowledge may be found in a wide variety of sources, such as correspondence, inventory reports, sales reports, research reports, trip reports, monographs, periodical articles, trade literature, and advertisements.

C. "Retrieval"

"Retrieval," as used in the phrase "mechanized information retrieval," has come to mean more than the standard dictionary denotation, that is, looking through or exploring thoroughly in order to find something. Today *any mechanized processing of recorded knowledge* has been considered, for better or for worse, to be "mechanized information retrieval." The processing may merely speed accession, or it may lead to an orderly arrangement of recorded knowledge so as to provide more convenient access by future human users.

D. "Mechanized Information Retrieval"

Effective development and use of any system must be based on a clear understanding of the material and the problems that the system is to handle. Experience in mechanized information retrieval indicates that, in general, it must handle these types of material:

1. Large files, usually containing more than a few documents.
2. Complex subject matter, usually containing many subjects of potential interest.
3. Scattered information, usually requiring selection from among many documents and subsequent correlation.

Recognizing these as the proper materials of the system, we may accept as its purpose the identification of documents according to various criteria. The system may now be divided into its component operations, for the purpose of analysis and study. Each of these functions, or "unit operations," comprises an area of discussion in this book. In each of these areas, machine techniques may be exploited to a greater or lesser degree, with more or less advantage. Therefore, in this book, "mechanized information retrieval" will designate *the use of mechanized or other nonconventional tools in connection with any one or more unit operations.*

VII. THE UNIT OPERATIONS

An information-retrieval system may be characterized in terms of a number of unit operations, which are carried through in order to place before interested people the material that they may consider useful and relevant.

It is assumed, for purposes of this discussion, that information has been generated and recorded in some form (e.g., printed page, film, or magnetic tape recording). This information (called *source material* in the following) is then a candidate for acceptance into an information retrieval system. The source material is processed through a series of *input* unit operations, involving:

1. *Acquisition (and accessioning).* The location, selection, ordering, and receiving of source materials for a collection.

2. *Analysis.* Perusal of source materials and selection of analytics (e.g., index entries, subject headings, keywords, and descriptors) that are considered to be of sufficient probable importance to warrant the effort of rendering them searchable in the system.

3. *Terminology (or vocabulary) control.* Establishing arbitrary relationships (e.g., cross references and thesaural associations) among analytics.

4. *Recording results of analysis on a searchable medium.* Use of a card, tape, film, or other medium onto which analytics are transcribed.

5. *Storage of source materials.* Involving the physical placement of the source materials in some location, either in its original form or transcribed or copied (in full or reduced size) onto a new medium.

Once these input unit operations have been completed, the information-retrieval system is ready to be consulted, and a set of *output* unit operations may then be carried through.

1. *Question receipt and analysis,* involving:

    a. The expression of a question or a problem.

    b. The selection of analytics relating to the question or problem.

    c. The expression of these analytics in terms of the particular information-retrieval system to be searched, involving use of:

      i. The same philosophy and procedure of analysis as was used to input source materials into the system.

      ii. The same terminology control or standard headings as used during input to the system.

    d. The arrangement of analytics into a configuration that represents a probable link between the question, as expressed, and the source materials on file, as analyzed.

    2. *Conducting the search.* Involving the manipulation or operation of the search mechanism in order to identify source materials from the system.

    3. *Delivery of results of search.* Involving the physical removal or copying of source materials in order to provide it in response to a question.

    At the risk of excessive redundancy, let us look at these input and output unit operations as they have been carried out traditionally in relation to the functioning of libraries, in the handling of books and monographs, and without reference to mechanization:

    1. *Acquisition.* Involving professional staff or bibliographers perusing announcements of books published or requests made by library patrons and making decisions as to whether to order given source materials.

    2. *Analysis.* Involving cataloguers perusing the source materials on receipt in order to identify the subject matter that will be used to classify them in terms of a given system (e.g., Dewey Decimal, Library of Congress).

    3. *Terminology control.* Involving cataloguers consulting subject authority lists in order to determine appropriate subject headings to be used.

    4. *Recording results of analysis on a searchable medium.* Involving clerical personnel typing the subject headings on catalog cards, which are then filed, either alphabetically or in other arrays suitable for consultation by patron.

    5. *Storage of source materials.* Involving personnel placing books and monographs on shelves.

    6. *Question receipt and analysis.* Involving a reference librarian serving to aid patrons in locating relevant materials in terms of their interests by suggesting subject headings that were likely to have been used in analyzing the contents of these materials.

    7. *Conducting the search.* Involving a reference librarian consulting the catalog to identify subject headings which may relate to the patrons' interest.

    8. *Delivery of results of search.* Involving the patron or a staff member removing from shelves those books and monographs listed under the appropriate subject headings.

VIII. CHANGES IN NATURE OF QUESTIONS ASKED

    But the periodicals, which also are acquired by libraries, have not generally been subjected to analysis in the same way as books and monographs, in that the individual articles have not generally been catalogued separately and therefore are not separately identifiable through the library catalog along with books and monographs that may bear on the same topic of interest to the patron.

The patron has therefore been left on his own, in attempting to identify this type of source material. The periodicals often have provided independent indexes to their contents, and the patron has been forced to consult annual indexes, year by year, for each periodical of potential usefulness—a time-consuming and often frustrating task.

Various organizations have attempted to alleviate this problem by abstracting and/or indexing the contents of groups of periodicals and publishing them in single sources (e.g., Readers Guide to Periodical Literature, Chemical Abstracts Service, Engineering Index, Industrial Arts Index). But this, too, has led to frustrations, since the indexing provided for a large clientele often does not serve well the specific and idiosyncratic needs of specific patrons. Even when attempting to index for most of these specific needs, the cost of analysis has become unmanageable, since the resulting index and abstract publications have become more and more expensive, as the higher cost of production of these publications was amortized over the clientele population.

Another equally important problem has resulted from the increasing quantity of periodicals published, and the consequent subtle change in nature of questions asked by patrons. There was a time when it was possible for a person to read all or most periodicals of interest, soon after publication. Thus, when a question arose that involved consultation of an appropriate index, the patron could recall some of the subject matter covered in periodicals of interest and could frame a question in those terms.

But as the quantity of publications reached the point where it exceeded an individual's capability to read material of interest upon publication and as the tasks of reading for indexing purposes were delegated to various organizations, the nature of the question changed because the patron could no longer select subject entries to consult in an index which were based on recall of what he had read. The new type of question was expressed in terms of a number of *characteristics* of a problem he faced, which might have been selected as index entries by those who performed the analysis. Furthermore, the patron now wished to specify that all of the characteristics would have to be present before he wanted the source material brought to his attention. This led to difficulty in performing the search of the index by traditional methods.

An example of this problem will make it easier to understand. Let us take an apparently simple information-retrieval problem.

The personnel manager of a company wishes to hire a receptionist and places an advertisement in the local newspaper which leads to responses from 100 applicants for the position. Each person is asked to complete an application providing the following information:

Name
Typing ability

Dictation ability
Education
Work experience
Marital status
Appearance
Hair color
Age

A typical applicant might then provide the following information:

Name	Diane Carter
Typing ability	Poor
Dictation ability	Poor
Education	Junior high school
Work experience	4 years
Marital status	Single
Appearance	Good
Hair color	Brunette
Age	19

The personnel manager now decides that he would like to interview only those applicants with the following characteristics:

Some typing ability
Some dictation ability
Work experience of more than 2 years
High school graduate
Single or divorced
Red hair
Over 20 years of age but less than 30
Excellent appearance

Since it would be very time consuming to peruse every application in order to determine which applicants met all of the qualifications, he asks one of his assistants to prepare an index of the applications, which is then given to him (Figure 1-1).

The personnel manager, in attempting to use this index to select applicants with the desired characteristics, would encounter frustrations in comparing the applicant numbers listed for each of nine index entries in order to determine those that refer to the same applicant.[14]

It is problems of this type that led to the consideration of how automation might be employed to overcome some of the difficulties involved in developing indexes and in retrieving information from them.

---

[14] Why not try it yourself to see how frustrating it really is.

Characteristic	Applicant Number
AGE	
Under 20	— 1, 6, 7, 12, 15, 17, 18, 21, 28, 29, 30, 32, 33, 36, 39, 40, 41, 42, 44, 45, 47, 48, 53, 55, 56, 57, 59, 61, 65, 68, 70, 75, 77, 79, 81, 84, 85, 88, 89, 90 92, 95
20-29	— 2, 3, 8, 10, 13, 16, 19, 22, 31, 37, 46, 50, 52, 58, 62, 64, 71, 72, 78, 80, 83, 86, 91, 93, 98, 99
30-39	— 4, 5, 14, 20, 25, 26, 27, 35, 38, 43, 51, 63, 66, 73, 76, 82, 94, 97
40-49	— 9, 23, 34, 49, 54, 67, 69, 74, 87, 96
50 or over	— 11, 24, 60, 100
APPEARANCE	
Excellent	— 2, 5, 7, 10, 11, 15, 27, 33, 39, 47, 52, 55, 60, 65, 71, 76, 79, 80, 91, 95, 100
Good	— 1, 3, 6, 8, 9, 12, 14, 16, 17, 18, 19, 21, 22, 23, 25, 26, 28, 29, 31, 32, 34, 35, 36, 38, 40, 41, 42, 43, 45, 46, 48, 50, 51, 53, 54, 56, 57, 58, 59, 62, 63, 64, 66, 68, 69, 70, 72, 74, 75, 77, 78, 83, 84, 85, 87, 88, 93, 96, 97, 99
Poor	— 4, 13, 20, 24, 30, 37, 44, 49, 61, 67, 73, 81, 82, 86, 89, 90, 92, 94, 98
EDUCATION	
College	— 2, 8, 22, 46
Jr. college	— 3, 4, 13, 15, 16, 19, 20, 23, 24, 26, 28, 37, 40, 42, 48, 50, 51, 54, 57, 58, 63, 66, 71, 74, 76, 79, 83, 90, 91, 94, 100
High school	— 1, 5, 6, 9, 10, 12, 14, 17, 18, 21, 25, 27, 29, 30, 31, 32, 36, 38, 39, 41, 43, 44, 45, 47, 52, 55, 56, 59, 60, 64, 65, 67, 68, 69, 70, 72, 73, 75, 77, 80, 81, 82, 84, 85, 86, 87, 88, 89, 95, 97, 98, 99
Jr. high school	— 7, 33, 35, 53, 61, 78, 92
Other	— 11, 34, 49, 62, 93, 96
EXPERIENCE	
0-2 years	— 1, 2, 3, 6, 7, 8, 12, 15, 17, 18, 21, 28, 29, 30, 32, 36, 39, 40, 42, 44, 47, 48, 55, 56, 57, 59, 68, 70, 75, 79, 81, 84, 85, 89, 90, 95
3-5 years	— 9, 16, 22, 26, 33, 41, 45, 46, 53, 58, 61, 65, 71, 77, 80, 83, 86, 88, 91, 92, 93, 99
6-10 years	— 5, 13, 19, 24, 25, 31, 35, 37, 43, 49, 50, 62, 63, 72, 73, 78, 97, 98
Over 10	— 4, 10, 11, 14, 20, 23, 27, 34, 38, 51, 52, 54, 60, 64, 66, 67, 69, 74, 76, 82, 87, 94, 96, 100

DICTATION ABILITY
Excellent   — 2, 5, 13, 21, 24, 37, 43, 51, 62, 66, 75, 82, 93, 98
Good   — 3, 6, 8, 9, 14, 16, 17, 18, 19, 22, 23, 25, 27, 28, 30, 31, 32,
               34, 35, 36, 38, 41, 45, 47, 50, 52, 53, 55, 56, 61, 65, 68, 70,
               71, 72, 76, 78, 81, 83, 84, 87, 88, 89, 92, 94, 95, 96, 97, 99,
               100
Poor   — 1, 4, 7, 10, 11, 12, 15, 20, 26, 29, 33, 39, 40, 42, 44, 46, 48,
               49, 54, 57, 58, 59, 60, 63, 64, 67, 69, 73, 74, 77, 79, 80, 85,
               86, 90, 91

TYPING ABILITY
Excellent   — 2, 5, 8, 13, 17, 21, 24, 31, 32, 37, 38, 45, 50, 51, 52, 56, 61,
               62, 66, 68, 70, 72, 75, 78, 81, 82, 84, 87, 88, 92, 93, 96, 97,
               98, 100
Good   — 3, 4, 6, 7, 9, 11, 14, 16, 18, 19, 22, 23, 25, 27, 28, 29, 30,
               33, 34, 35, 36, 40, 41, 42, 43, 44, 46, 47, 48, 49, 53, 54, 55,
               58, 59, 64, 65, 67, 71, 73, 74, 76, 77, 79, 80, 83, 85, 89, 90,
               91, 94, 95, 99
Poor   — 1, 10, 12, 15, 20, 26, 39, 57, 60, 63, 69, 86

MARITAL STATUS
Single   — 1, 3, 6, 7, 12, 14, 15, 17, 18, 22, 28, 29, 30, 31, 32, 33, 37,
               38, 39, 40, 41, 42, 44, 45, 47, 50, 52, 53, 55, 56, 57, 59, 61,
               62, 64, 65, 68, 72, 73, 75, 77, 78, 79, 80, 81, 84, 85, 88, 89,
               90, 91, 92, 94, 95, 99, 100
Married   — 2, 5, 8, 10, 11, 13, 16, 19, 20, 21, 24, 25, 26, 27, 34, 35, 36,
               43, 46, 48, 49, 51, 54, 58, 63, 66, 67, 70, 71, 74, 76, 82, 83,
               86, 87, 93, 96, 98
Divorced   — 9, 23, 69, 97
Widowed   — 4, 60

HAIR COLOR
Red   — 6, 32, 58, 63, 94
Brunette   — 4, 5, 7, 9, 10, 13, 14, 18, 20, 21, 23, 26, 27, 29, 33, 34, 35,
               38, 40, 45, 47, 49, 50, 51, 54, 55, 57, 60, 64, 66, 68, 71, 74,
               76, 78, 82, 85, 86, 88, 91, 95, 96, 98
Blonde   — 1, 17, 28, 31, 36, 39, 41, 44, 46, 53, 59, 75, 81, 92
Black   — 2, 3, 8, 11, 12, 15, 16, 19, 22, 24, 25, 30, 37, 42, 43, 48, 52,
               56, 61, 62, 65, 67, 69, 70, 72, 73, 77, 79, 80, 83, 84, 87, 89,
               90, 93, 97, 99, 100

Figure 1-1.

Two

The Physical Tools

The textbook is organized in terms of the various unit operations that people do in relation to information-retrieval systems, with particular emphasis given on what might be amenable to the application of automatic methodology.

What is it then that people do in relation to information-retrieval systems?

1. They receive inputs to their brain through various senses—through reading, listening, and so on. This is related to a unit operation such as *analysis*, in which the text of the source material must be read by a cataloguer or indexer before a decision can be reached as to which analytic (e.g., subject heading) should be selected.

2. They remember (or use external aids to memory) criteria that they are to use to judge the significance or relevance of inputs received. This is related to a unit operation such as *terminology control*, in which a subject authority list (which enumerates "legal" subject headings) may be committed to memory by a cataloguer or indexer. (More often, the list is printed and is consulted, as an external aid to memory.)

3. They process information by comparing inputs with criteria stored in memory in order to determine whether they are identical. This is related again to a unit operation such as *terminology control*, in which an analytic selected by a cataloguer or indexer is checked against the subject authority list to determine whether it is present, in identical form, and is therefore "legal."

4. They produce outputs which display the results of comparison and processing, through writing or speaking. This is related to a unit operation such as *recording results of analysis*, in which a person types an analytic on a 3 by 5

inch catalog card (a searchable medium) after it has been checked against a subject authority list to determine that it is a "legal" heading.

Now, if machines were to perform these same functions, how would they accomplish them?

1. Machines receive inputs through electronic or electromechanical impulses provided to them. Thus, any information to be "read" or sensed by machines must be available or converted into machine-readable form. This conversion is accomplished by:

a. Keyboarding (e.g., keypunching) information so as to convert information from human-readable to machine-readable form.
b. Having machine-readable information available as a by-product of operations involved in generating human-readable information (e.g., punched paper tape produced as a by-product of monotype composition).
c. Optical scanning of printed pages to permit character recognition by machines.

2. Machines remember information by having it stored in various forms:

a. Perforated
    i. Unit records (e.g., Hollerith cards)
    ii. Continuous records (e.g., punched paper tape)
b. Magnetic
    i. Tapes
    ii. Discs
    iii. Core memory
c. Film
    i. Unit records (e.g., Filmorex and Minicard)
    ii. Continuous records (e.g., microfilm)

3. Machines compare and process information from multiple sources of stored information by

a. Sorting
b. Collating
c. Internal processing involving
    i. Addition
    ii. Subtraction

4. Machines output information by

a. Printing out on sheets for people to read.
b. Punching out so that other machines can read the output on

     i. Unit records (e.g., Hollerith cards)

    ii. Continuous records (e.g., perforated paper tape)

  c. Magnetizing tapes or other storage media so that other machines can read the output.

  d. Activating, in an appropriate way, a temporary display (e.g., cathode ray tube) so that people can read it or so that it can be photographed.

Now let us examine some of the machines or physical tools that are specialists in performing certain aspects of these functions.

1. The Tabulating Card is a specialist in storing machine-readable information. This is a unit record 7¼ by 3¼ inches into which may be recorded rectangular punches (Figure 2-1). Eighty columns of information may be recorded on this card. If a numeral is to be recorded, one punch is required; if an

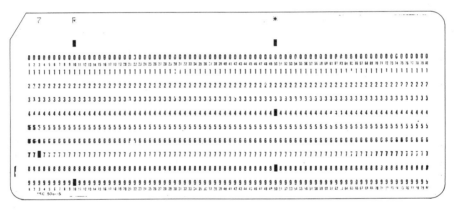

Figure 2-1

alphabetic character is to be recorded, two punches are required; if a special character is to be recorded, three punches may be required. The following are recorded in Figure 2-1: the numeral "7" in column 3; the letter "R" in column 10; and the special character "*" in column 50. The interpretation of the configuration of punches appears at the top of each column.

Another unit record of the same size (Figure 2-2) also may be used to store machine-readable information. Ninety columns of information may be recorded in this card by means of circular punches. As in Figure 2-1, the numeral "7," the letter "R," and the special character "*" are recorded in columns 3, 10, and 50, respectively.

2. The Keypunch is a specialist in recording information into Hollerith cards. The keypunch (Figure 2-3) has a typewriterlike keyboard (1) which is

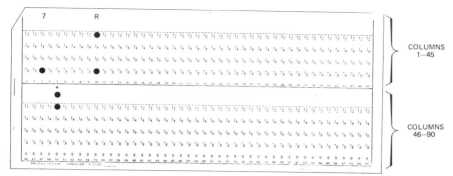

Figure 2-2

Figure 2-3

used for recording alphabetical, numerical, and special character information onto cards. Unpunched cards are inserted into the keypunch (2); they are fed automatically, column by column, past a punching head (3) which will make one, two, or three perforations in a particular column, depending on the letter of the alphabet, number, or special symbol that is to be represented.

Some keypunches are equipped to print automatically at the top of the card the letter, number, or symbol corresponding to the perforations in the body of the card.

When punching of a card has been completed, the card is automatically ejected and stored (4). Keypunches are available from various manufacturers. Although the resulting punches in the cards may be different in shape and positioning, the techniques for recording information are quite similar.

One of the advantages of cards, or unit records, is that errors in keypunching, once discovered, may be corrected by punching a new card accurately and inserting it in its proper location in a "deck" or file of cards.

Keypunches are also available for recording information on paper tape. The keyboard of such punches are also like typewriters. The resulting punches are recorded on a length of tape, rather than on a card unit record. Although procedures are indeed available for correcting mispunches on paper tape, there are some disadvantages in this procedure for some types of information-retrieval systems.

The Port-a-punch (Figure 2-4) is a hand-operated keypunch, which permits

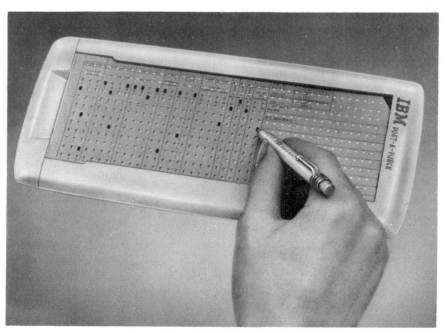

Figure 2-4

punches to be recorded into a Hollerith card using a stylus. This is a simple, inexpensive device for producing machine-readable cards when the amount of keypunching is very little.

3. The Verifier is a specialist in checking the accuracy of that which has been keypunched on a Hollerith card. The verifier has a typewriter keyboard just like that of the keypunch (Figure 2-3). Cards previously keypunched are inserted into the verifier and are fed automatically, column by column past a reading "head." If, when the key representing the numeral, letter, or special character that is supposed to be recorded in a given column is depressed and an error is detected, a notch is made directly over the column in which the error appears. Cards are notched on the right edge to indicate that they have been verified and are punched correctly.

4. The Reproducing Punch (Figure 2-5) is a specialist in preparing copies of Hollerith cards also in machine-readable form. This punch has two card-feed hoppers (1 and 2). The cards to be reproduced are placed in one hopper (1), and

Figure 2-5

blank cards are placed in the other (2). One unit of the machine reads the previously punched cards, while the other unit punches the blank cards that are to become copies of the original. During the reproducing operation, information punched in given columns of the original cards may be suppressed, so that only selected information is reproduced on the blank cards. The information may be punched in the same location as on the original card or it may be rearranged in any desired arrangement or sequence. The two decks of cards, after being processed, are stacked automatically (3 and 4).

5. The Interpreter (Figure 2-6) is a specialist in printing on the face of a card all or part of the information punched in that card. The machine accepts

Figure 2-6

punched cards in a hopper (1); one unit reads the desired information punched in given columns and another unit translates these punches into print which can be visually read.

6. The Accounting Machine (Figure 2-7) is a specialist in printing on a separate sheet all or selected parts of the information punched in cards. Cards

Figure 2-7

(1) are fed into the machine and are read by one unit, while another unit translates the punched information into print (2) which can be visually read. This machine can also summarize information contained in more than one card by adding or subtracting punched information and by printing the results in a report for visual reading.

7. The Sorter (Figure 2-8) is a specialist in arranging punched cards in an orderly sequence, either alphabetically or numerically. The cards to be sequenced are fed into a hopper (1), a selector control is set for a given column (2), and each card is distributed into one of thirteen receiving pockets. One of the more sophisticated sorters (the statistical machine) is able to sense all 80 columns at once, if necessary. In addition to the sequencing operation performed by the sorter, this machine can count cards, accumulate amounts punched in cards, edit the punched information (review, check, and approve a card before it is sorted or counted), and finally translate punched information into printed form for visual reading in a report.

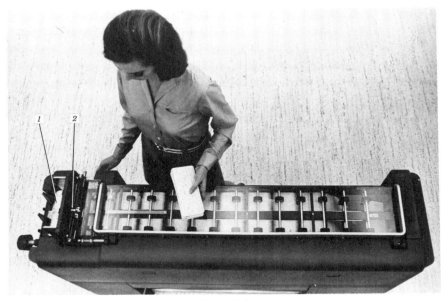

Figure 2-8

8. The Collator (Figure 2-9) is a specialist in comparing two sets of punched cards in order to merge them in a desired sequence (alphabetical or numerical). The two sets of cards are fed simultaneously from two hoppers (1 and 2), each holding one set of cards. One unit of the machine detects the punched information, while another unit matches the information punched in each of two cards. The machine can then merge the two files, or separate cards that do not match. There are four stackers (3 to 6) into which the cards may be separated, for example, into two groups of matched cards and two groups of unmatched cards. The collator may also be used merely to check sequence of cards (that is, to assure the accuracy of a sorting operation).

9. The Peek-A-Boo Card is a specialist in storing information in a form that permits further processing. This is a unit record that has been organized in such a way as to "dedicate" or reserve space for a given document number. Thus, a unit record may be organized in such a way as to reserve space for 100 document numbers, as shown in Figure 2-10. A given document number (e.g., 52) is recorded on the card by punching out the space dedicated or reserved for that number.

Each peek-a-boo card represents a given subject or index entry. Those document numbers in a file that are indexed for a given subject are punched out on the peek-a-boo card (also called an "optical stencil") for that subject.

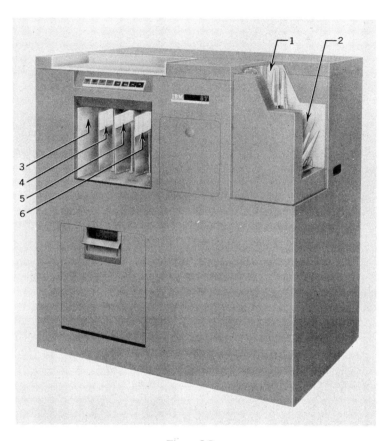

Figure 2-9

SUBJECT _____

1	2	3	4	5	6	7	8	9	10
11	12	13	14	15	16	17	18	19	20
21	22	23	24	25	26	27	28	29	30
31	32	33	34	35	36	37	38	39	40
41	42	43	44	45	46	47	48	49	50
51	●	53	54	55	56	57	58	59	60
61	62	63	64	65	66	67	68	69	70
71	72	73	74	75	76	77	78	79	80
81	82	83	84	85	86	87	88	89	90
91	92	93	94	95	96	97	98	99	100

Figure 2-10

Figure 2-11

39

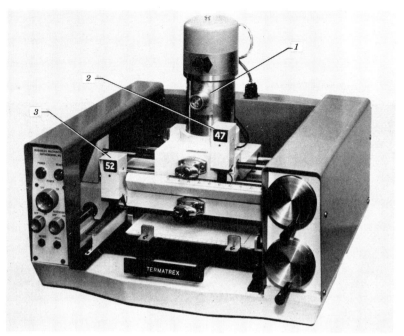

Figure 2-12

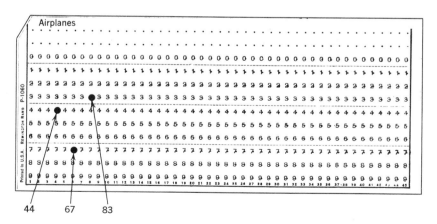

Figure 2-13

One commercial peek-a-boo card is the Termatrex card, which provides 10,000 dedicated spaces in a 100 by 100 matrix (Figure 2-11).

10. The Input Device for the Peek-A-Boo Card is a specialist in recording information on a card by drilling a hole in the reserved or dedicated space for a given document number. One such device, the Jonker 301 (Figure 2-12) may be positioned precisely over the space to be drilled. The drill (1) is actuated by push button. If more than one card is to be drilled in the same position, up to 25 superimposed cards can be drilled in one cycle. There is a visual display of the drill position number (2 and 3) for checking accuracy of recording. In the figure, the drill has been positioned over row *52* and column *47*.

Input may be accomplished in smaller systems by means of a hand punch. This punch has a pin that fits into a pinhole of a specially prepared card to assure that the hole punched out is in a precise position. Figure 2-13 illustrated a peek-a-boo card for one subject (*Airplanes*) to which applicable document numbers (44, 67, and 83) have been posted (recorded) by punching. (Note that the column number and position number determine the proper location of a particular document number. Thus, number "44" is recorded in column 4, position 4.)

11. The Peek-A-Boo Card Reader is a specialist in accurate visual identification of the position numbers of coinciding holes in superimposed cards. One such devise is the Jonker 52 reader (Figure 2-14), which accepts a number of Termatrex cards that have been previously punched. A light source in the base of the reader displays each coincident hole as a dot of light (1). A read-out scale (2) is provided, which permits ready identification of the coincident holes.

In smaller systems in which the holes are larger, the coinciding holes may be identified visually by merely aligning the relevant peek-a-boo cards and holding them up to any light source that is handy (e.g., an overhead light).

12. The Marginal Hole Punched Card is a specialist in recording information on a unit record (Figure 2-15). The card, as delivered by the manufacturers, has been drilled with one or more rows of holes around its periphery. Information is recorded by notching out one or more of the drilled holes (1).

13. The Groover is a specialist in notching marginal hole punched cards. The simplest such device is a hand punch (Figure 2-16) which is aligned over the hole to be notched, and clamped down to remove the cardboard above the drilled hole (Figure 2-15). Mechanical groovers are available which notch punch a large number of marginal-hole punched cards in one operation (Figure 2-17).

14. The Sorting Needle is a specialist in searching marginal-hole punched cards. The needle is inserted into a deck of cards at the position dedicated to a

Figure 2-14

Figure 2-15

Figure 2-16

Figure 2-17

Figure 2-18

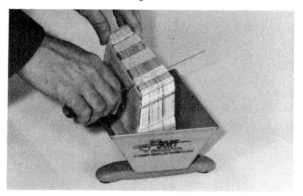

Figure 2-19

desired subject (Figure 2-18). It is twisted to one side in preparation for a fanning operation (Figure 2-19). The deck of cards to be searched is grasped firmly at the left as the sorting needle is twisted back to a position at right angles to the card face, thus forcing the cards to fan out (Figure 2-20). The sorting needle is then lifted (Figure 2-21*a*). This causes separation of the notched cards from the unnotched cards (Figure 2-21*b*). Thus, the cards left hanging on the sorting needle are unnotched and therefore do not contain the desired information, while the cards left behind are notched and represent the "answers" to the question posed.

15. The Flexowriter is a specialist in recording information into paper tape and printed onto a paper record. The punched tape is then readable by the Flexowriter and other machines (including some computers) permitting the information to be printed for human reading or used for further machine processing.

Figure 2-20

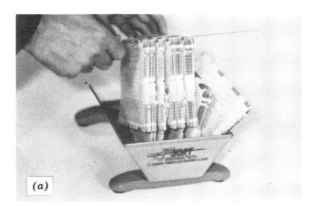

Figure 2-21a

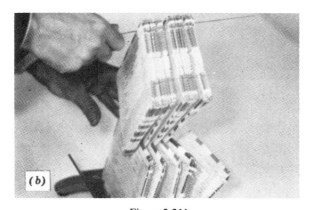

Figure 2-21b

45

Figure 2-22

A paper perforator operates from a typewriterlike keyboard (Figure 2-22). The depression of a key (1), which represents an alphabetical, numerical, or special character, perforates the tape (2) and advances the tape one space to be ready for the next keystroke.

16. Paper Tape is a specialist in storing machine-readable information. Depending on the type of equipment that is to be used to read the tape, configurations of holes (codes) may be stored in combinations of 5, 6, 7, or 8 holes perforated for a given number or letter of the alphabet. Examples of punched paper tape are given in Figure 2-23:

    a. 5-channel (5-hole combinations)
    b. 6-channel (6-hole combinations)
    c. 7-channel (7-hole combinations)
    d. 8-channel (8-hole combinations)

Small holes running through the center of each tape engage sprockets, which are used to advance the tape through the machine; they are not machine-readable and, therefore, are not counted as an extra "channel."

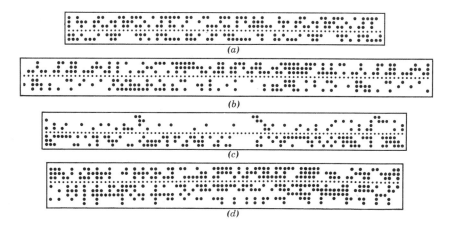

Figure 2-23

17. Magnetic Tape (Figure 2-24) is a specialist in storing information in computer-processible form. As with punched paper tape, information may be recorded in a number of ways, through keyboard action, or through card-to-tape, or paper tape-to-magnetic tape conversion. Information is recorded in binary form, that is, a given location is either magnetized or not. The description

Figure 2-24

of the state of magnetization of a given location on tape is generally represented by the number "1" to indicate magnetization, "0" for nonmagnetization.

18. The Digital Computer is a specialist in performing arithmetic tasks. In order that these tasks may be performed, the outside world must be able to communicate with the computer. Information and instructions communicated to the computer must be stored and moved about during processing. Finally, results of the computation must be communicated back to the world. The basic functional units of a computer are the following:

a. Input
b. Storage
c. Control
d. Arithmetic
e. Output

a. *Input.* This unit accepts information in the form of, for example, cards, punched tape, and magnetic tape. A typewriterlike keyboard may also be used to enter information directly into the computer. Some computers can accept printed information when equipped with suitable optical character recognition input units.

b. *Storage.* This unit, called memory, accepts data that arrive from the input unit, and instructions or commands that originate from a program, which specify the computing procedure. Data and instructions may be stored internally (magnetically polarized elements) or externally (punched cards, punched paper tape, and magnetic tape or other magnetically polarized elements).

c. *Control.* This unit accepts coded instructions from the computer program, decodes the instructions and sets up the computer circuitry in such a way that the operation called for may be carried out, or executed.

d. *Arithmetic.* This unit accepts data from the input unit or from the storage unit and, based on the instructions received via the control unit, executes the required computation.

e. *Output.* This unit displays the results of computation in such a way that a human can read them. The most common display is print on paper, which provides a permanent record for future reference. Another display, but more temporary, is a result shown on the face of a cathode ray tube. Alternatively, if the results are not of immediate interest, or if they are to be used in connection with further computation, they are stored (e.g., in magnetic form), ready for later printing or processing.

Information is stored magnetically in computers, and is generally represented in the form of binary numbers.

Computer programs are written in terms of a set of instructions that are general, in the sense that:

a. An operation is specified (e.g., addition).

b. The locations in storage (addresses) of the numbers involved in the operation are specified (e.g., whatever number is stored in location A is to be added to whatever number is stored in location B).

c. The next operation to be performed (e.g., printing the result of the addition) is specified.

There are four types of instructions that may be given in a program:

a. *Input and output.* Read information from one medium and store it somewhere, or transfer information from a location in the memory to an external medium.

b. *Arithmetic.* Perform a processing function, such as addition or subtraction.

c. *Internal.* Move or change information within the computer.

d. *Control.* Specify the performance of an instruction and the sequence in which a set of instructions are to be performed, relating to:

1. Input of instructions and data.
2. Performance of a given processing function on the data stored in given locations.
3. Transference of the result of the process in another given location.
4. Performance of another given processing function on the result stored in that location using data stored in still another location.
5. Output of the result in a form specified in a given instruction which is stored in a given location.
6. Stopping the computer.

The instructions given in a program are said to be "logical," in that two-way decisions are always involved, with a choice specified between two alternatives, depending on the outcome of a procedure made in the previous step.

An example might be related to a simple arithmetic function of addition, where the sum of numbers stored in two locations might be specified as a limit, with one instruction to be performed if the sum does not exceed that limit and another if it does exceed the limit.

If every machine function is covered in a program, it is said to be written in a low-level language and can be executed directly on the given computer for which the program was written. A high-level language, is written in such a way that it needs to be translated into the low-level language of a given computer before it can be executed. Fortran is such a high-level language; a program can be written in that language regardless of the computer to be used. However, there needs to be available for that computer a program into the low-level language peculiar to that computer. This translating program, called a compiler, is generally kept available to computer users, so that the instructions of the fortran program may be readily executed upon translation.

19. Film records are also specialists in storing information, either in binary form or as images. If in binary form, the individual unit of information is represented by a transparent or opaque spot on the film. If in image form an entire page of printed information may be recorded on film in reduced size. Examples of the latter form are as follows:

a. *Continuous film (microfilm).* A medium for storing document images at various reduction ratios on reels of film. Index codes relating to content may or may not be recorded, depending on the viewing equipment that is to be used.

b. *Unit record film.*

1. *Filmorex.* A film "chip," 2⅜ by 1⅜ inches, divided into two equal areas. One area holds microimages of up to two pages of text. The other area holds codes for subject headings relevant to the text. Each code is recorded in one of 16 rows on the card, and consists of a pattern of opaque and clear spots.

2. *Minicard.* A film "chip," ⅝ by 1¼ inches, on which can be recorded codes as opaque and clear spots, as well as microimages of some 12 pages of text.

3. *Microfiche.* A film unit record which holds microimages of text. One standard size is 105 by 148 millimeters (about 4 by 6 inches), containing images of up to 60 individual pages.

4. *PCMI* (the *p*olychromic *m*icro*i*mage). A trademark of National Cash Register Co. This is a film unit record that contains images of text reduced 150 times. A 4 by 6 inch record would contain 3200 pages.

c. *Mixed media.* Film is used together with tabulating cards (Figure 2-25)

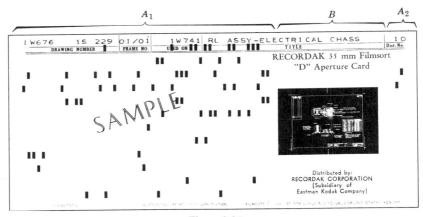

Figure 2-25

or marginal-hole punched cards (Figure 2-26) for storing text images along with searchable index information. In Figure 2-25, the card has been partially punched (A_1 and A_2), leaving an area (B) reserved for the insertion of a microimage. Similarly, in Figure 2-26, information may be recorded in full size (1, 2, and 3 in Figure 2-26a) or in microfilm inserts (4 and 5 in Figure 2-26b).

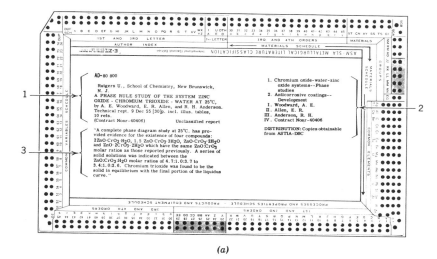

(a)

Figure 2-26a

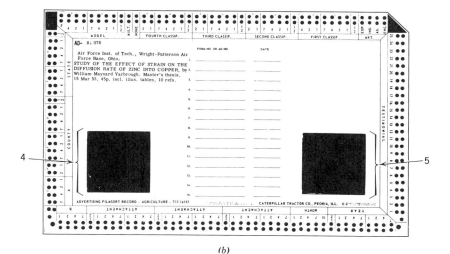

(b)

Figure 2-26b

Equipment is available for searching information recorded on film. Some examples are as follows:

a. *Filmorex (Figure 2-27).* This is a sorter of film chips (*A*) that separates those that contain desired codes.

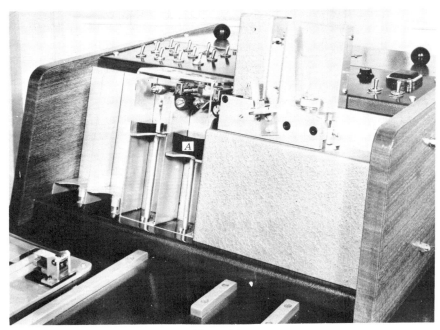

Figure 2-27

b. *Minicard.* This machine selects and sorts film records. The desired code(s) is scanned photoelectrically and is compared with data stored in memory. On the basis of this "compare" function, the film records are classified and relayed automatically to a given repository.

c. *Miracode* (*M*icrofilm *I*nformation *R*etrieval *A*ccess *Code*—Eastman Kodak Company). The basic unit is a 4 by 4 by 1 inch magazine consisting of 100 feet of 16 millimeter microfilm on which are recorded two types of images: reproducible images of documents; and, adjacent to each, an identifying code pattern. Questions are keyed into the console of the equipment, causing the film magazine to be scanned for the appropriate code pattern(s) relating to the question.

The appropriate document is displayed on a reader screen.

Equipment is also available for locating images recorded on film, as follows:

a. *SD 500.* A high-speed microimage storage and retrieval system that provides access to any one of many pages of stored information. The S/D-500 System consists of a microimage repository that can store intermixed micro-images of many sizes and formats, a remote television-style display terminal (Figure 2-28) connected by closed-circuit television to the repository and a 10-button keyboard control. The S/D-500 Data Storage and Retrieval System was developed as a result of a joint venture by Sanders Associates, Inc. of Nashua, N.H., and Diebold, Inc. of Canton, Ohio.

Figure 2-28

b. *HF Image Systems.* This is also a high-speed microimage storage and retrieval system, produced by H. F. Image Systems, Inc.

c. *COM* (computer output on microfilm). This equipment accepts information from magnetic tape, generates alphanumeric text, and records the information on microfilm.

d. *Microcite (Figure 2-29).* A matrix film on which is photographed, with suitable reduction, and recorded a microimage of an abstract or other text. Each

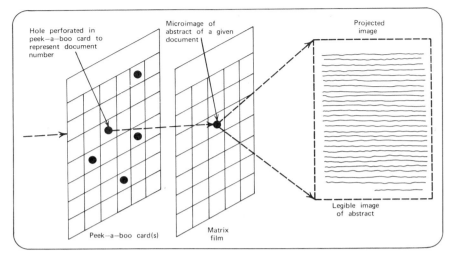

Figure 2-29

of these microimages is located on matrix film in the position dedicated to the corresponding document on a punched peek-a-boo card. This permits some portion of the original source material to be recorded in microform.

e. *Microfilm readers.* A wide variety of readers (and printers) are available from many manufacturers for the viewing (and printing) of text stored on microfilm. The threading of film to load the reader may be performed manually or automatically (when the film is stored in appropriate cassettes). The location of wanted images may be facilitated by various coding techniques.

20. Video Systems are specialists in recording images on magnetic tape in reduced size, analogous to what is done with film. An example of such a system is the Ampex Videofile. The electronic image of the document is recorded on television magnetic recording tape, along with an address designation. When the address of the document is entered into an appropriate keyboard, the reel of magnetic tape is searched until the desired image is located electronically. A duplicate of the desired image is transferred to another tape, which is used to display the text on a high-resolution television screen.

21. Terminal Digit Posting is a technique for recording document numbers in such a way as to facilitate their rapid location. A unit record, for example, a card, is reserved for each index entry to be used in a file. The card is arranged as shown in Figure 2-30. The serial numbers of documents indexed under a given entry are recorded in the appropriate columns of the card, depending on the last or terminal digit of the serial number. Thus, serial number 83 is recorded in column 3, while 206 is recorded in column 6. When a search is

INDEX ENTRY									
0	1	2	3	4	5	6	7	8	9
			83			206			

Figure 2-30

to be conducted for all documents indexed under three given entries, the appropriate cards are selected and the serial numbers are compared, column by column, to determine visually which are posted in common on all three cards (Figure 2-31). Thus document numbers *291, 2502, 104,* and *888* are found on each of the three cards.

GLASS

1	2	3	4	5	6	7	8	9	0
1	482	13	4	45	26	77	98	139	100
31	492	113	*104*	135	126	987	218	339	860
121	502	133	294	595	196	997	598	1799	870
281	922	473	654	605	356	1477	618	1819	1250
291	1132	983	664	655	426	1927	628	1919	1930
1111	1502	1013	934	2005	906	2227	868	2239	2000
1981	1902		954	2445	996		*888*	2659	
2501	2002		2004		1296		1208		
	2502				1506		1268		
					2716		1728		
							2008		

TEXTILES

1	2	3	4	5	6	7	8	9	0
11	12	43	94	5	636	47	28	99	40
121	492	93	*104*	165	826	87	458	569	320
291	522	863	1264	795	1656	367	848	1219	910
381	1802	1223	1654	1405	1666	1917	*888*	1449	1240
711	*2502*	2313	2354		1676		1218	1499	1770
1531					1906		2498	1769	2200
1781					2516			2729	
2701									

PROCESS

1	2	3	4	5	6	7	8	9	0
11	12	13	4	15	26	17	28	99	40
91	132	93	*104*	45	126	87	218	239	100
131	482	133	1264	795	356	97	848	569	910
161	632	473	2004	1405	426	997	868	1219	1010
211	792	863		2005	636	1367	878	1799	1250
231	882	1013		2445	826	2007	*888*	1919	1930
291	1512				1506		1818	2239	2200
951	2112				1906		2008	2729	2520
1221	*2502*				2516		2498		
1961	2622								
2001									

Figure 2-31

BIBLIOGRAPHY

1. R. R. Arnold, H. C. Hill, and A. V. Nichols, *Modern Data Processing*, John Wiley & Sons, Inc., New York, 1969.
2. C. P. Bourne, *Methods of Information Handling*, John Wiley & Sons, Inc., New York, 1963.

Three

Mechanization of Input Unit Operations

Let us now consider, more specifically, how some of the various physical tools may be applied in connection with the input unit operations of information retrieval.

I. ACQUISITION

Acquisition involves the location, selection, ordering, and receipt of source materials for a collection. The process consists of a number of tasks, such as:

1. Determination of current and probable future requirements of potential users of an information-retrieval system.

2. Formulation of a policy for acceptance of source materials as may be defined by subject coverage, publication type, source, or other criteria.

3. Comparison of available or incoming source materials with policy to determine which shall be included in the information-retrieval system.

4. Establishment of procedures to ensure that identified materials are ordered and received.

The application of data-processing equipment with regard to this unit operation has tended to emphasize the acquisition and accessioning of books in libraries, rather than documents and periodical articles in information centers.

57

One of the most convenient times to start applying data-processing equipment is when a particular item is selected for addition to a collection. Information relating to that item may be recorded on a unit record by keypunching information such as the following in specified areas of a tabulating card.

1. Author
2. Short title
3. Publisher code
4. Date
5. Edition
6. Volume
7. Price
8. Accession number
9. Jobber code
10. Copy marker

This record (Figure 3-1) may be sorted into any desired arrangement and collated with other information to automatically produce such items as:

1. Purchase order
2. Check and voucher
3. On-order list
4. New book list
5. Pocket label
6. Book card
7. Spine label
8. Expenditure records
9. Encumbrance records

In addition, the record may be used in searching to determine whether the book selected for possible acquisition is already in the collection.

Once an item has been acquired in a library, a new unit record may be generated, transcribing automatically, if desired, some of the information that was recorded in a unit record at the time of acquisition (using a reproducing punch). The type of information so recorded may include items such as call number, descriptive and subject catalog entries, that is, the same type of information that is available on the traditional catalog cards of a library. The unit records so prepared can be used to produce catalog cards mechanically. The same unit record can then be retained so that book catalogs may be prepared automatically and updated periodically.

Some additional items that may be produced quickly and economically include:

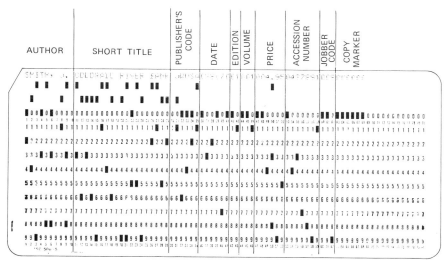

Figure 3-1

1. Shelf list.
2. Specialized bibliographies and listings, arranged by author, subject, language, form of publication, country of origin, or location in a library system, time of publication, time of acquisition.

When a machine-processible record has been prepared for each item in a collection, it is possible to contemplate the mechanization of many of the aspects of controlling the whereabouts of a collection. A necessary step, of course, is to create a machine-processible unit record for each transaction involving the movement or loan of an item in the library collection. This unit record should be generated, to the maximum extent possible, using already available machine-processible records. Thus a loan transaction involves a book and a borrower. If a unit record in machine-processible form exists which uniquely describes each book and each borrower, then these can be brought together on one unit transaction record, with only the additional information on time of transaction to be added.

Once this record has been created, it is possible to prepare mechanically lists, reports, and information as follows:

1. Overdue list and notices
2. Fine list and notices
3. Book inventory reports
4. Use studies (of books and users)
5. Replacement and weeding reports

Serials control represents a difficult problem in a library, because of volume, bibliographic instability, and user requirements.

The application of data-processing equipment to serials control has been effective in a number of libraries. One way in which a mechanized system may be developed is to center the procedures about an "arrival card," which is punched in anticipation of the arrival of issues of a serial. The cards contain, at a minimum, the following information:

1. Title
2. Destination
3. Volume and number of expected issue
4. Call (or other identifying) number

When issues of serials arrive, the appropriate arrival cards may be pulled, permitting the automatic printing of such information as destination packing lists, cumulative catalog of active serials, and binding instructions (using, for example, an accounting machine). The arrival cards not pulled may be used to produce, automatically, claims requests and "want lists."

II. ANALYSIS

Analysis involves the perusal of source materials and the selection of analytics that are considered to be of sufficient probable importance to warrant the effort of rendering them searchable in an information-retrieval system.

Graphic records are analyzed in order to produce indexes, classifications, abstracts, or other "raw materials" for an information-retrieval system. In general, analysis is performed by trained human personnel who have developed insight into both the subject matter of the graphic records and the needs of the clientele expected to make use of the analysis. Since machines have not yet been developed that can *economically* read the great variety of texts of graphic records and since computers have not yet been programmed to interpret their contents effectively in a way that is analogous to human interpretation, it may be anticipated that the use of machines for analysis of whole texts in large-scale retrieval systems will be limited for some period into the future.

Since, however, certain routine analytical operations can be programmed on a computer, it is foreseeable that these machine functions may become feasible if such limited analysis can be justified by its sufficiency and cost.

Two approaches to machine analysis are now being used or investigated:

1. The "permuted" index (variously called "Key-Word-in-Context," KWIC key-word index, or title index).
2. The "auto-abstract."

Techniques derived from these two approaches are discussed in Chapter Five. For consideration in the present chapter, the physical tools used in analysis may be grouped as follows:

1. Means for converting titles or text into machine-readable form. At the present stage of equipment development, it is necessary to use a key punch for this conversion.

2. Means for permuting a title to generate a "word index," or to determine the frequency of occurrence of key words in the text, so that sentences containing the greatest content of these words are selected for the "auto-abstract." A digital computer is generally used for these purposes.

III. VOCABULARY CONTROL

Vocabulary control involves the establishment of relationships among analytics, often on an arbitrary basis, but most usually based on the prediction of those relationships that may facilitate identification of all source materials in a system relating to a given subject regardless of how the source materials have been indexed.

Whenever the analysis of a graphic record has been completed, the results are recorded as a part of an index, a catalog, a classification system, or a coding system for a mechanized retrieval system. However, the words selected to express the results of the analysis are seldom recorded in their "raw" form. In indexes and catalogs designed for a retrieval system, it is advantageous to impose constraints on the vocabulary used. This may be done by employing a subject authority list or a coding system, which helps to delimit the scope of permissible use of each retrievable entry. When a classification system is used, the meaning of entries selected from documents is delimited by recording for search the appropriate classification headings.

In most "manual" retrieval systems, and in many mechanized systems, the selection of appropriate subject headings or classification headings is made by the analyst of the graphic record. However, the authority list or classification system may be so complex that analysts must take an inordinate length of time to consult listings and to choose appropriate headings. Also, it becomes increasingly difficult for analysts to maintain consistency in their choice of headings. It then becomes advantageous to consider using mechanical aids for all or part of this control of vocabulary.

Let us consider an example of how this process works when mechanical aids are not used.

The designer of an information-retrieval or library system may decide that the term "philatelist" is an acceptable "standard" heading that would represent the most likely term to which a user of the system might refer if interested in obtaining information on that subject. However, the system designer could recognize that the term "stamp collector," which is generally considered to be synonymous with "philatelist," might be selected by an analyst as an appropriate subject heading when indexing a particular document whose author used the term "stamp collector" in his text.

In order to control the usage of the two alternative terms, the system designer might have a heading in a standard authority list, as follows:

Stamp Collector, see (or *use*) Philatelist

implying that "stamp collector" should not be used as a heading, and that the appropriate heading to use is "philatelist." Also, there would be provided an entry in appropriate alphabetical position, as follows:

Philatelist

implying that "philatelist" is indeed a "standard" heading.

Conventional library and information-retrieval practice would require the analyst to refer to the standard subject heading list whenever a term is selected on examination of a source material. Thus the analyst choosing "stamp collector" would record "philatelist" after following normal procedures.

In order to mechanize the control of vocabulary, it is necessary to collect a "dictionary" of words or phrases that are likely to be selected by analysts, together with accepted or standard headings for the terms. This information may be recorded on punched cards by means of a keypunch. Then, the words or phrases actually selected in the process of analysis may also be keypunched onto similar cards, called detail cards.

After the detail cards are punched, they are compared mechanically with the file of dictionary cards in order to match each term with the authorized word or phrase. This comparison may be performed with a collator. The appropriate, accepted heading may then be transferred to the detail card, using a reproducer. The set of detail cards is now ready for the next appropriate processing step of the particular retrieval system.

As an example, let us assume that for a given retrieval system the decision had been reached that the two terms *philatelist* and *stamp collector* are synonymous and that all documents indexed under either should be indexed under the "standard" heading "philatelist." This decision would involve the preparation of two dictionary cards (Figure 3-2). The asterisk following the term means that it is a standard term (Figure 3-2*a*); the absence of an asterisk following the term means that it is not a "legal" term, and that another term is to be used instead (Figure 3-2*b*).

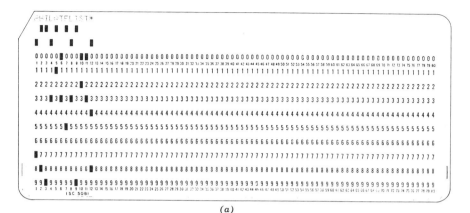

(a)

Figure 3-2a

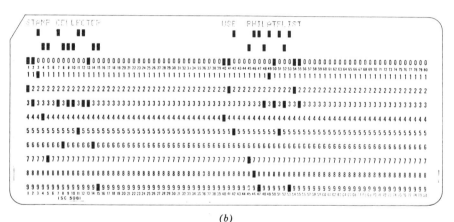

(b)

Figure 3-2b

Let us further assume that two documents (1 and 2) are indexed for this file, one under *philatelist* and the other under *stamp collector*. This would be recorded in machine-processible form by the preparation of two detail cards (Figure 3-3). It will be noted that an asterisk has been recorded in each detail card immediately following the index terms. The reason will become obvious in a moment.

The detail cards (Figure 3-3) may now be compared with the dictionary cards (Figure 3-2) by means of a collator. The program board of the collator may be wired appropriately so that cards are compared in certain columns, in this case, columns 1 to 20. Thus when the detail card for document 1 is

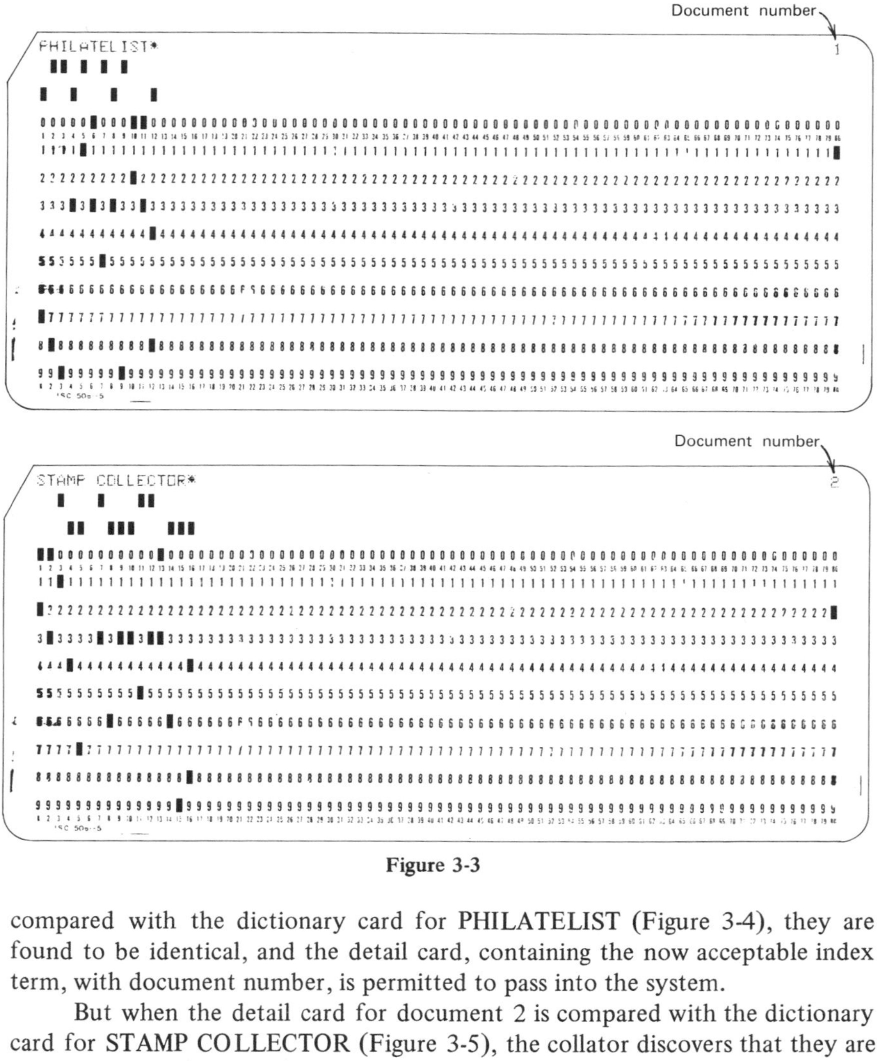

Figure 3-3

compared with the dictionary card for PHILATELIST (Figure 3-4), they are found to be identical, and the detail card, containing the now acceptable index term, with document number, is permitted to pass into the system.

But when the detail card for document 2 is compared with the dictionary card for STAMP COLLECTOR (Figure 3-5), the collator discovers that they are different. It is the asterisk following the term that makes the difference.

The final step is taken when a card reproducer is used to create a new detail card, which picks up the legal term PHILATELIST from the dictionary card and the document number from the original detail card (Figure 3-6).

If a term is not found anywhere in the dictionary (neither as a standard nor as a nonstandard term), the detail cards for which no match at all was found by the collator are given to a subject specialist who must decide whether the new

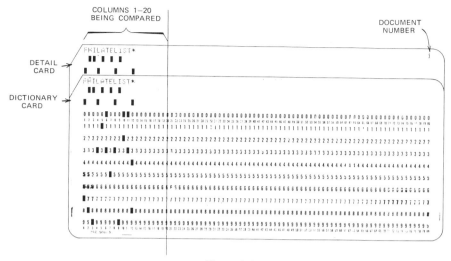

Figure 3-4

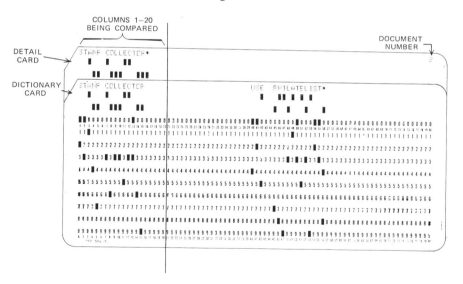

Figure 3-5

term should be a standard one, or whether an existing standard term should be used in its stead. In any case, an appropriate dictionary card is prepared and filed with the others, so that the decision made is available for the future.

It is perhaps obvious that the application of the data-processing equipment

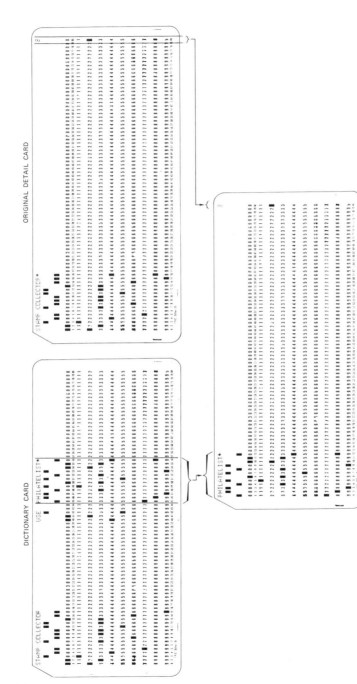

Figure 3-6

66

described above is not practical for the checking of a subject authority list with reference to one heading or one document, but rather that batches of some size must be available before such an approach should be even considered.

Also, all of the processing steps described above, which involve the use of several pieces of equipment, could be accomplished with a computer program.

IV. RECORDING RESULTS OF ANALYSIS IN A SEARCHABLE MEDIUM

A. Introduction

After standardization of vocabulary, the next step in the processing of a graphic record is to record the results of analysis onto some medium that can later be searched. For a cataloging operation, this record is usually a 3 by 5-inch card on which a subject, corporate, or other entry is displayed as a heading, and which serves as one means of identifying the original document. Analogs of the 3 by 5-inch card in the various mechanized systems as well as the tools used for recording information and for manipulation during a search are described below.

Two systems for recording the results of analysis have been described in the literature: *document* and *aspect* systems. The *document system* (sometimes called *item entry system*) presumes that a discrete record—e.g., a marginal-hole punched card, a machine-sortable punched card, a piece of film, a length of tape—represents a single document and contains, in searchable form, all the results of analysis of a single document. The aspect system (sometimes called *inverted* or *term entry system*) assumes that a discrete record represents a single subject (or aspect) and contains, in searchable form, information as to which documents in a file have this subject in common.

Let us return to the information-retrieval problem discussed at the end of Chapter 1 to illustrate the two types of systems. The problem is related to the selection of receptionists, based on an index to applications given in Figure 1-1. A simple *document* system, employing a marginal-hole punched card, would involve the use of a discrete record for each applicant and a recording of all of the characteristics of a given applicant, through notching of the appropriate holes, on that record (Figure 3-7). Thus, the characteristics of applicant number 5, Diane Carter, are recorded as: under 20 years of age, good appearance, junior high school education, 3-5 years of work experience, poor dictation ability, poor typing ability, single, and brunette. Alternatively, the same characteristics may be recorded on a tabulating card (Figure 3-8). In both of these examples, a discrete record is reserved for each "document" (i.e., applicant), and all of the index entries (i.e., applicant characteristics) are recorded on that record.

A simple aspect system would involve the use of a discrete record for each characteristic and all the applicant numbers would be recorded on that record.

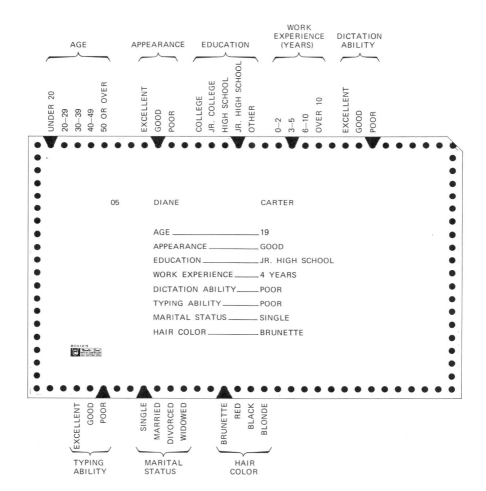

Figure 3-7

68

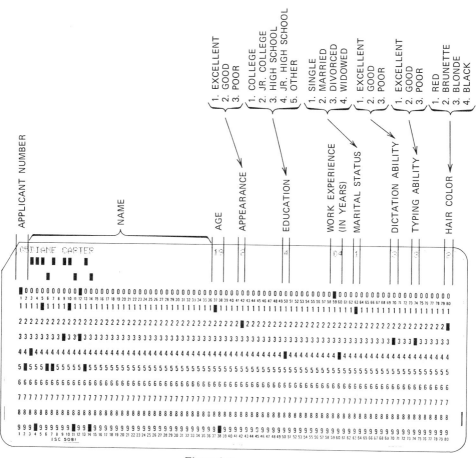

Figure 3-8

One type of aspect card, most closely associated with the Uniterm retrieval system, is shown in Figure 3-9, in which all applicant numbers for brunettes are recorded. Another type of aspect card, the "peek-a-boo" type, involves the

BRUNETTE									
0	1	2	3	4	5	6	7	8	9
10	21	82	13	4	5	26	7	18	9
20	51		23	14	35	66	27	38	29
40	71		33	34	45	76	47	68	49
50	91			54	55	86	57	78	
60				64	85	96		88	
				74	95			98	

Figure 3-9

punching out of the portion of the card reserved (or "dedicated") for that number. In Figure 3-10, an aspect card for BRUNETTE has been punched for each of the numbers of the applicants who claimed to be brunettes. Thus, the fifth punch down in the first column at the left (reserved for applicant numbers 0-9) again represents our would-be receptionist, Diane Carter (number 5).

One way of visualizing the differences between the document and aspect systems in terms of common experience is to consider the following analogies.

In conventional library practice, there is a main entry catalog card prepared for each source material processed. This card contains all the "tracings" (or entries) under which the same source material is filed in the catalog. In a way, then, this main entry card may be considered analogous to a unit record in a document system.

In conventional indexing practice, index entries are listed in alphabetical array, each entry followed by a series of page references that indicate where references to the entry may be found. In a way, then, each index entry with

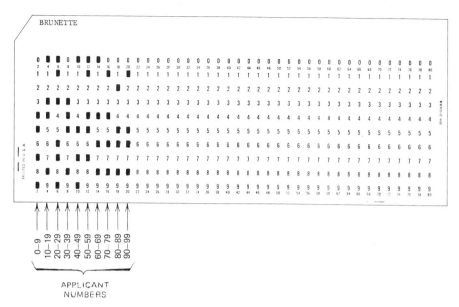

Figure 3-10

appropriate page references may be considered analogous to a unit "record" in an aspect (or inverted) system.

The differences between *document* and *aspect* systems were quite clear as long as only single, discrete records were used to record all characteristics relating to a document (for a document system) and all document numbers relating to a characteristic (for an aspect system). However, application of the principles involved, but using other tools, has led to modifications of the following types.

1. *Use of Hollerith card files for aspect systems.* In order to permit the use of card sorters for searching, the information recorded on discrete records in aspect systems may be ecorded in sets of cards, each set representing a characteristic, and each card in the set representing a document number. Two such sets of cards are illustrated in Figure 3-11, one representing the aspect "brunette," and the other representing the aspect "single." If a search were to be conducted for all *single brunette* applicants, the card set for each characteristic would be withdrawn from the file and sorted into document number sequence (see Figure 3-12). Visual inspection of the cards when fanned out, would make it easy to identify which document numbers are common to both characteristics (i.e., applicant numbers 40 and 47).

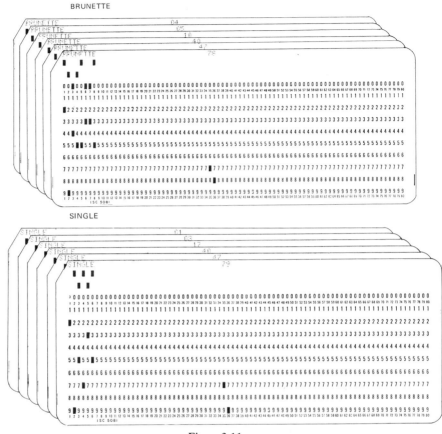

Figure 3-11

2. *Use of magnetic tapes for aspect systems.* In order to permit the use of digital computers for searching, the information recorded on discrete records in aspect systems may be recorded on magnetic tapes, each tape representing a characteristic, and all appropriate document numbers recorded[1] on that tape (Figure 3-13). A program could then be written which would compare the numbers recorded on each tape in order to identify those that are common to the characteristics involved in the search (applicant numbers 40 and 47).

But using a separate magnetic tape for each characteristic is wasteful, and therefore the discrete record principle has generally been diluted by recording on a single tape the characteristic and relevant document numbers, one following

---

[1] Information is stored magnetically and is generally represented in the form of binary numbers. Nevertheless, for purposes of exposition, information will be represented in terms of natural language and decimal, Arabic numbers.

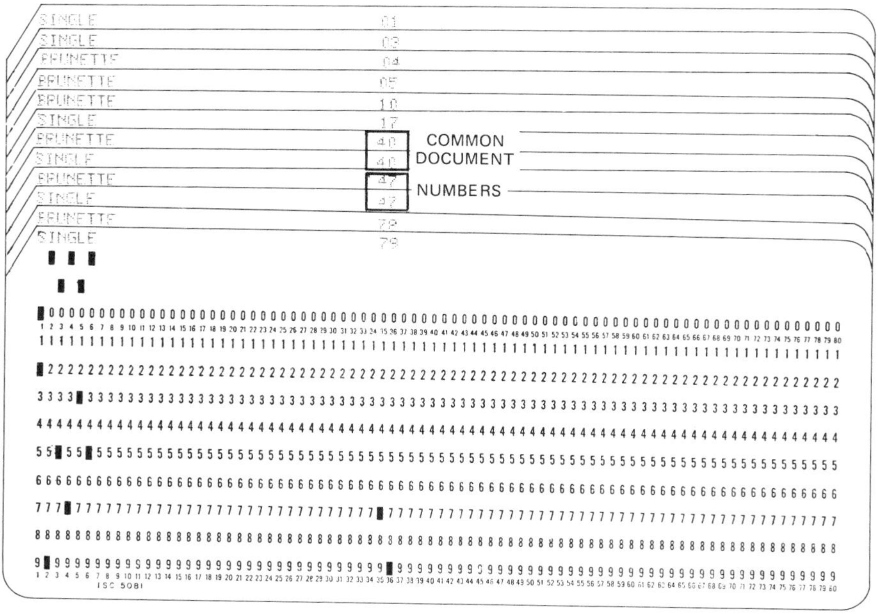

Figure 3-12

the other, as shown in Figure 3-14. Here, a program may be written first to identify the characteristics that are to be searched, and then to compare the numbers that follow.

An analogous principle may be used when discs or other mass storage devices are available with the digital computer.

3. Use of magnetic tapes for document systems. In order to permit the use of digital computers for searching, the information recorded on discrete records in document systems may be recorded on magnetic tapes, as shown in Figure 3-15. Here, the applicant number is recorded first, followed by all of the characteristics of that applicant; then the next applicant number is recorded, followed by all of her characteristics; and so on. A program may then be written which would involve a search of the entire tape in order to identify those applicants who have the desired characteristics.

B. Other Media for Recording Results of Analysis

There are many other media that may be used for storing the results of analysis, including punched paper tape, film records, and magnetic drums. It is beyond the scope of this textbook to provide details regarding these media; it should be noted, however, that the principles involved are analogous to those already discussed.

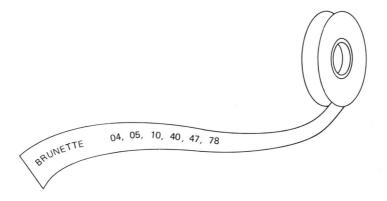

BRUNETTE   04, 05, 10, 40, 47, 78

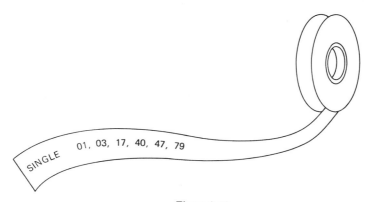

SINGLE   01, 03, 17, 40, 47, 79

Figure 3-13

74

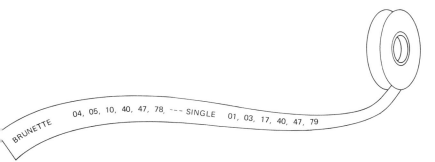

Figure 3-14

Figure 3-15

V. STORAGE OF SOURCE DOCUMENTS, EXTRACTS, ABSTRACTS, AND BIBLIOGRAPHIC REFERENCES

A. Introduction

The analysis of a graphic record has now (hypothetically) been completed, and the results of this analysis have been recorded on a medium that is suitable for subsequent searching. It is still necessary to provide a means for delivering on demand more information about the record than is conveyed by the "index" to its contents. The user of graphic records usually expects one or more of the following items as the product of a literature search:

1. The original record
2. A copy of the original record
3. A suitable extract from the record
4. An abstract of the contents of the record
5. A bibliographic reference to the record

This material may be stored either on the same medium as the index to it, or on another medium. The decision as to choice of storage medium is made on the basis of the convenience of delivering and using the copies, and the cost of storing and delivering copies. If the record is not stored together with the index to it, then a common serial number is used to relate the two in their respective storage media.

Obviously, the decision to store source documents on the same medium as the index to it can be made only when a document system is being used. The aspect system, providing only space for recording document numbers on a card or other medium, leaves no convenient, economical opportunity for storage of even a part of the source material.

B. Marginal Hole Punched Cards

These cards are often used to record bibliographic references, extracts of data, or abstracts, or any combination of these, as products of a search. The information may be recorded in directly readable form (Figure 2-26*a*) or in microform (Figure 2-26*b*).

Such information may be recorded for direct reading (Figure 2-26*a*) as:

1. Bibliographic reference to the source document
2. Analytics (e.g., catalog headings)
3. Abstract of the source document

When a microform insert is used (Figure 2-26*b*), one or more pages of the source document (4 and 5) may be stored.

Obviously, there are a variety of methods available for recording information on the face of such a card (e.g., handwriting, typewriting). Often, there is a desire to create a replica of a file of cards for one purpose or another. Generally some process such as photography or electrostatic printing is considered for such a purpose. However, it is sometimes forgotten that merely replicating the image of the card does not replicate any notches that have been physically made to record index entries. Indeed, the image of the notch can be replicated, but of course, the sorting for index entries requires that the notch be physically present.

C. Aspect Cards

These cards, because of their basic design as an "index" searching tool, are not used for storage of documents, abstracts, or even bibliographic references.[2]

Only document numbers are "stored" (e.g., as holes in cards). Therefore, documents associated with an aspect system of searching are numbered appropriately, and are stored, separate from the index, often in accession number order.

D. Tabulating-Type Punched Cards

This type of card can be used for the storage of information in four basic ways.

1. Recording by Perforation. First, alphabetic and numeric characters can be recorded by perforation of the card according to a set pattern in a form that is readily reproducible by machine. With the Hollerith-type card, 80 columns are available, and with the Remington Rand card, 90 "columns" are available for the recording of symbols. Thus, any or all of the following information about a document can be recorded on one or more such cards:

   a. Accession number
   b. Author's name
   c. Title
   d. Source (name of journal, issuing agency etc.)
   e. Other bibliographic information (volume of journal, year of issue, page references, etc.)
   f. An abstract
   g. The complete text of the document

Information once recorded in this way may be reproduced or may be printed without further human transcription effort. However, there is obviously a severe limit to the amount of reproducible and printable information that can be recorded on an 80- or 90-column card. (See Figure 3-16.)

In Figure 3-16*a*, a bibliographic citation has been recorded, with author names in columns 1-22, journals in columns 24-45, volume numbers on columns

---

[2] However, one proposal has been made by personnel at the Office of Basic Instrumentation at the National Bureau of Standards, in connection with the peek-a-boo system.

In this system, there is associated with the peek-a-boo search cards a matrix film (Microcite) on which is photographed, with suitable reduction, and recorded a microimage of an abstract or a bibliographic citation. Each of these microimages is located on matrix film in the position dedicated to the corresponding document on the punched aspect cards. This permits some portion of the original source material to be recorded in microform, in a sense, as part of the aspect card. (See Figure 2-29.)

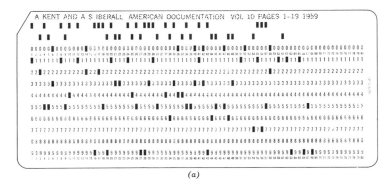

(a)

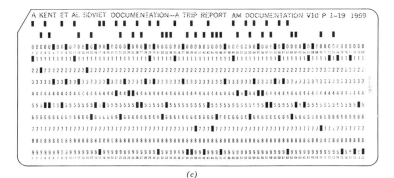

(b)

(c)

Figure 3-16

47-52, and page numbers and years of publication in columns 54-63 and 65-68, respectively. The space limitation is obvious, since the article title (Soviet Documentation—A Trip Report) could not be recorded on the same, single card. The article title would have consumed 34 more columns, which could have been used only at the expense of other information (see Figure 3-16*b*). Thus, journal title could have been abbreviated, co-author could have been listed as et al. But still the full title could not fit within the 80-column limitation, unless other abbreviations were made (Figure 3-16*c*).

Another problem arises when a significant number of characters, such as all of those contained in an abstract or in the text of a document, are to be recorded. A large number of cards must be used, and each set must be maintained in a predetermined sequence in order to be used meaningfully. The proliferation of cards necessary for a large collection would lead to surprisingly high costs for recording, "housekeeping," and exploiting the material.

Therefore, as a general rule for tabulating-type punched cards, it is wise to avoid recording for mechanical reproduction and printing more information than can be punched into a single card.

2.   *Recording Information Without Perforation.* If it seems advantageous to maintain a single card for each graphic record, a problem arises when it is necessary to record additional information about the document. A second means may be used to preserve information on the punched card: we may type such information directly on the face of the card (Figure 3-17). Of course, if the card is reproduced mechanically, only the keypunched information will appear on the new card; the other information will have to be typed again or otherwise transferred to the reproduced card.

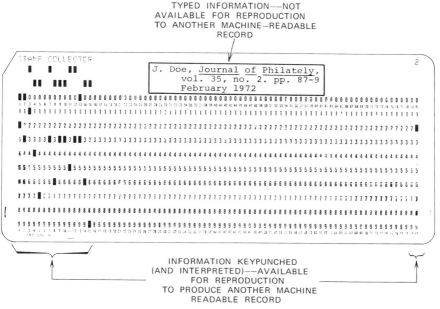

Figure 3-17

3.   Recording Information Photographically. Microfilm "windows" provide a third method of storing information on punched cards (Figure 2-25). All of the information on such "aperture" cards can be reproduced mechanically (where information has been keypunched) or by photographic or analogous techniques (where microfilm has been inserted).

It should be evident again, that if a replica of an aperture card is desired, a two-step process is required: (a) the aperture card with microimage must be reproduced and (b) the perforations must be replicated. For single replications this two-step process is not too much of a chore. However, when files of significant size are to be processed in such a way repetitively, annoyances may tend to develop.

4.   Recording Information Magnetically. A fourth method of recording information has been developed commercially: printing with magnetic ink which, upon detection, can activate the electrical or mechanical recording of the information (Figure 3-18). Here a bank check has information recorded at A, which illustrates a machine language that is also readable by the human. An

Figure 3-18

analogous method uses a mark-sensing medium (Figure 3-19); a graphite pencil is used to make marks on the face of the card. (Darkened oval spaces have been "marked" with such a pencil). This permits original information to be recorded manually. After the manual recording is completed, the card can be processed automatically so that the graphite marks may be translated into punches.

E. Film

In this type of medium, abstracts or documents are recorded, usually in microform, on a sequential medium, or on unit records. When unit records are employed, either the film alone is used as a record, or it is combined with another medium, such as punched cards.

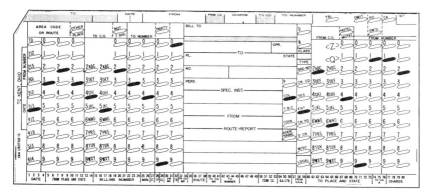

Figure 3-19

F. Other Media

Documents, abstracts, and other information may also be recorded on magnetic media. It is quite convenient to reproduce data from these sources electronically. Information stored as magnetic impulses can provide printout in other forms, such as by electric typewriter or display on a cathode ray tube.

A development was announced that permits the storage of documents in a medium, such as Videotape, and that permits scanning and display through television techniques.

VI. SUMMARY

Some representative physical tools which may be used to perform input unit operations have been described and discussed. The presentations do not intend to imply that economical, technological, or intellectual advantages accrue when mechanical or other nonconventional aids are used in connection with the performance of these operations. Nor is it indeed possible to reckon such advantages until the unit operations are fitted together to become a total system, since it is the effectiveness of the total system, rather than only one of the individual unit operations, that permits rational evaluation.

Four

Mechanization of Output Unit Operations

I. INTRODUCTION

A considerable capital investment must be made when establishing an information-retrieval system, particularly in loading the system, involving the performance of the input unit operations. Obviously, output operations cannot be conducted unless there is material available in the system that may be exploited. Accordingly, it is often found that considerable expense is incurred in acquisition of materials, their analysis, the recording of analysis results on a searchable medium, and the storage of the source materials, before the first amortization of this capital expense is possible through use of the system.

As in Chapter 3, physical tools are discussed in terms of the basic unit operations, but in this chapter the concern is with the output unit operations: question analysis and search strategy development, conducting of search, and delivery of search results.

Question analysis and search strategy development involve the expression of a question or problem, selection of analytics (subject headings, index entries, descriptors) in terms of a particular search requirement, and an arrangement of the analytics into a configuration that represents a probable link between the question as expressed and the records on file as analyzed. Therefore, this operation is quite analogous to that of analysis as an input unit operation. And this should have been anticipated, since it was suggested in Chapter 3 that analysis calls for the selection of information which it is predicted will provide useful reference points to facilitate the identification or selection of desired source materials after they have been stored.

Conducting the search involves manipulation or operation of the search mechanism in order to identify records in the file.

Delivery of search results calls for physical removal, copying, or otherwise making available an image of those records identified during a search, in order to provide it in response to a question.

II. QUESTION ANALYSIS AND SEARCH STRATEGY DEVELOPMENT

This unit operation may be considered in terms of five functions, even though they are not always carried out consciously:

1. *Statement of question.* The desire for information is verbalized in the form of a question or inquiry, so that it may be examined in a formal manner, and in order that the information-retrieval system may be activated to yield responses.

2. *Question analysis.* The question or inquiry is interpreted in order to identify its "essential features," which may be used as reference points during a search.

3. *Terminology control.* The terms used to express the elements of the question are standardized so that terms known to have been used during input are used in the same fashion.

4. *Question negotiation.* The question statement is adjusted, if necessary, both in scope and in mode of expression, in order to increase the likelihood that the material of potential interest may be located.

5. *Strategy determination.* The question is expressed formally as a logical statement in terms of the configuration predicted to most likely identify source material of importance. Alternative expressions (or logical statements) of the question may be considered so that these may be used if the preferred strategy yields no significant response.

It is instructive to examine the five functions of this output unit operation to determine how physical tools might facilitate their performance.

The first function, question statement, must obviously originate with a human being, at least for the types of information-retrieval systems that are considered in this textbook. The only physical tools available to facilitate the performance of this function are essentially communication systems which can transmit a question, as stated, from the asker to the operator of the information-retrieval system. On the other hand, the advent of time-sharing computers, which can provide a console at the desk of the question asker permits the question statement, if it is in proper form, to be transmitted directly to the computer for search.

The second function, question analysis, generally is also one performed by human beings. It is difficult to imagine the machine analysis of any very sophisticated question, at least in the present state of systems and equipment development. However, it need not follow from this generalization that some information-retrieval inquiries may not be subject to automatic analysis. It is reasonable to expect that if automatic analysis of the text of documents (Chapter 5) is found to be satisfactory, automatic analysis of questions may be equally satisfactory.

The third function, vocabulary control, may indeed be facilitated occasionally with the aid of automatic devices. After the analyst determines the basic aspects of a question, he must guess which words, synonyms, or near-synonyms were recorded by the specialist who analyzed the original document. In attempting to develop a search strategy that will increase the probability of his identifying useful information, the question analyst often finds it helpful to consult thesauri, dictionaries, and indexes in order to locate terminology related to that found or implied in the statement of the question. In several systems, mechanical methods have been used to arrange the results of terminological analysis.

The keypunch may be used to record words and their relationships onto machine-processible cards. Sorters arrange the cards in any desired order, and an alphabetical accounting machine may then be used to print the information contained in the cards in the form of a listing that is convenient to use, such as an authority list or a thesaurus (Chapter 8).

The fourth function, question negotiation, is again a task for people in that a dialog between the question asker and system operator ensues, which is not amenable to mechanization in the strictest sense. However, a dialog between the human and a time-sharing computer may be developed to facilitate the negotation process. An example of such a dialog is exhibited in Figure 4-1. The effective participation of the computer in this dialog is based, of course, on the advance storage of a number of alternative statements in computer memory, the appropriate one being chosen on the basis of the human participant's input.

The fifth function, strategy determination, is again a human function. However, a more hopeful note may be sounded by the expectation that digital computers will be able to store the strategies of successful searches. The "association trails" of such prior machine searches will serve to expedite the processing of a new question and to make a useful response more probable.

Discussions in the literature point to the development of inductive reasoning machines designed to make a logical analysis of questions as well as of the text of documents, and to provide machine aids in this direction; however,

Please state your question:

>Any articles on automatic indexing techniques for use in automated retrieval systems.

You must now decide on subjects to be searched and terms which express them. When you finish putting in terms, type "DONE".

      TERMS=>
>automatic

>indexing

>information retrieval

>done

Terms listed below are either misspelled or are not included in the index to our collection, or are variant forms of terms which are in the index.

      B = indexing

Do you mean:

      index?

TERM	NUMBER OF DOCUMENTS REFERENCED
A = automatic	
C = information retrieval	2
D = index	3
	2

Now create a logical strategy for searching the file. Use A, B, C, etc. to represent each term. Use any or all of the following terms. Unused terms will be considered as deleted.

      A = automatic, C = information retrieval, D = index

Go ahead=>
>axcxd

The terms you chose and the strategy you devised retrieved 1 document reference.

Do you want the bibliography printed out now?
>yes

Document No. 6617705
Walston, C.E.
INFORMATION RETRIEVAL—A NEW TECHNOLOGY?
In AROD Proc. of ARO Working Group on Computers, Feb. 1965, p. 367-373

      * * * *   End Bibliography   * * * *

Figure 4-1. A search program which uses a guiding or prompting technique to help the novice user. User input indicated by > at beginning of each line. (Example from the search program used in the experiment: "An Experiment To Determine The Effectiveness Of An Interactive Tutorial Program, Implemented On The Time Sharing IBM System 360, Model 50, In Teaching A Subject-Oriented User To Formulate Inquiry Statements To A Computerized On-Line Information Retrieval System", D. E. Caruso, University of Pittsburgh, August 1969.)

such devices are not yet operational, and discussion will have to be postponed to a still later edition of this volume.

III. CONDUCTING THE SEARCH

A. Introduction

The conducting of a literature search has been the historical target of all efforts toward mechanization of the documentation process.

The general problem can be formulated, in practical terms, as involving the selection of a relatively small number of documents from a collection containing a relatively large number of documents. The selection is based on various analytics, relevant to a question or inquiry, that have been made available for search and correlation during input, when the analysis unit operation was conducted.

The choice of physical tools for mechanized information retrieval depends, in any particular situation, on the method by which the results of analysis of documents have been recorded. And these matters have been discussed in some detail in Chapter 3. Further, the search principles involved for each tool have been covered in Chapter 2. Accordingly, this section will necessarily be very brief and is presented chiefly for review purposes.

The emphasis in the following will be placed on physical tools that must be manipulated in some way in order to conduct a search. However, it should be remembered that mechanized systems may involve the use of various tools for performance of input unit operations, with arrangement and storage of the resulting file in such a way as to facilitate exploitation by human beings.

An example of such a case is when unit records are stored in alphabetical or classified order as shown in Figure 4-2.

A mechanical file (Diebold, Inc. Super Elevator file) permits an operator to select a specific bank of trays (A), by depressing the appropriate button of a keyboard (B). The bank of trays is brought to the operator automatically. The equipment is entirely neutral regarding the way in which information may have been arranged and placed in search-ready condition.

B. Marginal-Hole Punched Cards

A simple tool used for searching is the marginal-hole punched card (Figure 2-15). Once the results of analysis have been recorded on the card by notching, they can be retrieved by means of a sorting needle which is used to select cards on the basis of information notched along their edges.

As discussed in Chapter 2, the needle is inserted in the hole position of a

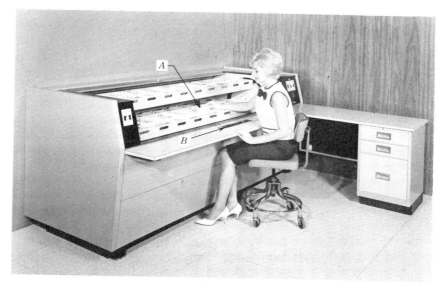

Figure 4-2

file of cards that corresponds to the desired subject. The cards are fanned to facilitate the physical selection of those cards notched at the hole position dedicated to the desired subject. All these cards that represent documents containing the desired subject have been notched, and are not held by the needle so they drop out of the file.

Of course, the determination as to which hole or combination of holes is to be searched in connection with a given question depends on the meaning that had been ascribed previously to each particular hole or set of holes. Thus, for the example shown in Figure 3-7, the personnel manager who was left with the problem of finding a receptionist with the appropriate set of desirable characteristics (e.g., some typing ability and some dictation ability) would be able to conduct a search by inserting a sorting needle, successively, in each appropriate hole of the card, so that the presence or absence of a notch would indicate that each desired characteristic was or was not present for a given applicant.

C. Aspect Cards

1. Number Posted for Visual Comparison. It will be recalled that this technique involves the posting of numbers of documents on subject (or aspect) cards (Figure 2-30). When a search is to be conducted for all documents that are characterized by the coincidence of two or more subjects (aspects), the following procedure is used. The appropriate aspect cards are selected from the file (Figure 2-31), and are examined so that a determination may be made as to which document numbers appear on all cards. The documents so identified may then be withdrawn from another file where all documents are arranged in accession number order.

It may be obvious that it is difficult to compare more than two such cards at a time. Therefore, for questions that require the comparison of many such cards, it may be cumbersome to consider such an approach.

2. Peek-A-Boo Principle. A search is conducted with aspect cards employing the peek-a-boo principle by superimposing cards corresponding to the subject of the inquiry, and holding them up to a source of light. Wherever light shows through, there is a coincidence of document-number punches that identifies those documents that meet the search criteria (see Figure 2-14).

But not all kinds of searches are performed conveniently using this principle. Let us return to the problem of selecting a receptionist from a group of applicants whose characteristics have been organized in a peek-a-boo file. If the question posed to the file involves characteristics, all of which must be present before an applicant is of interest, there is no problem. Thus, if we wish to have all applicants who are (1) brunette, (2) single, and (3) have good typing ability, the three relevant peek-a-boo cards are withdrawn from the file and are superimposed so that we can discover which applicant numbers have the three characteristics in common.

However, let us now seek a receptionist who is (1) single *or* (2) widowed *or* (3) divorced, *and* who has either (4) good typing ability *or* (5) good dictation ability. For this question, the five relevant peek-a-boo cards would be withdrawn from file, but superimposing all to discover applicants having *all* five characteristics is not what was prescribed in the question.

D. Tabulating-Type Punched Cards

Punched cards may be used for searching, in both document and modified aspect systems. In document systems, each card, or unit record, generally represents a single document, all of the "index" information being recorded on that card. In order to locate a document based on the information recorded on a card, we may either use a sorter or a collator to physically select the desired cards or we may use an alphabetic accounting machine to print selectively from cards or portions of cards as they are scanned.

If machine-sorted punched cards are used in modified aspect systems, an entire subfile of cards may be used to represent a single aspect of information, while the documents that contain this aspect of information are so identified by having merely their serial numbers punched in separate cards of the subfile. When a search is to be conducted for documents that have two aspects in common, the appropriate subfiles for these aspects are compared in a collator in order to identify the desired documents. Alternatively, the cards representing aspects may be sorted in numerical order, according to document numbers punched in them, bringing together coincident numbers which may be identified visually (Figure 3-12).

More and more, tabulating cards are being used for the original recording of information that is then to be fed into a digital computer, and less and less for searching per se.

E. Punched Paper Tape

Some digital computers use punched paper type as input. Some of these computers may be useful in special situations for conducting literature searches, but in general they have had no major impact.

Several special-purpose machines utilizing punched paper tape have been developed for literature searching. One of these, the Western Reserve University Searching Selector, was designed and constructed at the Center for Documentation and Communication Research, and was in operation during 1956-1961. (In 1961, the machine was replaced by a high-speed computer.)

F. Magnetic Tape

Most general-purpose digital computers can be programmed to conduct literature searches with lesser or greater efficiency, depending on the design parameters of the equipment. Searches for both the document and aspect systems can be programmed on this equipment and files can be organized according to these systems and recorded on magnetic tape that can be searched at considerable speed. The basic logical operations conducted by this equipment during a search are analogous to those used in tools of lesser speed and versatility. The search is conducted by having information recorded on magnetic tape "read" into a high-speed memory of the computer, where search criteria are stored. If this information matches the search criteria (or question), there is a printout or another means of indicating that a response has been found.

The primary advantages of this type of equipment are the high speed and low unit cost of searches. A special-purpose (The GE-250)[1] was designed, but could not compete during design studies in effective search speed or economic feasibility with a general-purpose computer (GE-225) having special programming features.

---

[1] See Allen Kent, Ed., *Information Retrieval and Machine Transition,* Interscience, New York, 1960, Part 1, Chap. 21.

G. Film Records

Filmed documents are available for search either in strips and continuous reels or as unit records (Chapter 2). The index information is recorded as a pattern of opaque and transparent spots on film which is generally scanned by photoelectric or analogous techniques.

The searching of the encoded "index" to the contents of documents recorded on continuous film is essentially a scanning operation, in which the equipment is conditioned to recognize a particular pattern of opaque and transparent spots. Once the particular pattern has been identified, various machine actions may be triggered. For example, the machine may be instructed to stop its scanning operations so that a "readout" device may make a record of the response. Alternatively, the machine may photograph index information while the search continues.

When unit film records are searched, the scanning operation is conducted in a manner analogous to the sorting of cards: the film can be directed to various storage locations in the machine, depending on the search criteria. Two unit-film record scanners are the Filmorex (Figure 2-27) and the Minicard.

The result of a search of unit films is the physical separation of the records, the reproduction of the record on new film, or the preparation of "hard" copy for delivery to the user.

The IBM Walnut System (IBM 9603 Image File) involves the use of strips of microfilm stored in bins. Retrieval is achieved by mechanically selecting a strip of film, with appropriate images copied from the strip onto aperture cards.

H. Other Media

The searching of other media, such as random access discs, magnetic drums, core memories, or other specialized media, is accomplished using specialized equipment such as digital computers. Even Addressograph plate-selecting equipment may be considered to constitute a mechanized search system. However, most of this equipment has been developed primarily for purposes other than information retrieval, and its adaptation for this purpose will not be discussed here.

IV. DELIVERY OF RESULTS

The delivery of the results of a search implies the provision of one or more products:

1. *A serial number* that is meaningful to the patron, and that provides entree to a file of information that is organized so that the last step of identification and withdrawal from file may be performed readily. In most aspect systems, in many machine-sorted punched-card systems, and in many digital computer systems (where storage space with high-speed access is expensive) the most condensed reply—a unique serial number, or numbers—is provided in response to a question. Usually, the serial numbers of documents identified during a search are typed out or punched automatically onto a suitable medium.

2. *A bibliographic reference* that provides entry to freely available sources of graphic records. If this reference is not recorded in the search medium in machine-readable and machine-reproducible form, then it is necessary to have a human being copy or photograph this information.

3. *A suitable abstract or extract* from the source record. As with the bibliographic reference, if this information has not been recorded in machine-readable and machine-reproducible form, then it is necessary for a human being to copy laboriously the required information or to use a photographic or other aid to copying.

4. *A copy of the original document.* Usually there is so much information in a source document that it is not economical to record the full text on a high-speed storage and printing device. It is common to use microphotographic techniques for inexpensive storage of graphic records. If this is the practice, copies may be made photographically or electronically. If the documents are stored in their original form, in full size, then various well-known copying techniques may be used to duplicate the original record.

V. SUMMARY

It may be obvious from the discussions in this chapter that the physical tools used for output unit operations are quite dependent on the physical tools used for input unit operations presented in Chapter 3. In other words, the level of analysis, and media used for recording of results of analysis and for storage of source materials determine what may be obtained once an information-retrieval system is queried and results are to be provided to the inquirer.

Five

Principles of Analysis

I. INTRODUCTION

It will be recalled that the purpose of a mechanized information-retrieval system like that of any system of information retrieval, is to facilitate the identification of those records in a collection that have one or more common characteristics: a certain set of features that are pertinent to a given question. Such features are determined by the person who specifies a configuration of information requirements peculiar to his special interest at a particular time.

In order to organize the information contained in graphic records in such a way as to facilitate its identification on demand, it is necessary to analyze the records in an attempt to: (a) infer the intentions of sources who are not present (the authors of the records); and (b) infer the requirements of readers who are not present (the potential users of the records).

In order to meet both of these requirements it would apparently be necessary to avoid *any* analysis of a record prior to its storage in a file or library, but rather to require that the record be read in its entirety (either by humans or by machines) each time the collection is to be searched. This procedure would presumably be feasible if the value of the search results were sufficiently great to warrant such a "total" search. However, experience has indicated that the value of most search results is not sufficiently great to warrant such a massive effort. On the other hand, experience also shows that many search results are of sufficient importance to warrant analysis, and organization of the results of analysis, in the form of a catalog, an index, a classification system, or a mechanized retrieval system, in anticipation of requirements for searches. Principles for such analysis of graphic records are the subject of this chapter.

Strictly speaking, the principles of analysis are basically the same, whether the retrieval system used is mechanized or nonmechanized. The basic techniques may be adapted to achieve a suitable "depth" of penetration into the subject matter of the graphic record. Or they may take advantage of the special features of some particular retrieval device, in order to save money or time, or to facilitate effective searching. Inevitably, some variations in analysis techniques are introduced in order to overcome or to mask one or more deficiencies of a particular retrieval device.

Each analytical method is developed from a traditional procedure used in librarianship. However, all mechanized retrieval systems share a nontraditional characteristic. They tend to rely on a "multidimensional" approach to analysis of source records and to retrieval. They characterize source records from more than one point of view, and they retrieve information by combining more than one aspect of subject matter—by applying clerical, mechanical, or electronic means to perform operations of selection and correlation.

Even the simplest records are multidimensional, in this sense, and it is usually difficult to predict which point of view (or dimension) will be pertinent in a particular search. As an example, consider a basic problem in analysis, a "simple" problem perennially confronting the telephone company in any large city. The company wishes to serve a physician who wants to be located by potential patients who desire his services.

In the classified section of the telephone directory of a large American city, for example, there is a heading for "Physicians and Surgeons," under which are listed alphabetically the names, addresses, and phone numbers of doctors of medicine. Whoever desires the services of a doctor may locate him, if he has a particular doctor in mind.

But thinking of a particular doctor may not mean finding him, especially if that "particular doctor" has a name such as:

Braun, E. J.

or

Brown, E. J.

or a name like Cohen, of which they are four possibilities in the directory of one large American City:

Cohen

Cohn

Cowen

Kohn

In these cases, it is necessary to know how the name of the physician is *spelled*.

However, the spelling itself may not be enough, because there are 11 listings for Brown, 11 listings for Smith, 8 listings for Thomas, 8 listings for

Johnson, and 6 listings for King. In these cases it is necessary to know the *initials* of the M.D. in order to narrow the search.

However, if the M.D.'s name happens to be

J. E. Brown

or

M. A. Thomas

the ailing searcher is still out of luck, because there are two of each in the directory. It is finally necessary to know his *address* in order to locate the right man!

Now, consider the plight of the prospective patient who forgot the name of the M.D., but only remembers that the address of his office is

10515 Carnegie Avenue

Since this is the address of a large medical building in an American city, it is listed for about a hundred doctors. The classified telephone book has become progressively less useful as a retrieval device, and at this point it resists yielding up its information. The names of doctors are not grouped according to their street addresses, nor according to their suite numbers within individual buildings. Even if the company did anticipate such a need—and it has probably done so—it would be sure to decide that the distribution of such a "reverse" listing would not repay, in subscriber use, the extra effort and expense in preparation and the extra bulk in use.

And small wonder that the telephone company cannot afford to provide for every possible need. Doctors can be considered from an unlimited number of points of view, as, for example, area of specialization, school of medical training, year of degree, school of premedical training, city or country of birth, and marital status.

Each of these points of view may be of extreme importance to a particular person at a particular time. But even if it ignored practical considerations, the telephone company probably would not be able to predict every possible point of view from which its classified pages would be approached, or every possible demand that would be made of that particular record.

On the basis of this glance at a specific problem in retrieval, we can make the following general statement:

No analysis, no matter how detailed, will be as exhaustive as a separate total search made by each interested individual.

And its corollary:

No analysis can predict every possible point of view or use that might be demanded of any graphic record.

II. ANALYSIS TECHNIQUES

A. Introduction

The term *content analysis* is usually reserved for situations in which a written or spoken message is analyzed in an attempt to infer the intentions of a source (author) who is not present. If we assume, as is usually the case, that the author has selected values (or meanings) for the message variables, then the job of the content analyst is to discover those values. Only then can he properly interpret the message. Experienced analysts do this implicitly as they keep in mind the alternatives open to the author for each variable. If an analyst is faced with the problem of interpreting a Russian statement on the political situation in India, he will try to guess the communicative situation as it is perceived by the Russian source. Whether the destination is defined by the source as the Indian public or the Russian Politburo will have considerable effect on the meaning of the statement. His problem is to infer the author's intentions from his judgment of the communicative situation and the messages available to him. This provides a basis for the analyst's real interest as he seeks to determine the effects that the source is interested in obtaining.

Common experience suggests, and experiment confirms, that a person does not always make the same choice when faced with the same options, even when the circumstances of choice seem in all relevant respects to be the same.[1]

This statement summarizes one of the basic problems of conducting consistent content analysis (indexing, classification, etc.) to serve the purposes of an information-retrieval system. It is not possible for a single analyst, much less a team of analysts, to achieve absolute consistency in the way in which they conduct analyses of graphic records.

An example that may serve to illustrate this point has been developed from a class exercise in which a graphic record was presented to a group of students, who were asked to provide five index entries for the record. The graphic record was a cartoon, shown in Figure 5-1.

Four examples of sets of index entries provided are as follows:

Student "A"
1. Mr. Mum
2. Ladies
3. Kangaroos
4. Baby
5. Reverse situation

---

[1] D. Davidson and J. Marschak, "Experimental Tests of a Stochastic Decision Theory," Technical Report No. 17 on Contract Nonr 225(17), ASTIA Document No. 201, 285, Stanford University, July 25, 1958.

Figure 5-1. Reprinted by permission of The Hall Syndicate, Inc.

Student "B"
    1. Cartoon
    2. Mr. Mum
    3. Zoo
    4. Kangaroos
    5. Mother

Student "C"
    1. Infant exchange
    2. Humor, mother's preoccupation
    3. Observer's reaction
    4. Kangaroo mother's reaction
    5. Gossip

Student "D"
    1. Animals, care of
    2. Rabbit
    3. Cage
    4. Zoo
    5. Carriage

The differences among these sets of index entries are as follows:

1. Students choose different ideas as being important for retrieval purposes.

2. Students use different terms to express the same ideas.

It is perhaps obvious that these inconsistencies would lead to considerable uncertainties in later retrieval.

Absolute consistency may be achieved only if machines are used to scan the complete texts of natural languages and to perform analytical decisions based on instructions (programs) developed by human beings. However, this absolute consistency brings with it no guarantees whatever that the resulting analysis meets any of the purposes that are to be served by an information-retrieval system.

This discussion has been provided as a prelude to the description of various analysis techniques that have been proposed or are in use in the field of mechanized information retrieval. By this time it will be evident that no analytical method may be considered "perfect." Some means must be considered for overcoming the effects of inconsistency, either through the use of some redundancy[2] in analysis, through the use of a coding or a cross-reference system that is superimposed after analysis (see Chapter 9), or through the use of alternative strategies of searching (see Chapter 6).

Any form of content analysis can be used in connection with a mechanized information-retrieval system—some forms more effectively than others for one machine or another, or for one purpose or another. In general, content analysis is performed by humans, but considerable research is being conducted in the use of computers to aid in the work of analysis; and some results are being applied in operational situations. Regardless of whether humans or machines perform all or part of the analysis of documents, the procedures can be considered under the following categories: indexing, classifying, abstracting, and processing of full texts.

B. Indexing

An index may be defined as a device that serves as a pointer or indicator, most often an alphabetic list that includes subjects and names of people or places that are considered to be of special pertinence in a graphic record.

---

[2] Redundancy may be defined as the quantity of transmitted information in excess of the necessary minimum.

The process of indexing involves a selection of words[3] or ideas from a graphic record on the basis of well-defined rules. The purpose of indexing is to facilitate the identification or selection of desired documents after they have been sorted and shelved or stored. As in any form of content analysis, some value judgments are made in selecting aspects of subject matter as important for inclusion in an index.

It will be evident that, from many points of view, the terms "indexing" and "subject cataloging" are synonymous. The principles of analysis required to conduct cataloging and indexing appear to be identical—certainly with regard to basic objectives.

The various indexing techniques can be discussed under two headings: (1) word indexing and (2) controlled indexing.

1. Word Indexing. The form of indexing that is simplest to apply is the one that assumes on the part of the indexer the least amount of subject-matter background and the least amount of technical skill in indexing. Of course, the fact that it is the simplest form of indexing to apply does not indicate that it can be exploited effectively. Nevertheless, it happens to represent the type of indexing that a machine can perform with precision and consistency.

a. CONCORDANCES. The concordance is an alphabetic index of *words* in a document in exact context. No discrimination is exercised in preparing this type of index. Each word that is present in the text is an index entry. Therefore the decisions that must be made in conducting such an indexing operation are not very difficult and can be performed very well by machines.

If a sentence of text were to be recorded in machine-processible form, then a suitable computer program[4] would be written which would prepare automatically an index of every word in that sentence. This would require that the beginning and ending of every word be recognized automatically.

One machine technique that has been used[5] in making a concordance of a continuous text involves the following steps:

---

[3] Variously called descriptors, key words, descriptions, index entries, aspects, uniterms, subject headings. Each term used may imply a different level of "control" of use of words, but the definition of each is not yet a matter of common agreement, particularly among the "coiners" of the various terms.

[4] G. Salton, *Automatic Information Organization and Retrieval*, McGraw Hill Book Company New York, 1968.

[5] R. Busa, "The Use of Punched Cards in Linguistic Analysis," R. S. Casey. J. W. Perry, A. Kent, and M. M. Berry, *Punched Cards* 2nd ed., Reinhold, New York, 1958, pp. 357-373. See also R. Busa, "Concordances" in *Encyclopedia of Library and Information Science* Vol. 5, Marcel Dekker, Inc. New York, 1971.

1. A scholar marks the text to indicate how it should be recorded on punched cards, noting the beginnings and endings of paragraphs and sentences, and so forth.

2. Each line of text is keypunched into cards, with identifying reference to its place in the text. Words are not split between cards; rather, a word is started on a new card if it will not fit on the preceding one.

3. The keypunching is verified and errors are corrected.

4. The running text is divided into single word cards by using a Cardatype[6] machine which prints the context of a total card on the reverse of each card for a single word.

5. The single word cards are sorted into alphabetic order and printed if desired, providing a concordance index ready for use by a scholar.

As was mentioned earlier, the preparation of a concordance by machine requires that the entire text must be "readable" automatically to be processed. Three approaches may be used: (1) keypunching of the entire text; (2) having available tapes prepared as an intermediate step in the original composition of the text; and (3) automatic optical recognition of the text (character recognition). The concordance procedure described above involves the first of these approaches.

If a concordance were to be prepared for the titles of two documents:

1. Visual and Photographic Inspection of Sites
2. A Description of Space Programs

The resulting index of words would be as follows:

Word	Document number
A	2
And	1
Description	2
Inspection	1
Of	1, 2
Photographic	1
Programs	2
Sites	1
Space	2
Visual	1

---

[6] The Cardatype (card-operated typewriter) reads cards and causes a typewriter to transcribe the punching onto some record.

From examination of this index, it is perhaps obvious that it might be a more useful tool if the context of each index entry were given along with the index word.

Word	Context	Document number
A	*A* description of space programs	2
And	Visual *and* photographic inspection of sites	1
Description	A *description* of space programs	2
Inspection	Visual and photographic *inspection* of sites	1
etc.		

Alternatively, the index word at the left could be omitted, if it could be consulted in context. The index word may be printed in a given position on a page, showing the context as shown in Figure 5-2.

Since the selection of index words in preparing a concordance requires no discriminative ability other than recognition of beginnings and endings of words, no subject matter knowledge is required for the performance of this task in special situations.

   b. KEY-WORD-IN-CONTEXT (KWIC), OR PERMUTATION, INDEX. The making of a Key-Word-in-Context (KWIC),[7] or Permutation, index, like concordance making, requires little in the way of subject-matter knowledge, and therefore is amenable to mechanization.

The rationale behind this approach to automatic analysis, or more specifically to automatic indexing follows.

Since it may be too expensive in the long run to convert whole texts (particularly of technical reports and journal articles) into machine-readable form, it is suggested that the title alone of the source material may be converted to such form (by keypunching) at little expense. It is hypothesized that the author of the source material has expended considerable effort in preparing an informative title, particularly for scientific and engineering publications. It is therefore hypothesized that many of the "key" words that would normally be used by human indexers are available in the title.

It is further observed that when human indexers are under considerable pressure to analyze large numbers of source materials rapidly, they may often tend to consult only the titles of these materials. Accordingly, it is suggested that very often the automatic and human indexes may be quite similar.

---

[7] H. P. Luhn, "Keyword-in-Context Index for Technical Literature," *American Documentation*, **11**, 288-295 (1960).

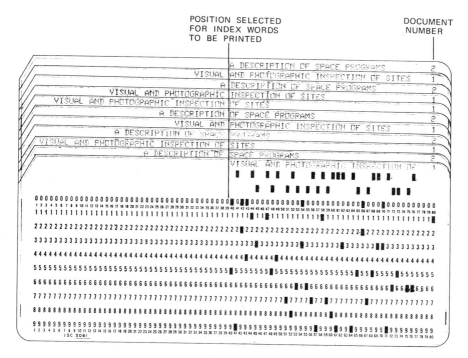

POSITION SELECTED
FOR INDEX WORDS
TO BE PRINTED

DOCUMENT
NUMBER

Figure 5-2

Stated in another way, the rationale for KWIC indexing has been given as follows:[8]

The usefulness of an index depends upon the manner in which index entries have been organized. The establishment of categories by subject or other appropriate characteristics is the conventional means by which such organization is accomplished. The establishment of categories and the assignment to such categories of index entries is a matter of judgment and experience and constitutes a considerable part of the intellectual effort involved in the manual compilation of indexes. Various indexers will usually differ in their approaches to this task

---

[8] H. P. Luhn, "Keyword-in-Context Index for Technical Literature (KWIC Index)," ASDD Report, RC-127, International Business Machines Corp., Yorktown Heights, New York, August 31, 1959, p. 6.

and will also differ in their interpretation of the material to be indexed. While there may be differences of opinion as to the effectiveness of this or that scheme, the important fact seems to be that any reasonable scheme or ordering, if understood, will save time in locating desired information.

In striving for a speedy method of organizing an index, the question arises as to which of various possible schemes is adaptable to fully automatic processing. Clearly, some means of ordering is required that is based on criteria extracted from the text itself rather than assigned in accordance with human judgment.

Just as with the preparation of concordances, KWIC indexing is based on cyclic permutations of words. However, unlike most concordances, not all words are used in KWIC indexes. Rules have been established in an attempt to differentiate between words in titles that are significant and those that are probably not useful for retrieval purposes. Since significance is difficult to predict by skilled humans, much less by machines, it was decided to omit from the KWIC index all "nonsignificant" words—those that do not carry a heavy semantic burden in indexing, for example, articles, conjunctions, prepositions, auxiliary verbs, certain adjectives, and a few nouns. This list of words (called "stop list" or "exclude list") is stored in computer memory.

The title of a document is keypunched, and each word of the title is compared automatically with each word in the "stop list." Those words *not* on the list are considered to be significant and would be ready for further processing as "index" or "key" words.

Thus, if the "stop list" were to include terms such as: a, and, of; and if the titles:

1. Visual and Photographic Inspection of Sites
2. A Description of Space Programs

were keypunched and subjected to this type of processing, seven index words would be identified as significant, one for each of the terms not included in the "stop list" (that is, VISUAL, PHOTOGRAPHIC, INSPECTION, SITES, DESCRIPTION, SPACE, and PROGRAMS).

Each such word would be placed automatically in a given position on the machine record (for example, starting with column 40 of a Hollerith card). For example, in Figure 5-3, the word "photographic" of title 1 is punched starting in column 40. Now, in order to carry along the context of that word, the remainder of the title is punched as shown in Figure 5-4. Some of the context words may precede the index word and some may follow, depending on the position of the index word in the original title. It should be noted that words on the "stop" list (e.g., and, of), although dropped from consideration as index words, are still retained for context purposes.

POSITION SELECTED FOR
BEGINNING OF INDEX
WORD TO BE PRINTED

DOCUMENT
NUMBER

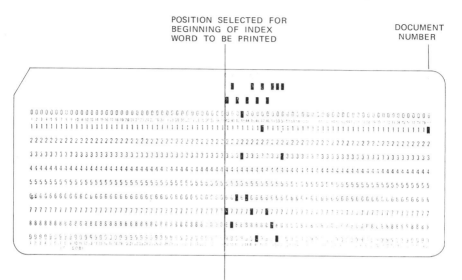

Figure 5-3

CONTEXT
WORDS

INDEX
WORD

CONTEXT
WORDS

DOCUMENT
NUMBER

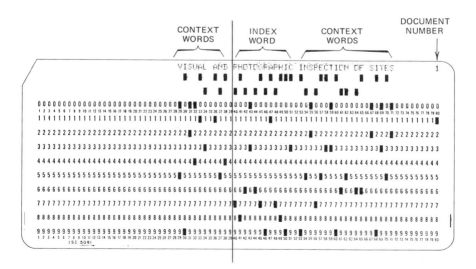

Figure 5-4

When the index word VISUAL is placed in the index position, the remainder of the title needed to provide context does not fit into the available space, as shown in Figure 5-5. Some KWIC programs merely omit whatever context does not fit as has been done in this illustration. Other programs take the missing context and place it at the beginning of the machine record, as shown in Figure 5-6. The choice of program is a matter of taste.

The resulting machine records are then automatically arranged alphabetically, by index words, as shown in Figure 5-7, and may be printed, ready for consultation.

Also provided is a list of titles, arranged by document number (Figure 5-8), in order to provide full bibliographic information once a reference is found to be of possible interest through consultation of the KWIC index.

Since there has been some difficulty encountered in conditioning those who refer to indexes to use such an unusual format, a modification has been employed in some applications. For example, the "Keywords Index to U. S. Government Technical Reports," produced by the Office of Technical Services, U. S. Department of Commerce, used the same techniques for deriving key words as above, but has printed the resulting index in another format (Figure 5-9) which lists the key word at the left, followed by a more intelligible citation. This has been called a KWOC index, the acronym representing *Key Word Out of Context*.

Regardless of format, two basic questions remain with regard to the effectiveness of this type of index.

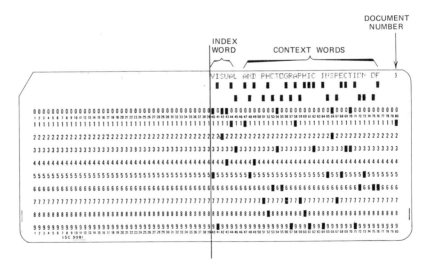

Figure 5-5

1. Are enough key words provided that approach the "depth" of indexing normally performed by humans?

One approach to investigating this question may be to examine man-produced indexes to determine whether the entries selected would indeed have been identified using the KWIC procedures.

A segment of the subject index (man-prepared), selected from the August 15, 1964, issue of the *Technical Abstract Bulletin* (produced by the Defense Documentation Center) shows the following subject entries and titles:

Subject Entry	*Report Title*
Aerial cameras, air-to-space	Development leading to astrographic camera system
Aerial cameras, photographic reconnaissance	Operational test and evaluation KA-4, KA-5, KA-30, and CAX-12 cameras
Aerial photography, display systems	Experimental double image enhancement viewer
Airburst, meteorological parameters	Handbook for prediction of air blast focussing
Alkaline cells, performance (engineering)	Alkaline battery evaluation
Antennas, guidance	Fixed antenna guidance techniques

Figure 5-6

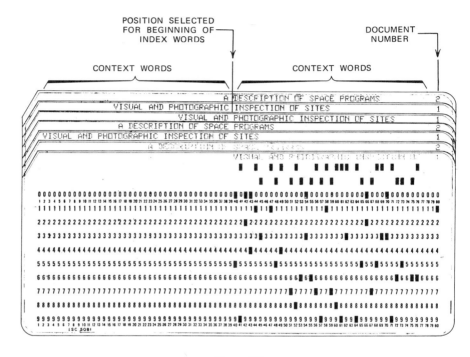

Figure 5-7

It may be obvious from the above example that few of the man-selected index entries would have been identified by the KWIC processing of titles. This observation leads to the second question.

2. Can the user of the KWIC index overcome the problems of coping with synonyms and variations in word usage and spelling that result from the unedited product of automatic processing?

---

1. J. BENNETT, "VISUAL AND PHOTOGRAPHIC INSPECTION OF SITES."
   TID-18458 (K) $4.60 0664.

2. R. GROSS, "A DESCRIPTION OF SPACE PROGRAMS."
   N63-14591 (K) $7.60 0175.

Figure 5-8.

```
INSPECTION          VISUAL AND PHOTOGRAPHIC ON-SITE INSPECTION.
                                       TID-18458(K)   $4.60 0664
INSTABILITIES       PENETRATION OF AN ELECTRON BEAM THROUGH A PLAS
                    MA. PART I. ELECTROSTATIC INSTABILITIES.
                                       AD-401 123(K)   $2.60 0661
INSTABILITIES       SOME INVESTIGATIONS OF PLASMA INSTABILITIES IN
                    ONE-DIMENSIONAL PLASMAS,
                                       MATT-152(K)    $1.00 0599
INSTABILITIES       THE BOUNDING OF INSTABILITIES OF THE PIC DIFFE
                    RENCE EQUATIONS.    LA-2414(K)    $1.50 0387
INSTALLATION        PRELIMINARY HANDBOOK FOR INSTALLATION INSTRUCT
                    IONS. VOLUME 5.    AD-400 311(K)   $7.60 0325
INSTRUCTION         INSTRUCTION MANUAL FOR THE FLUX RESPONSIVE TAP
                    E REPRODUCER,     PB 163 122(K)   $4.60 0086
INSTRUCTION         STAIR (STRUCTURAL ANALYSIS INTERPRETIVE ROUTIN
                    E) INSTRUCTION MANUAL.
                                       AD-400 280(K) $12.50 0421
INSTRUCTIONS        PRELIMINARY HANDBOOK FOR INSTALLATION INSTRUCT
                    IONS. VOLUME 5.    AD-400 311(K)   $7.60 0325
INSTRUMENT          AGE ASTROINERTIAL INSTRUMENT TEST SET 7842353.
                                       AD-400 342(K)   $3.60 0530
INSTRUMENTAL        INSTRUMENTAL VARIABLES IN FACTOR ANALYSIS,
                                       AD-401 393(K)   $2.60 0615
INSTRUMENTATION     SPACE PROGRAMS SUMMARY NO. 37-20, VOLUME III F
                    OR THE PERIOD JANUARY 1, 1963 TO FEBRUARY 28,
                    1963. DEEP SPACE INSTRUMENTATION FACILITY.
                                       N63-14591(K)   $7.60 0175
```

Figure 5-9

The developers of this indexing system assume that the expert in his field is familiar with such variations and is resourceful enough to overcome this problem, as he has done in the past without the help of machines.[9]

Realistically, the question remains unanswered, since significant controlled experiments in this regard have not been conducted. Furthermore, it should be remembered that the "key" words are selected during automatic processing because they are not included in a list of "nonkey" or "nonsignificant" words. Therefore, the use of the term "key words" seems inappropriate; rather they might be called "non-nonkey" words.

In an attempt to overcome some of these difficulties, another variation of the KWIC index has been introduced in some operational settings. This is called, the KWAC index, or *Key Word Augmented in Context*. This involves the addition of index words to the title of a document by a subject specialist. The thought is that this augmentation of the title would permit better penetration of the subject matter of the document than is often possible by using the author's title alone. In one system, this augmentation is called a "notation of content."

C. UNITERM INDEXING.[10] Uniterm indexing, as described a number of years ago, involves the analysis of the contents of graphic records in terms of key words that represent the content of the record that is being indexed. These key words include not only single common English words, but also serial numbers and other symbols, if they are found in the text and if, in the judgment of the

---

[9] H.P. Luhn, *op. cit.,* p. 6.

[10] M. Taube, et al., "The Uniterm Coordinate Indexing of Reports," B. H. Weil, Ed., *The Technical Report,* Reinhold, New York, 1954, p. 319 ff.

Mallinckrodt Chemical Lab., Harvard U., Cambridge, Mass.
THE MATRICES D^{-1} AND G^{-1} IN THE THEORY OF MOLECULAR VIBRATIONS, by S. R. Polo.   May 55, 15 pp. (Rept No. 6; OSR-TN-55-153)
(Contract AF 18(600)590)   Unclassified report   UNITERMS

A vector method is given by which to determine the elements of the matrices D^{-1} and G^{-1} which occur in the study of the vibration-rotation spectra of polyatomic molecules. D^{-1} is the matrix of the transformation giving the mass-weighted Cartesian displacements in terms of the internal coordinates, and G^{-1} has as elements the coefficients in the expression of the vibrational kinetic energy in terms of the velocities. The determination of the elements of D^{-1} is reduced to finding by inspection a set of displacement vectors to which is added an appropriate rigid translation and rotation of the whole molecule. The D^{-1} matrix elements are obtained from the equation	Matrix D^{-1} G^{-1} Theory Molecular Vibration Vector Polyatomic

Figure 5-10

indexer, they represent the significant content of the record (Figure 5-10). Here a government report has been analyzed, and the "uniterms" at the right-hand column selected.

The indexer is not required to create or to maintain a list of approved headings, since the list is generated as the indexing operation proceeds. It is seldom necessary for the indexer to consult the list of headings accumulated during previous analyses, at the time when uniterms are being selected for a new document. Because it is not necessary to consult the headings, the indexer can freely add to the list of uniterms rather than changing it or being restricted by it.[11] In addition, the indexer does not specify the order of key words or the relationships among them.

It was hypothesized that these short cuts would provide dramatic savings in catalog space and in cost of indexing, and would not significantly affect the integrity of the system.

Here, as in other "word indexing" procedures, one crucial assumption is

---

[11] More recent writings on this subject suggest that the use of this system does not obviate the need for appreciable subject background on the part of the record analyst nor for a considerable degree of terminology control. However, the earlier directions are still being used in some organizations.

being made. The user of such an index must be sufficiently familiar with the subject matter of his search that he can provide a control over the words used in the Uniterm index, a control that the indexer was instructed to omit (or was not instructed to take into account). In other words, the user must somehow compensate for the missing order, relationship, or representation of meaning among the words used in the Uniterm index.

The word *Uniterm* has been used loosely over the years, and in many persons' minds it has been equated to: keyword; index entry, descriptor, subject, analytic, and so on.

2. *Controlled Indexing.* Controlled indexing, as opposed to "word" indexing, implies a careful selection of terminology used in indexes in order to avoid, as much as possible, the scattering of related subjects under different headings.

Proponents of these approaches to exploiting the literature believe that the most attractive feature of the index is its ability to identify specific aspects of information that may be discussed in a document. But there is likewise a desire to combine some of the advantages of classification approaches, that is, group-related subject headings. In attempting to reconcile these two approaches in an index, there is a tendency to impose more and more "control" over the use of "permissible" language in recording the results of the analysis of a graphic record.

Various methods are used for imposing "control" over the indexing operation: (a) in the subjects that may be chosen; (b) in the number of aspects that may be chosen; and (c) in the language used to express the results of analysis.

a. CONTROL OVER WHICH SUBJECTS ARE CHOSEN (Figure 5-11). This type of control may be imposed on the basis of two criteria: (1) predicted or actual subject interests of those who are potential users of the index, and (2) nature of the graphic records that are analyzed.

The first criterion may be imposed by the establishment of a subject-authority list that provides the "acceptable" points of view and the required form in which these must be expressed. Examples of such authority lists are given in Figures 5-12 and 5-13. The control implied by this list may be imposed in several ways:

1. The human indexer may be asked to use the list as an absolute authority for decisions as to the recording of indexing selections.

2. The human indexer may be permitted to record index entries at will, with decisions as to authority and relationship recorded in the form of a dictionary, which is consulted either clerically or with machine aid (see Figure 5-13).

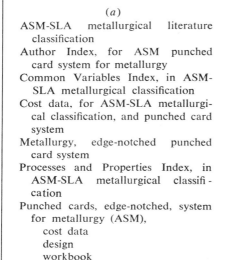

(a)
ASM-SLA   metallurgical   literature
classification
Author Index, for ASM punched
card system for metallurgy
Common Variables Index, in ASM-
SLA metallurgical classification
Cost data, for ASM-SLA metallurgi-
cal classification, and punched card
system
Metallurgy,   edge-notched   punched
card system
Processes and Properties Index, in
ASM-SLA   metallurgical   classifi -
cation
Punched cards, edge-notched, system
for metallurgy (ASM),
    cost data
    design
    workbook

(b)
American Society for Metals, development of classification and literature searching system
Bibliographic   literature   searching
system for metallurgy
Classification system, for metallurgical terminology

Figure 5-11. An article in the field of documentation on "An Edge—Notched Punched—Card System for Metallurgy" is indexed from two different points of view (*a* and *b*), both useful, but serving different clienteles; (*a*) in a book on mechanized information retrieval; and (*b*) in a metallurgical journal.

Another means of imposing the first criterion is called "probabilistic indexing."[12] Here, it is decided during an indexing operation that there is only a probability that a user will find that the document in question is relevant to a certain subject. Conventional indexing consists in having an analyst decide, on a yes-no basis, whether or not a given term is applicable to a particular document; either an entry is applicable or it is not—there is no middle ground. However, experience warns that there is considerable uncertainty associated with all indexing. It may be much more reasonable and realistic to make the decision on a probabilistic basic, that is, to assert that a given entry may hold to a certain degree or with a certain weight. By developing the ability to "weight" index entries, the indexer can characterize more precisely the information content of a document. The indexer may wish to assign a low weight such as 0.1 or 0.2 to a term, rather than to say that the term does not hold for the document.

---

[12] M. E. Maron and J. L. Kuhns, "On Relevance, Probabilistic Indexing and Information Retrieval," *Journal of the Association for Computing Machinery,* 7, 216-244 (1960). See also G. Salton, *Automatic Information Organization and Retrieval*, McGraw-Hill Book Company, New York, 1968.

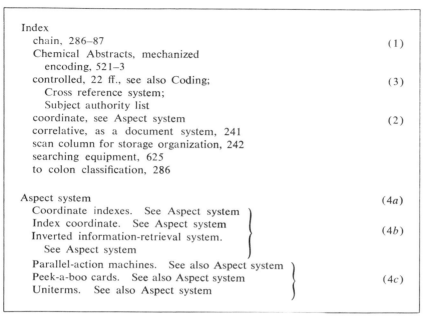

Index
    chain, 286–87   (1)
    Chemical Abstracts, mechanized
      encoding, 521–3
    controlled, 22 ff., see also Coding;   (3)
      Cross reference system;
      Subject authority list
    coordinate, see Aspect system   (2)
    correlative, as a document system, 241
    scan column for storage organization, 242
    searching equipment, 625
    to colon classification, 286

Aspect system   (4*a*)
    Coordinate indexes.   See Aspect system
    Index coordinate.   See Aspect system
    Inverted information-retrieval system.   (4*b*)
      See Aspect system
    Parallel-action machines.   See also Aspect system
    Peek-a-boo cards.   See also Aspect system   (4*c*)
    Uniterms.   See also Aspect system

Figure 5-12. Subject authority list. (1) Acceptable heading; (2) unacceptable heading, indicated by "see" reference to the acceptable heading; (3) acceptable heading, with potential relationship indicated through "see also" reference. Acceptable main heading (4a) together with "see from" listings, showing which unacceptable headings have been referred to, and should be included under this heading (4b); and "see also" listings, showing which acceptable headings having potential relationships were referred to the main heading (4c).

Conversely, the indexer may wish to assign a high weight of 0.8 or 0.9 to a term, rather than to say that it definitely holds for a document. Thus, using weighted indexing, it is possible to more accurately characterize the information content of a document. This weighting can then be exploited during a machine search.

    Another method for controlling the subjects chosen during analysis is based on the frequency of occurrence of key words in the running text, those occurring most frequently being considered, *prima facie,* to be most significant for analysis of the texts.[13]

    This type of analysis may be conducted by keypunching the entire text of a document so that it may be scanned by machine, and compiling statistics as to the frequency of occurrence of various key words. The words found by scanning the keypunched text are compared with a word list that provides instructions as

---

[13] H. P. Luhn, "The Automatic Creation of Literature Abstracts," *IBM Journal of Research and Development,* **2** 59-165 (April 1958).

Name	Code
Fish	FASH·001
Clam	FASH·003
Lobster	FASH·005
Mussel	FASH·006
Oyster	FASH·007
Porpoise	FZSH·008
Seal	FZSH·009
Shellfish	FASH·010
Shrimp	FASH·011
Whale	FZSH·014

Figure 5-13. Dictionary used in conjunction with subject-authority lists. The code combination F-SH means "marine creature." The only difference between this type of list and the index shown in Figure 5-12 is that here less burden is placed on the subject analyst, since all probable alternative expressions of a given idea (marine creatures, in this instance) are listed in the dictionary, so that little or no judgment need be exercised in order to identify a subject heading that is permissible. A clerk with no subject knowledge may perform this "look-up" operation, or a machine may be used if the amount of dictionary look-up is sufficiently great to make this economical (see Chapter Three).

to which words are not sufficiently discriminatory, that is, are too common to be significant, in the analysis of a document; when these are disregarded, the frequency of occurrence of the remaining terms may be used as a basis for "controlling" indexing.

The probabilistic indexing approach has also been used to explore automatic assignments of index entries.[14]

An experimental file of the text was selected from a group of abstracts in the field of computer technology indexed to 32 subject categories. This text was keypunched to permit automatic processing.

As with KWIC indexing common words such as articles and prepositions were first excluded. Next, words occurring less than three times were purged and words such as "data" and "computer" were also rejected because they occur so frequently in this literature. Approximately 1000 words remained after these purging operations. After sorting the source documents to their most appropriate subject categories, statistical frequencies were obtained for the co-occurrences of the candidate clue words [key words] with the categories and the resulting listings manually examined to determine which words peaked in a particular category. Eventually, 90 such words were selected.

The occurrence of one or more of the 90 clue words in the text of new

---

[14] Report of work of M. E. Maron et al., in M. E. Stevens, *Automatic Indexing: A State-of-the-Art Report,* National Bureau of Standards Monograph 91, U.S. Government Printing Office, Washington, D.C., March 30, 1965.

documents was then used to predict the subject category to which the new item should belong. Tests were run with two groups of documents, one consisting of the source items from which the statistical frequency and word list data had been obtained, and the second group consisting of 145 genuinely new items. For the latter group, twenty documents contained two or more clue words; the results of the computer assignment program were predictions of the correct category in 44, or 51.8 per cent, of the cases. Results using the source documents were significantly better, as expected, with 84.6 per cent accuracy of category prediction for 247 items. Results were also related to the number of clue words that occurred in the test items, with a prediction accuracy of only 48.7 per cent for items with a single clue word, rising to 100 per cent probability of correct assignment if six or more clue words occurred.

The second criterion for controlling subjects chosen is imposed by permitting the graphic records "to index themselves." This expression implies that the nature of the subject matter encountered will dictate the development of controls in indexing. To a certain extent, any "mature" index is developed by permitting the documents "to index themselves" at the start. It is only after a representative collection of index entries has accumulated that the probable subject matter of the file can be discerned and indexing policy can be formulated or evolved.

b. CONTROL OVER NUMBER OF SUBJECTS CHOSEN. A text on cataloging and classifying makes this summary statement:

A catalog card is planned to give a concise description of a single book or set of books. Because the space on a standard card is small, the description is limited to certain important items, is given in conventional terms, and is arranged in a specific form. The items usually given are these: (1) the call number which locates the book on the shelves; (2) the name of the author; (3) the title of the book, including such items as the edition and the name of the editor or illustrator, but not necessarily all the words on the title page; (4) the name of the publisher, name of place and date of publication; and (5) description of the book, giving the number of pages (or volumes, if it is a work in more than one volume), mentioning illustrations, maps, and portraits, and indicating the height of the book. Sometimes other information is added.
A good catalogue will enable the seeker to find the book he wants from any one of the several avenues of approach.[15]

Although the application of machine methods to information retrieval has provided some relief with regard to how many "avenues of approach" may be selected during an indexing or cataloging operation, there is usually *some*

---

[15] *Syllabus for the Study of Cataloguing and Classification,* 2nd ed., School of Library Service, Columbia University, New York, 1937, p. 11.

practical, economic limit to how many points of view will be selected and therefore made explicit as reference points for searching.

Artificial limits may be established as to how many index entries may be chosen, either on an absolute basis or as an average. Once such a decision has been made, however, it is often difficult to enforce. Arbitrary inclusion or exclusion of index entries may result because of the lack of uniformity in subject content of different graphic records that may be included in a collection.

This burden of human decisions is alleviated by the use of computers to conduct indexing operations on the basis of frequency of occurrence of key words, or to limit the number of entries by the same means. The consistency of this method is commendable but its quality may be impaired.

c. CONTROL OVER LANGUAGE USED. Another independent variable in controlled indexing is the language used to record the results of analysis of graphic records. In many ways this variable is completely analogous to the control of subjects chosen. In the latter, various means are used to limit the subject matter that is made explicit during indexing. This may be thought of as providing an index with a special "point of view." For example, a document on literature retrieval in metallurgy may be indexed independently from both the documentation and the metallurgical points of view. As a result, the document may have two totally different, but useful, sets of index entries (Figure 5-11).

Independent of the control of subjects chosen, or the "point of view" of the indexer, it is considered helpful to regularize the manner in which index entries are expressed. Some of these methods are identical with those used to control choice of subjects (the subject-authority list: see Figure 5-12); however, careful examination of the subject-authority list sometimes makes it possible to discern the degree of subject control versus language control inherent in it. Control over choice of subjects is evidenced by the referring of synonymous, nearly synonymous, or related headings back to a single heading; control over language is evidenced by relating only synonymous headings to a single heading, while other relationships are noted by "see also" references.

Control over language is achieved by using various other techniques. For example, subject-authority lists may incorporate "scope notes." These notes provide a description of the limits of subject matter, or scope, of each permissible heading.

Another technique that has been used to describe the limits of subject matter of each permissible heading is the "role indicator," (alternatively called *role, role factor, or role director*). These techniques have been used in various machine systems and are quite analogous to the "modifications" used with index entries in conventional retrieval systems. These indicators are useful for limiting the area of meaning of the index entry, according to the "role" which that entry plays in a particular contest.

Let us consider a document which discusses the ways in which iron ore is processed in order to produce the pure metal. An analyst in perusing this document might provide an index entry:

Iron ore, use in preparation of pure iron, 78

The term "Iron ore" would be considered to be the *main entry*, while the phrase "use in preparation of pure iron," would be considered to be the *modification* to the main entry. (The number "78" refers to the document number in which the subject is discussed.) Someone referring to the index entry would then be guided in deciding whether to refer to document 78 in terms of his specific interests by the modification given.

If the analyst were applying role indicators in indexing, he would still select the term "Iron ore" as his main entry, and might assign to that entry a role indicator "starting material," which would specify the particular point of view from which "Iron ore" is treated in the given document [Figure 5-14].

More will be said about role indicators later in this chapter.

3. Citation Indexing. The rationale behind the citation index is the assumption that the author of a paper citing someone else's work in a reference has discerned some relationship between the subject matter of the cited work and that of his own. Therefore, all references cited in the literature are brought together in a directory, each reference accompanied by a list of citing source documents. The primary arrangement of the index may be by author of the

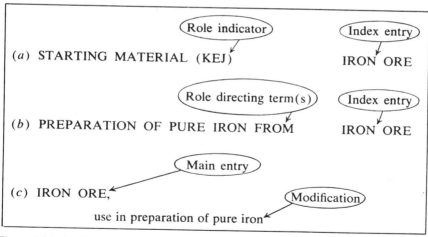

Figure 5-14. (*a*) Use of *role indicator* in systems of analysis developed at Western Reserve University (KEJ is a code representation of "Starting Material"), (*b*) use of similar technique, called *role directing term* in system developed at Linde Company (the role directing term and its corresponding index entry has been called a *structerm*); (*c*) technique analogous to use of role indicators is employed in conventional subject indexing by means of a *modification* of the main index entry.

reference, creating an author citation index; by publication in which the reference appeared, creating a journal citation index; or by date of publication of the reference, creating a chronological citation index.

For example, a paper by Richard Roe:

R. Roe, *J. Biol. Chem.,* **6**, 103 (1968).

cited by John Doe in an article published in *J. Chem. Biol.,* **7**, 55 (1969), would appear in an author citation index, listed under:

Roe, Richard

and with the citing author (John Doe) listed immediately following, together with any other authors who may have cited his work. The bibliographic citation(s) for each such entry would be provided as well.

The full bibliographic citation, coupled with a reference to the paper in which the citation appeared, recorded in machine-processible form, permits ready manipulation by computer to produce listings ready for human consultation.[16]

Shepherd's Citations, which is prepared using the citation indexing principle described above, has been used for many years as a convenient tool for searching for precedent in the legal profession.

C. Classifying

Classification may be defined as the systematic arrangement of items according to a definite plan, or in a definite sequence. More specifically, it may relate to a system for the arrangement of books or other library materials according to subject or forms. Said in another way, classification may involve arrangement or placing in a class or classes on the basis of resemblances.

A *class,* in logic, may be defined as consisting of *any* specified elements. *Anything whatsoever* may be the element of a class. For example, we may have such classes as:

1. The class of foods that are colored green.
2. The class of foods that contain more than 10 percent protein.
3. The class of foods that cause me to break out with hives.
4. The class of green objects that are edible.
5. The class of proteins that are edible.
6. The class of skin irritations that are caused by foods.

Some classes may have so little in common that their association appears ridiculous, for example, the class of football players and mining equipment.

---

[16] E. Garfield, " 'Science Citation Index'–A New Dimension in Indexing," *Science* **144**, 649-654 (May 8, 1964). See also M. Weinstock, "Citation Indexing," in *Encyclopedia of Library and Information Science*, Vol. 5, Marcel Dekker, Inc., New York, 1971.

A class may be defined even before it is possible to determine whether any of its elements exist or not, for example, the class of planets aside from Earth on which life exists.

It is also possible to recognize the existence of a class that is made up of *no* members, for example, the class of women over 30 feet tall.

Furthermore, one class may be a member of another class, for example:

1. The class of tempered steels.
2. The class of tempered steels whose properties are influenced by silicon.
3. The class of tempered steels whose properties are influenced by the addition of silicon and beryllium.

The point of this discussion is that there is no such thing as a "logical" or "universal" classification of things. In an early text of classification,[17] a very useful operational definition was provided:

Classification being the putting of things together according to likeness, there may be as many kinds of classification as there are kinds of likeness.

Likeness may be in respect of mass or weight, it may be likeness of form or shape . . . , likeness of color . . . , in hardness . . . , in brittleness . . . , in elasticity . . . , in conductivity . . . , in transparency, specific gravity, radiating power . . . .

The likeness may be one of position and space (geographical), or position in time (chronological), or of origin (genetic), or power (dynamic).

The series in likeness which is formed may be in respect of quality (better or worse), quantity (more or less), extent or duration (longer or shorter), position (far or near) . . . .

The object of classification is thus economy and increase in efficiency in the use of books. "Use" is the watch word of book classification as "truth" or "truth order" is of theoretical classification. Any variation whatever from the scientific order is permissible if so be it promote this end of use—the motive of the whole process is "getting together the books most used together."

Two types of classification approaches have been in use: the rigid, or monodimensional, classification; and the nonrigid, or multidimensional, classification.

1. Rigid Classification. Rigid classification, often called a "pigeonhole" classification, involves the characterization of each record from a single point of view. When a record is to be stored, and only a single copy is available, a pigeonhole, or a single physical location, must be provided for this record. Of course, it is recognized that records are generally multidimensional in nature.

---

[17] E. C. Richardson, *Classification: Theoretical and Practical,* Scribner, New York, 1901.

Hence, the physical classification of records often tends to assume the characteristics of a rigid classification.

2. Multidimensional Classification. Multidimensional classification involves the characterization of each graphic record from more than one point of view. This can be accomplished for the physical placement of records only when more than one copy is available for filing in more than one physical location.

However, many classification systems are employed as guides to a physical collection of records. For example, in a classified catalog, copies of catalog cards, each one representing a graphic record, are filed in appropriate locations within the classification system. Each card represents a single graphic record, but one such record may be represented by several cards. Thus it is convenient to file as many cards for a record as there are "dimensions" to the classification (see Figure 5-15).

Experimental attempts have been made to classify materials automatically, involving as a first step the generation of machine-readable information.[18] The rationale for these efforts is that: (a) content analysis is a complex task involving the analysis of meaning; (b) statistical analysis of the words of documents provides some clues as to its content. In an example provided by Borko,[19] he asserts that:

. . . a document that contains the words "boys," "girls," "teacher," "school," "arithmetic," "reading," etc., probably deals with *education*.

Accordingly, an effort was made to:

a. Construct an empirically based mathematically derived classification system;

b. Devise a set of procedures by which documents can be automatically classified into their categories; and

c. Determine the accuracy of the classification by comparison to a criteria [sic].

A collection of abstracts was used for an experiment in automatic document classification.

Classification categories were derived by means of a factor analysis technique. This technique involved sorting the words in the abstracts by computer program into an order which reflected their respective frequencies of

---

[18] See, for example, F. B. Baker, "Information Retrieval Based on Latent Class Analysis," *Journal of the Association for Computing Machinery*, **9**. 512-521 (1962).

[19] H. Borko and M. Bernick, "Automatic Document Classification," *Journal of the Association for Computing Machinery*, **10**, 151-162 (1963).

538.114:669.245.3

COLLECTIVE ELECTRON FERROMAGNETISM III. NICKEL AND NICKEL–COPPER ALLOYS

Wohlfarth, E. P., *Proc Roy. Soc.* (London) A195, 434–62 (1949); cf. *C. A.* 33, 3683; *C. A.* 43, 4941.

The theoretical implications of the overlap of the d and a electronic bands are considered. The dependence of the electron distribution on temp. is discussed. Calcns. are carried out for the transfer effect and the influence of thermal expansion is considered. The theory is applied to the temp. variation of susceptibility above the Curie point. For Ni-rich alloys satis. agreement with expt. is obtained. For Cu-rich alloys the high-temp. variation is accounted for, but the low-temp. is discussed also. Its variation with compn. is satis. accounted for with the Ni-rich regions, but again discrepancies appear at the low-temp. range of the Cu-rich alloys.

WKJ:njh

Figure 5-15. Example of abstract of document which has been characterized by the Universal Decimal Classification (modified), from several points of view. The U.D.C. number is given at the upper left corner of the illustration. This number is a combination of two separate classification numbers, 538.14 and 669.245.3 separated by a colon. The applicable sections of the U.D.C. are:

538.114		
	538.	magnetism, electromagnetism
	538.1	theory of magnetism and electromagnetism
	538.11	general laws of magnetic action. Fundamental theories
	538.114	special theory of ferromagnetism. Magnetization curves
669.245.3		
	669	metallurgy
	669.2	nonferrous
	669.24	nickel and its alloys
	669.245	nickel alloys
	669.245.3	nickel-copper alloys

occurrence in the texts of the abstracts. Frequency of *co-occurrence* of most frequently occurring words were analyzed mathematically to produce the classification categories. Then, the texts of new abstracts were analyzed to determine the frequency of occurrence of words, and were "classified" automatically.

It was determined that 48.9 per cent of the new abstracts were placed into their "correct" categories by this procedure. It was suggested that additional experimentation could improve the accuracy of the automatic classification technique.

It may be obvious that automatic classification techniques are still under experimentation. Furthermore, the techniques have not yet been tested against the criterion of usefulness. That is, controlled experiments have not been described which determine whether users of classifications so produced are led to information relevant to their particular requirements, and that information irrelevant to their interests are withheld.

D. Abstracting

Traditionally, an abstract has been considered to be "that which comprises or concentrates in itself the essential qualities of a larger thing, or of several things." An abstract is a summary of a publication or article accompanied by an adequate bibliographical description to enable the publication or article to be traced. In recent library and documentation literature, it is possible to identify three types of abstracts: (1) traditional; (2) extracts; and (3) stylized. To these must be added the "stylized index," which is closely related to the stylized abstract.

1. Traditional Abstracts. In practice, two general types of traditional, literary-style abstracts may be distinguished: the descriptive (or indicative, or annotative) type and the informative type.

The *descriptive* abstract embodies a general statement of the nature and scope of a document. It is not pretended that this type of abstract can serve as a substitute for reading the original document; it merely presents several clues as to whether or not the information being sought might be contained in the original record. The *informative* abstract, on the other hand, has the purpose of presenting (concisely) information of high probable significance contained in the original record. Ideally, the informative abstract will obviate the necessity of referring to the original.

Examples of a descriptive and an informative abstract of the same article are given in Figure 5-16.

The *descriptive* abstract often consists only of a single sentence or phrase, elaborating on the title of the document. In some instances, when dealing with subjects of considerable complexity, and in order to make the abstract meaningful, reference is made to some of the procedures, conclusions, and results of more significant investigations.

The *informative* abstract is written in order to provide a concise but comprehensive summary of the significant contributions to knowledge contained in a document. One set of rules used for preparing an informative abstract is as follows:

a. Indicate scope and objective if not evident from the title.

b. Summarize or cite all new information.

c. State principles, essentials of novel methods or equipment, and the conclusions, but not the fine details.

    d. Cite special or novel applications.

    e. Be factual; do not be critical.

    f. Be specific and informational, not vaguely general.

    g. Be brief, but retain value, especially indexing value.

A review of abstracting instructions from many indexing and abstracting services, led to the following general criteria for an adequate abstract:[20]

Purpose:	A statement on the goals, objectives, and aims of the research or reasons why the article was written. This statement should be included in both the *informative* and *indicative* abstracts.
Method:	A statement about the experimental techniques used or the means by which the previously stated purpose was to be achieved. If the techniques are original or unusual, or if the abstract is *informative*, more detail should be included.
Results:	A statement of the findings. The *informative* abstract tends to be more quantitative than the *descriptive* abstract.
Conclusions:	A statement dealing with the interpretations or significance of the results.
Specialized Content:	Certain subject-matter fields require that the abstract contain specialized information. Medical journals, for example, require that the abstract contain details of diagnosis and treatment, drug dosages, etc., where applicable. In writing or evaluating abstracts in these fields, the specialized requirements must be considered.

Although it is convenient to differentiate between descriptive and informative abstracts, the division is quite artificial, since an abstract is seldom strictly one type or the other. Actually, abstracts comprise a continuous spectrum, varying from a poor title at one extreme, through a good title, a one- or two-line annotation, a longer annotation, and so forth to the other extreme of a highly informative abstract.

A third type of traditional abstract, the *pseudo* abstract, was identified by the late T. E. R. Singer in a private communication. The pseudo abstract is described as an abstract of a paper that has not yet been, and may never be, written. It originates from the practice of inviting speakers before professional associations to submit abstracts of their papers for publication prior to delivery

---

[20] Harold Borko and Seymour Chatman, *American Documentation,* **14,** 149-160, No. 2 (1963). (Bibliography contains 30 references.)

"A new fusion welding process is carried out by bombardment with a beam of electrons in a high vacuum chamber. Basic elements are a tungsten cathode to emit a large number of electrons; a high potential, several thousand volts, between the cathode to the plate to accelerate the electrons; a focusing system to form the electrons into a beam; a vacuum chamber and pumping equipment to maintain a pressure of 5×10^{-3} mm. of mercury. Most of the work has been directed toward the development of welding procedure for Zircaloy–2 tubing, although some attention has been paid to welding tungsten, molybdenum, titanium, nickel, and stainless steel alloys."

(b) "Fusion welding of Zircaloy–2 by means of a beam of electrons in a high vacuum chamber. Technique has also been applied to alloys of tungsten, molybdenum, titanium, and nickel and to stainless steel."

Figure 5-16. Examples of informative (a) and descriptive (b) abstracts of the same article (W. L. Wyman, "High-Vacuum Electron-Beam Fusion Welding," *Welding Journal,* 37, 49s-59s, February 1958).

of the full paper. Often, these papers are delivered ex tempore and may never be reduced to full text form. Accordingly, an abstract of this paper remains in the literature—the pseudo abstract of a paper that has never been published nor otherwise recorded. In Figure 5-17, a pseudo abstract is compared with descriptive and informative abstracts.

The three functions that traditional abstracts have served are as follows:

a. *Current awareness.* To aid a reader in keeping informed concerning new developments and in acquiring new technical information.

b. *Reference.* To provide a back file of accumulated information which may be consulted as required.

c. *Indexing (or classifying).* To serve as a basis for indexing a record. The abstract is prepared after a decision has been made regarding the important aspects of a record; this same analysis can be used to provide those important aspects that should be incorporated into an index or other searching tool.

Another way of considering the functions of a traditional abstract is as follows:

a. To serve as a substitute for reading the full source material.

b. To serve as a means of predicting whether the original, full source material is worth reading; that is, to serve to separate materials that are relevant from those that are irrelevant to the particular interests of the reader.

It is the second of these functions that is most often considered when information retrieval systems are designed. For example, many such systems provide a set of abstracts to a requestor of information. It is expected that review of these materials will permit determination as to which full source materials are really relevant.

PSEUDO
> Painless dentistry is becoming increasingly significant. Newer methods of anaesthesiology will be discussed.

DESCRIPTIVE
> A method for painless tooth extraction was discovered.

INFORMATIVE
> A wooden mallet struck on the head was used instead of anaesthesia in tooth extractions. Three taps of a one-pound mallet was effective in 95% of the cases.

Figure 5-17. A pseudo abstract is compared with descriptive and informative abstracts.

The usefulness of abstracts as predictors of the relevance of full documents has been questioned in an experiment conducted with motivated users of information-retrieval systems in medicine.[21]

The results suggest that abstracts are undistinguished as predictors of relevance. First and last paragraphs of documents, extracted clerically, consistently predicted relevancy to a higher degree than abstracts and bibliographic citations.

2. Extracts. An extract is analogous to an abstract in that it represents what is considered by an analyst to be the important subject matter of a graphic record that has been selected for quotation.

Some feel that the use of direct quotations, or extracts, provides more effective service to a reader than an abstract. However, it may be argued that an abstract is able to present, usually in more concise form, a more complete indication of the contents of a record than can any extract taken out of context.

Extracts may be selected by human analysts, or by the application of machine techniques. When machines have been used for extracting, the resulting product has been called an "auto-abstract."[22]

The techniques used by humans to prepare extracts are subjective, and involve the exercise of judgment by an analyst in order to determine which portion of a document is of sufficient potential significance to warrant

---

[21] A. Kent et al., "Relevance Predictability in Information Retrieval Systems," *Methods of Information in Medicine*, **6**, No. 2, 45-51. *(April 1967)*.

[22] H. P. Luhn, "The Automatic Creation of Literature Abstracts," *IBM Journal of Research and Development,* **2**, No. 2, 159-165. (1958). See also G. Salton, *Automatic Information Organization and Retrieval,* McGraw-Hill Book Company, New York, 1968.

recording. When a machine is used for extracting, the entire text of a record is converted to machine-readable form. It is then scanned by a digital computer. It is assumed when applying these methods that the frequency and distribution of key words (and their synonyms) in the text can be used as the basis for determining the relative significance of sentences in the text. Following this assumption, the sentences that are highest in "significance" (as determined by their high content of key words) are printed out to produce an extract (or auto-abstract, see Figure 5-18).

It may be noted from Figure 5-18, that the auto-abstract of the New York Times article would read:

Two major recent developments have called the attention of chemists, physiologists, physicists and other scientists to mental diseases: It has been found that extremely minute quantities of chemicals can induce hallucinations and bizarre psychic disturbances in normal people, and mood-altering drugs (tranquilizers, for instance) have made long-institutionalized people amenable to therapy.

This poses new possibilities for studying brain chemistry changes in health and sickness and their alleviation, the California researchers emphasized.

The new studies of brain chemistry have provided practical therapeutic results and tremendous encouragement to those who must care for mental patients.

This "extract" does not seem too bad a representation of the article from which it was derived.

In an early description of this approach to analysis, it was stated that a primary objective of the program was to develop a system "that would take full advantage of the capabilities of a modern electronic data-processing system such as the IBM 704 or 705, while at the same time keeping the scheme as simple as possible." The rationale for this approach was the premise that an analyst is influenced by his background, attitude, and disposition; these may tend to bias his interpretation, or lead to inconsistent results. The analysis by machine would be based on the unbiased selection of those words that are repeated by a writer as he advances the argument of his paper, and elaborates on various aspects of a subject. Proponents of this system assume a direct relationship between the frequency of occurrence of words and the significance of the sentences that provide their context.

Since the auto-abstracting experiments were used first with a journalistic type of source material (e.g., newspaper articles), it is perhaps not too unrealistic to assume some relationship between word occurrence frequency and significance of context sentences. It may be recalled that embryonic journalists are taught to repeat the basic message of their story three times: concisely in the first paragraph; developing the theme in the next few paragraphs; and expanding the theme and providing background in the last part of the story. (This, of course, permits the editor to cut stories to desired length without having to

SCIENCE IN REVIEW

Chemistry Is Employed in a Search for New Methods to Conquer Mental Illness

By ROBERT K. PLUMB

By coincidence this week-end in New York City marks the end of the annual meeting of the American Psychological Association and the begining of the annual meeting of the American Chemical Society.

Psychologists and chemists have never had so much in common as they now have in new studies of the chemical basis for human behavior. Exciting new finds in this field were also discussed last week in Iowa City, Iowa, at the annual meeting of the American Physiological Society and at Zurich, Switzerland, at the Second International Congress for Psychiatry.

Two major recent developments have called the attention of chemists, physiologists, physicists and other scientists to mental diseases: It has been found that extremely minute quantities of chemicals can induce hallucinations and bizarre psychic disturbances in normal people, and mood-altering drugs (tranquilizers, for instance) have made long-institutionalized people amenable to therapy.

Money to finance resreach on the physical factors in mental illness is being made available. Progress has been achieved toward the understanding of the chemistry of the brain. New goals are in sight.

At the psychiatrists meeting in Zurich last week, four New York City physicians urged their colleagues to broaden their concept of "mental disease," and to probe more deeply into the chemistry and metabolism of the human body for answers to mental disorders and their prevention.

Blood May Tell

Dr. Felix Marti-Ibanez and three brothers, Dr. Mortimer D. Sackler, Dr. Raymond R. Sackler and Dr. Arthur M. Sackler cited evidence that the blood chemistry of victims of schizophrenia is different from that of normal people. Perhaps multiple biological factors are responsible for this chemical change, they suggested.

Mental disease is a "developmental process" and long duration of a disorder may result in "permanent alteration of anatomy and physiology," they said. They urged that trials of new drugs which affect the brain should be concentrated on complex studies of the mechanism of action of the drugs. The variety of substances capable of producing profound mental effects is a new armory of weapons for use in investigating biological mechanisms underlying mental disease, they said.

The sources of behavioral disturbance are many and they may come from external as well as internal forces, the four reported. This concept has already proven practical, for instances, when it enabled psychiatrists to predict that the administration of ACTH and cortisone could produce psychosis.

"It led some years ago to the development of a blood test which was 80 per cent accurate in the identification of schizophrenic patients," they said. "It permitted us on physiologic grounds to deny that the psychoneuroses and the psychoses were lesser and greater degrees of the same disease process, and, in fact, to affirm that they represented opposite and even mutually exclusive directions of physiologic disturbances," they said.

Chemicals now available should be used not only to bring relief to the mentally sick but also to uncover the biological mechanisms of the disease processes themselves. "Only then will the metabolic era mature and bring to fruition man's long hoped for salvation from the ravages of mental disease," they reported.

Chemistry of the Brain

At the psychologist's meeting here, a technique for tracing electrical activity in specific portions of the animal brain was described by researchers from the University of California at Los Angeles. They reported that deep brain implants in cat brains were used to record electrical discharges created as the animals respond to stimulations to which they had been conditioned. In this way the California group was able to track the sequence in which the brain brings its various parts into play in learning. Specific areas of memory in the brain may be located. Furthermore, the electrical pathways so traced out can be blocked temporarily by the use of chemicals. This poses new possibilities for studying brain chemistry changes in health and sickness and their alleviation, the California researchers emphasized.

The new studies of brain chemistry have provided practical therapeutic results and tremendous encouragement to those who must care for mental patients. One evidence that knowledge in the interdisciplinary field is accumulating fast came last week in an announcement from Washington.

This was the establishment by the National Institute of Mental Health of a clearing house of information on psychopharmacology. Literature in the field will be classified and coded so that staff members can answer a wide variety of technical and scientific questions. People working in the field are invited to send three copies of papers or other material — even informal letters describing work they may have in progress — to the Technical Information Unit of the center in Silver Spring, Md.

Figure 5-18. Article from *The New York Times* for which auto-abstract has been prepared. The auto-abstract consists of sentences selected in toto from the original article, based on their greatest content of key words, as determined by scanning of the entire text and computation of frequency of occurrence of words. The sentences selected for the auto-abstract are encircled. (Reprinted from *The New York Times,* September 8, 1957, p. 11, by permission of the copyright owner.)

rewrite completely.) The tendency, then, is for words and terms in the basic message to be used several times over. The frequency of occurrence of these words would be detected during automatic scanning of text.

It should be recalled, of course, that any hopeful results obtained in dealing with newspaper articles may not necessarily transfer to professional papers written for specialized audiences. Authors in these fields do not necessarily employ the same rules for exposition.

3. Stylized Abstracts

a. INTRODUCTION. In an earlier section, abstracts were discussed in terms of their being read by humans for various purposes. The following sections will present discussions of some of the effort that has been directed to the development of highly stylized "abstracts" in order to do the following:

1. Increase the consistency with which abstracts are prepared.
2. Facilitate their comprehension by readers.
3. Serve as an "index," particularly for mechanized information-retrieval systems.

b. FORMATTED ABSTRACTS. The manner in which stylized abstracts have evolved may perhaps be seen from Figures 5-19 to 5-23.

A traditional abstract written in narrative form is given in Figure 5-19. It is instructive to attempt to write an abstract of a paper and to discover how difficult it is to decide just what is of sufficient significance to be included, and to write it succinctly. How much easier it would be if it were not necessary to be faced with a totally blank sheet on which the abstract is to be inscribed, but rather to have some guide headings.

The abstract shown in Figure 5-20 provides the same information as in Figure 5-19. But some general guides are given (purposes, procedures, findings) that are used as headings about which to group information discussed in the source material.

These headings may serve as checkpoints in the mind of the abstractor, thus avoiding some omissions that might occur under production pressures. Also, when several abstractors may be at work, consistency of analysis efforts may be enhanced, at least to the extent of their having available a format within which to organize their thinking. It will be noted that use of the format has not altered the nature of the abstract—that is, it is still an indicative rather than an informative abstract.

The format of Figure 5-20 may be particularized considerably, as in Figure 5-21, in which much more in the way of headings and therefore content guidance is provided to the abstractor.

From Figure 5-21, it becomes evident that when a highly detailed format is provided, information may not be available in connection with each heading. Also, the source material to be processed by the analyst must be quite similar in character and form to make feasible the use of such an articulated format.

c. "TELEGRAPHIC" ABSTRACTS. Another step in the evolution of stylized abstracts might be identified as the "telegraphic" abstract. In this type of abstract there is provided a set of "headings," or *role indicators*, to be used in

S-0128. Ronald J. McBeath. *A Comparative Study on the Effectiveness of the Filmstrip, Sound Filmstrip, and Filmograph for Teaching Facts and Concepts.* NDEA Title VII Report, Project no. 462, University of Southern California, 1961. 22 pp.

> Experiment with 558 sixth grade pupils from Los Angeles County, grouped according to IQ, age, sex, and socio-economic status of father. Preparation of social studies lesson by means of silent captioned filmstrip, captioned filmstrip with recorded narration, sound filmstrip and 16 mm. sound filmograph. Administration of pre-test, post-test and retention test; analysis of results by variance and Tukey test. Effect of sex and IQ on achievement, and interaction between sex and presentation method.
> 56 refs.

Figure 5-19. Traditional abstract of an indicative or descriptive nature.

S-0128. Ronald J. McBeath. *A Comparative Study on the Effectiveness of the Filmstrip, Sound Filmstrip, and Filmograph for Teaching Facts and Concepts.* NDEA Title VII Report, Project no. 462, University of Southern California, 1961. 22 pp.

Purpose of Study

> To compare the effectiveness of several media for teaching facts and concepts.

Procedures

> A social studies lesson was prepared by means of silent captioned filmstrip, captioned filmstrip with recorded narration, sound filmstrip, and 16 mm. filmograph; pre-test, post-test, and rentention tests were administered to 558 sixth grade pupils from Los Angeles County, grouped according to IQ, age, sex, and socio-economic status of father. Results were analyzed by variance and Tukey test.

Findings

> The effect of sex and IQ on achievement, and interaction between sex and presentation method are discussed.

Figure 5-20. Abstract of Figure 5-19, stylized somewhat.

conjunction with subject matter selected by analysts from source materials. However, unlike the format illustrated in Figure 5-21, which is not flexible in arrangement, any one or more of a set of role indicators may be used in any order that the analyst may consider appropriate for the specific source material at hand.

Let us consider a set of role indicators (or headings) specifically selected to have bearing on education research:

1. Population

    a. Population (subject of study)
    b. Attributes given for population
    c. Environmental or geographical location

2. Process

    a. Major process being carried out in relation to the population
    b. Media (or agent of process)
    c. Attribute given for the media
    d. Subject matter taught

3. Findings and achievements

    a. Attribute or behavior found or influenced
    b. Factor influencing population
    c. Product
    d. Attribute of product

4. Design and conditions of study

    a. Type of literature
    b. Location of research
    c. Source of financial support

Using role indicators as required, an analyst might prepare a "telegraphic" abstract of the source material abstracted in Figure 5-19, as follows:

Role indicator	Description
Type of literature	Research
Source of financial support	National Defense Education Act
Population (subjects of study)	Students (558)
Location of research	Intermediate elementary school in Los Angeles County
Attributes of subjects of study	IQ
	Age
	Sex
	Socioeconomic status
Subject matter taught	Social studies
Media	Filmstrip
	Filmograph
Attribute of media	Captioned
	Narration
	Sound
(etc.)	

S-0128. Ronald J. McBeath. *A Comparative Study of the Effectiveness of the Filmstrip, Sound Filmstrip, and Filmograph for Teaching Facts and Concepts.* NDEA Title VII Report, Project no. 462, University of Southern Californa, 1961. 22 pp.

Purpose of Study

To compare the effectiveness of several media for teaching facts and concepts.

Description of Procedures

1. General methodology (e.g., survey, experiment)
     Experiment
2. Academic subject area
     Social studies
3. Teaching methods or devices
     Silent captioned filmstrip, captioned filmstrip with recorded narration, sound filmstrip, and 16 mm. sound filmograph.
4. Characteristics of population
     a. Size, 558
     b. Location, Los Angeles County
     c. Grade Level, 6th
     d. Age (not given)
     e. Other significant characteristics (not given)
5. Sampling Procedures
     Population selected from groupings according to IQ, age, sex, and socio-economic status of father.
6. Experimental treatments
     Lesson administered and pre-, post , and retention tests were administered.
7. Methods of data analysis used
     Variance and Tukey test

Findings and Effects

1. Findings relevant to purposes
     The effect of sex and IQ on achievement, and interaction between sex and presentation method was determined.
2. Correlation obtained
     (Not available)
3. By-product findings
     (Not available)
4. Major conclusions
     (Not available)

Figure 5-21. Abstract of Figure 5-19, more highly stylized.

If the role indicator-description combinations are punctuated, and read in sequence, the reason for the term "telegraphic" abstract[23] might become apparent:

Type of literature—research; source of financial support—National Defense Education Act; subject of study—students (558); location of research—intermediate elementary school in Los Angeles County; attributes of subjects of study—IQ, age, sex, socioeconomic status; subject matter taught—social studies; media—filmstrip, filmograph; attribute of media—captioned, narration, sound; etc.

---

[23] More recently, a collection of index entries and role indicators, arranged as here, has been called a "mini" abstract.

It is perhaps also apparent that the telegraphic abstract is also a detailed index to a graphic record. It is composed of (1) significant words selected from the document; (2) *role indicators* which supply a context for the selected words; and (3) punctuation symbols which separate and group the words and role indicators into various units in somewhat the same fashion as conventional punctuation does.

Telegraphic abstracting, as developed at Western Reserve University,[24] is a method for recording important characteristics of information contained in documents so that the characteristics further processed for machine input will serve the function of an index enabling the document to be identified by machine in response to requests for information. The design of the telegraphic abstract was part of an overall logic that also dictated the design of the code into which the words are encoded, and the design of the strategy and program by which the information is searched. The telegraphic abstract, the encoded terms, and the search program taken all together comprise a mechanized information-retrieval system. The purpose of the telegraphic abstract, then, was to provide "input" to the machine in a consistent and predictable form so that the machine could be programmed to search for certain predictable arrangements of information within this input.

Certain assumptions formed the basis for analysis by this system, which was used for a number of years in a mechanized information-retrieval system in the field of metallurgy:

1. The names of *materials,* their *properties, processes* which they undergo, and the *conditions* of these processes can usefully be selected as index terms. Words designating these four concepts can be taken from the records being indexed.

2. Certain roles which the words designating *materials, properties, processes,* and *conditions* can play in the context of the subject matter of the graphic record are also important in indexing the subject matter. For example, it is useful for an index to tell whether a *material* is discussed in a document as a starting material for further processing, or as a final product. The devices for designating the role of a word in a context are called *role indicators.*

3. It is also useful for an index to show how the words designating *materials, properties, processes,* and *conditions* are grouped together into certain larger blocks of information. For example, it is important that words designating a material, its chemical composition, the form or state it is in, and any important properties it may possess are shown as relating to each other and not to another material, composition, form or state, or set of properties. The devices to achieve

---

[24] J. W. Perry and A. Kent, *Tools for Machine Literature Searching,* Interscience, New York, 1958.

grouping of information units into larger units are called *links* or *punctuation symbols.* The units of information are called by analogy *syllables, words, subphrases, phrases, sentences,* and *messages.*

4. The words used in the record itself to name *materials, properties, processes,and conditions* can be encoded into an artificial language that will act as a thesaurus to show the areas of meaning which various words partake of, so that in using the index, if the words of the question mean the same thing as the words in the index, the document will be found. The device used to achieve a thesaurus function for the words selected is called the *semantic code.*

The first three assumptions listed above enter into the technique of indexing a document to make what is a telegraphic abstract, so they must be well understood by the abstracter. The fourth assumption has led to the development of an encoding process which is carried out automatically after the telegraphic abstract has been made. It is then ready to be used by a machine to find documents in response to questions.

An example of a portion of a telegraphic abstract is given in Figure 5-22. It is obvious that in order to prepare abstracts of this type three things must be

Role Indicator	Description
1. . . KEJ,	2. Rod
3. . KUJ,	4. Alloy
5. . KUJ,	6. Aluminum
7. . . KAM,	8. Annealing

Figure 5-22. Portion of a telegraphic abstract. This telegraphic abstract indicates that the document being indexed contains information about *rod, alloy, aluminum,* and *annealing.* This information is conveyed by the words listed on the right side of the form under the heading, "Description." The information given on the left side of the form, under the heading "Role Indicator," tells what *roles* these words assume in the context of the article, or how they relate to each other, and how they are grouped. In box 1 we find ". . .KEJ,". KEJ is a role indicator. It is written into this space to show that the word, "rod," which follows it, is the name of a material that is acted upon by a *process.* KEJ is followed by a comma. This is a punctuation symbol or grouping device. It tells us that KEJ is one unit of information (a word) and that the word "rod" is another unit of information. (After it is coded into the semantic code it will be a *word* made up of one or more *syllables.*) KEJ is preceded by two dots. The dot is another punctuation or grouping symbol. It tells us that KEJ+rod is also a unit of information (a subphrase), more complex than either KEJ or rod considered separately. A brief explanation of the rest of the information given in the example is that rod is shown as being composed (KUJ) of an *alloy* whose major constituent (KUJ) is *aluminum* and that this aluminum alloy rod is being subjected to the process (KAM), *annealing.*

learned by an analyst: (1) what kinds of words to select for indexing and how to write them down; (2) how to assign role indicators and how to organize them; (3) how to assign the punctuation symbols.

d. SCHEMATIC ABSTRACTS. Another evolutionary step in the formatting of abstracts but in a flexible manner is the "schematic" abstract. This is quite similar to the telegraphic abstract in basic philosophy. The differences are in format, definition of the role indicators, and the symbolism used to represent them. Accordingly, we may consider the following role indicators:

Role indicator	Symbolic representation
Direction of reaction	⟶
Affects, influences	⟶
Does not affect	—O→
Increase	↑
Decrease	↓
Related	∿
No correlation	੪
Equal	=
Not equal	⊖
Minus, absent	—
Plus, and	+
Greater than	>
Less than	<

Obviously, this set of role indicators is not the same as that given earlier, nevertheless they serve the same function: to suggest the context of index entries.

For the schematic abstract, the arrangement of index entries and role indicators is such as to attempt to provide more accurate and rapid understanding of relationships discussed in a source material (see Figure 5-23).[25]

---

[25] After A. Lazarow.

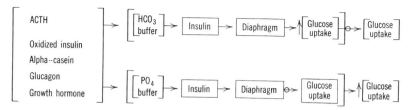

Figure 5-23. Schematic abstract for article selected from literature on diabetes.

3. Stylized Indexes

a. INTRODUCTION. Just as abstracts have been stylized to increase consistency with which analysis may be conducted, to increase reliability with which exploitation may take place, and to enhance automatic processing potentialities, indexes have become somewhat more stylized for analogous reasons. The stylized indexing approaches have borrowed heavily from the stylized abstracting techniques.

The rationale for stylized indexing may be derived from the problems encountered increasingly as "indexing in depth" came into vogue and as simple nonconventional information retrieval systems were placed into operation. As may be obvious from the term, "indexing in depth" implies the selection, during analysis of source materials, of as many entries as may be considered useful later as reference points in searching. The nonconventional information retrieval systems involve the ability to search conveniently on a multidimensional basis.

Let us develop an example of a problem that was encountered.

Three documents in a retrieval system contain the following information:

Document 1 discusses the breeding of sheep in Australia.

Document 2 discusses the breeding of horses in the United States.

Document 3 compares the breeding of sheep in Australia with the breeding of horses in the United States.

An analyst might index these documents as follows:

Document 1	Document 2	Document 3
Breeding	Breeding	Breeding
Sheep	Horses	Horses
Australia	United States	Australia
		Breeding
		Sheep
		United States

A conventional alphabetical index for the three documents might be listed as follows:

```
Australia
   Breeding
      of horses,      3
      of sheep,       1
Breeding
   Horses
      in Australia,          3
      in United States,      2
   Sheep
      in Australia,          1
      in United States,      3
Horses
   Breeding
      in Australia,          3
      in United States,      2
Sheep
   Breeding
      in Australia,          1
      in United States,      3
United States
   Breeding
      of horses,      2
      of sheep,       3
```

If one were to consult this index in order to determine in which documents breeding of sheep in Australia was discussed, it would be possible to refer, alternatively, to the headings

```
Australia
Breeding
   or
Sheep
```

and quickly come to the conclusion that only document 1 was of interest in that regard.

On the other hand, if a marginal-hole punched card was designed for this hypothetical information-retrieval problem, the holes dedicated for particular information might be as shown in Figure 5-24.

The three documents would be notched as shown in Figure 5-25. Now, if it were desired to discover in which documents the breeding of sheep in

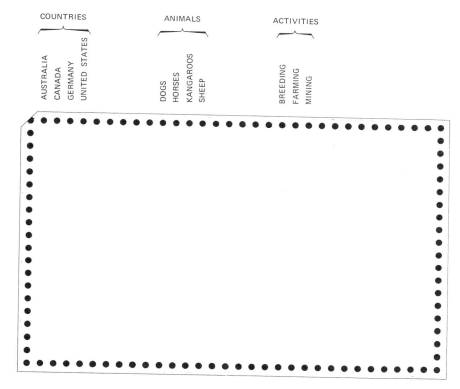

Figure 5-24

Australia was discussed, document 1 would be identified as before; but document 3 would also be identified even though it does not contain a proper response to the question posed.

It is perhaps obvious that in recording the index entries for document 3 (i.e., breeding, horses, Australia, breeding, sheep, United States) on this type of searchable medium (the marginal-hole punched card), there is no ready way to record the fact that the document discussed:

The breeding of horses in Australia
and
the breeding of sheep in the United States
but not
the breeding of sheep in Australia
nor
the breeding of horses in the United States

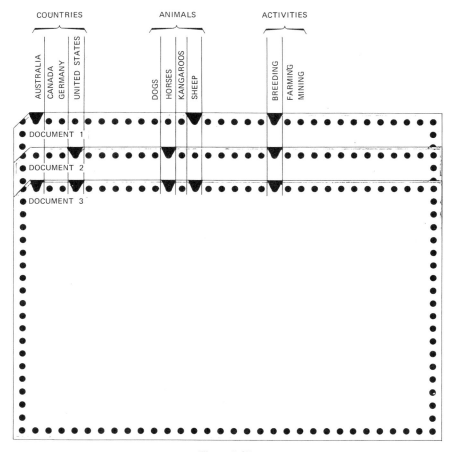

Figure 5-25

If an aspect system were to be used for recording the index entries, the situation would be no better. The aspect cards for the five index entries used for the three documents are shown in Figure 5-26. The appropriate document numbers are recorded on the aspect cards. If a search were conducted for those documents with index entries on Australia, breeding, and sheep, it is obvious that documents 1 and 3 are again both identified.

Nor would it be possible to eliminate the identification of the unwanted document 3 if the index entries were to be recorded on other media, such as magnetic tape, and searches were conducted by computer.

Thus, if a document system were involved, the information recorded in sequence on magnetic tape would be

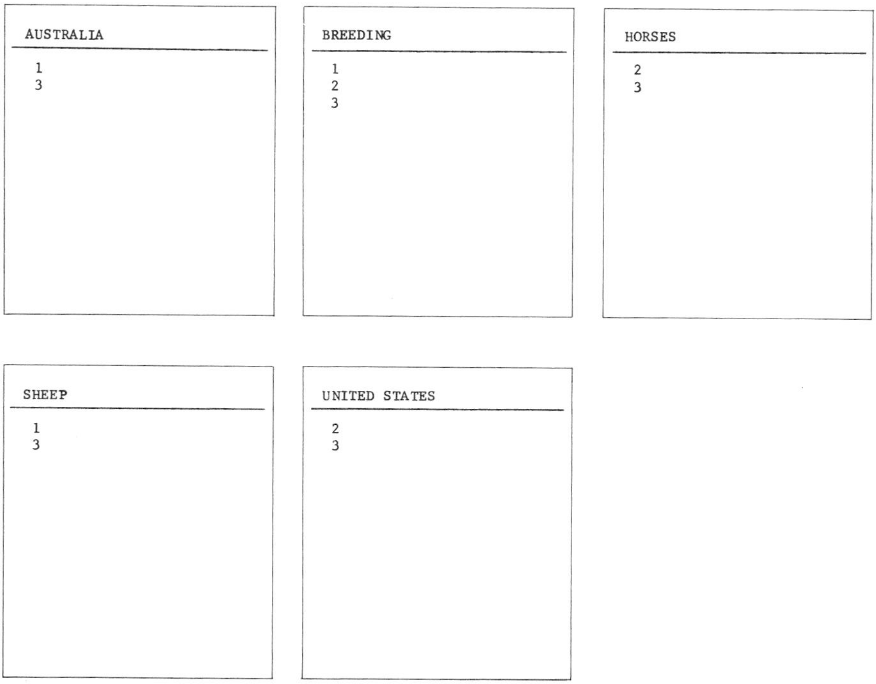

Figure 5-26

1; Breeding; Sheep; Australia. *2*; Breeding; Horses; United States. *3*; Breeding; Horses; Australia; Breeding; Sheep; United States.

A computer program could not be written which would permit searching of the tape to identify document *1* and not *3* in relation to the question (see Figure 5-27).

If an aspect system were involved, the information recorded on magnetic tape would be as follows:

Breeding; 1; 2; 3. *Sheep;* 1; 3.
Australia; 1; 3. *Horses;* 2; 3.
United States; 2; 3.

A computer program could not be written here either, which would fail to select document 3 while identifying document 1.

Techniques have been developed to control this type of "noise" (or identification of unwanted documents) when operating nonconventional retrieval systems based on deep indexing.

1. Store *criteria*:
   a. Index entries: breeding, sheep, Australia.
   b. All these index entries must be present in a document.
2. Read in the next entry from tape.
3. Is it an index entry?
   a. *If not*, it must be a document number, in which case, erase any document numbers and index entries stored previously, and store the new document number, and go back to instruction 2 (read in the next entry from tape).
   b. *If yes*, go on to instruction 4.
4. Compare index entry with each of the three index entries stored under instruction 1a.
   a. *If it matches none of these*, return to instruction 2.
   b. If it matches one of these, store the matched index entry.
5. Check to see if all three criterion index entries (1a) have already been found and stored.
   a. *If not*, go back to instruction 2.
   b. *If yes*, read out document number, as answer to question.

Figure 5-27

b. LINKS. One form of stylized indexing proposes to control this type of noise in retrieval operations by a technique calling "linking." This technique, analogous to the "punctuation" of the telegraphic abstract, provides a method for recording the fact that in document 3, the *breeding* of horses in *Australia*, is discussed separately from the *breeding* of *sheep* in the *United States*. This might be recorded as follows:

Index Entry	Link Identifiers	
Breeding	A	B
Horses	A	
Sheep		B
Australia	A	
United States		B

If this were to be recorded on magnetic tape for search by computer, as follows:

3; Breeding–A, B; Horses–A; Sheep–B; Australia–A; United States–B

it would then be possible to program a computer to search for the three desired index entries (Breeding, Sheep, and Australia), but with the added requirement that each must have an identical "link identifier," which would now suppress document 3.

This linking technique may also be exploited in manual retrieval systems. In the example given above, *Breeding, Horses,* and *Australia* would be considered to be index entries for *subdocument* 3a; while *Breeding, Sheep,* and *United States* would be considered to be index entries for *subdocument* 3b. In aspect systems each subdocument number may be considered as if it were an independent document number. When computers are used, subdocument numbers need not be used; rather, the links may be exploited through programming, as mentioned above.

c. ROLES. As discussed earlier, it is perhaps obvious that index entries may have several different roles in documents. For example, an index entry "Wiring" may represent the material that is used for *wiring* purposes, or the process by which *wiring* is accomplished. Also, the index entry for a particular chemical may represent the chemical compound when it is discussed as a raw material or when it is presented as a final product.

As an additional example, the name of a personality mentioned in a document may be indexed by name alone regardless of the role of this personality in the particular document. This personality may be author of the document, he may be subject of the document, or he may be discussed by another personality who is the main subject of the document.

If a search is to be directed to the name of that personality, it may turn out that many inappropriate references may be identified if the questioner wishes to locate only those references to the particular personality in which he has a specific function or role.

In these instances it may be economically feasible to establish an analysis procedure which identifies roles of index entries made explicit during analysis.

One set of empirically derived role indicators has been promoted aggressively by the Engineers Joint Council,[26] together with encouragement to use these roles in conjunction with links. Some of the role indicators suggested are the following:

1. Principal subject
2. Raw material
3. Product
4. Waste or by-product
5. Possible applications
6. Environment

---

[26] *Information Retrieval—The Problem . . . Coordinate Indexing—A Solution,* Engineers Joint Council, New York, 1964.

7. Cause
8. Effect
9. Means to accomplish primary objective
10. Bibliographic and other source identifying data.

To illustrate how the role indicator might be used, let us assume that an article compares the open-hearth process for making steel from iron and traces of bauxite, with the Hall process for producing aluminum from bauxite, and which aluminum may be coated with steel to produce light weight building blocks. The index entries chosen, with appropriate role indicators, might be as follows:

Index entry	Role Name	Role Number
Steel making	Principal subject	1
Iron	Raw material	2
Steel	Product	3
Open hearth	Process—or means to accomplish primary objective	9
Aluminum production	Principal subject	1
Bauxite	Raw material	2
Aluminum	Product	3
Hall process	Process—or means to accomplish primary objective	9
Aluminum	Raw material	2
Coating	Process	9
Steel	Raw material	2
Building blocks	Product	3

Of course, the role indicators could be used in conjunction with links, to produce the following.

Index entry	Link - role	Link - role	Link - role
Steel making	A - 1		
Iron	A - 2		
Steel	A - 3		C - 2
Open hearth	A - 9		
Aluminum production		B - 1	
Bauxite		B - 2	
Aluminum		B - 3	C - 2
Hall process		B - 9	
Coating			C - 9
Building blocks			C - 3

E. Processing of Full Texts

1. For Information Retrieval. A full text may be considered to be "processed" for retrieval purposes whenever it has been read and indexed, classified, abstracted, extracted, or otherwise analyzed. In general, such processing implies that certain subjects and points of view have been selected from the text by human or machine analysis in order to record decisions as to what in the text of a document is of greatest probable importance for retrieval purposes.

However, some research has been aimed at recording for retrieval purposes essentially everything that is available in the full text of a source document. The rationale behind this approach is that potential needs are so diverse that only the recording of essentially an entire document would provide adequate services.

A U. S. Patent Office procedure[27] typified the approaches that use an intermediate "ruly" language for encoding documents. The presumption is that some regularized synthetic language can more accurately convey meaning (particularly within a mechanized system) than can a natural language. V. H. Yngve took the contrasting point of view[28] that English represents a highly regular language, very well "engineered" for the purpose of conveying meaning within an information-retrieval system.

Another approach, followed at one time in research at Itek Corporation[29] seemed to be an attempt to use any available syntactic information about English to regularize natural language documents. By this means, it was claimed, unwanted information is eliminated and implicitly conveyed information is added or is more expressly defined. Others, however, are ultimately concerned with making automatic analysis of English documents in such a way that the intended meaning of the message is preserved or conserved. Needless to say, to accomplish this objective, many difficult syntactic problems must be considered. What is lacking, of course, is an unambiguous set of structural rules governing the operation of the language.

It should be recognized that the approaches to recording of full texts for retrieval purposes make the assumptions that:

a. The text will be "read" by machine, or that the text will be made available by publishers in machine-readable form (for example, monotype tape).

---

[27] S. M. Newman, "Linguistic Problems In Mechanization of Patent Searching," U. S. Patent Office Research and Development Report No. 9, 10 pp., 1957.

[28] V. H. Yngve, "In Defense of English," in A. Kent, Ed., *Information Retrieval and Machine Translation,* Interscience, New York, 1961, Part 2, Chapter 40.

[29] T. M. Williams, "Language Engineering," J. H. Shera, A. Kent, and J. W. Perry, Eds., *Documentation in Action,* Reinhold, New York, 1956, pp. 330-337. See also A.C.F. Industries, "Translations from Ordinary Discourse into Formal Logic," ARCRC Report TN-56-770.

It is not yet evident that the full range of type fonts, styles, and reproduction techniques now in use will permit effective and economical programs for machine recognition of text. Otherwise, it is necessary to keyboard all text into machine-readable form, in order to make it available for further processing.

　　b. It will be economical to search by machines the tremendous full texts volume of produced even in restricted fields, without attempts to "compress" the available material by a "probabilistic" approach to analysis of the document.

　　c. Most questions can be analyzed so precisely that an equally precise selection of matching information in the full text of a document will provide useful results. It is anticipated that the major problem to be faced is that "normalization" or syntactical analysis of running text by machine may well yield answers to questions from trivial mentions of a "subject," as well as from those that are more significant.

　　d. It is tacitly assumed that requests for searches will be based on *recognition memory* rather than *recall memory*. In the former pattern, the formulation of a request for a search is based on the way in which a requester remembers, or believes he remembers, the text of a record that he has seen before. In the latter, a request for a search is based on recalling some subject that is of interest, whether or not it may have been seen before. In this latter case, the resources of natural language are sufficiently great so that the alternate clues that would have to be provided when formulating a question are sometimes staggering.

　　2. Mechanical Translation. In seeking a reasonable conclusion to the question of determining feasibility (economically, technically, emotionally) of automatic processing of full texts for analysis purposes, it is perhaps wise to examine the progress made in automatic processing methods in a related field—*mechanical translation.*

　　At a "Conference on Mechanical Translation" at Massachusetts Institute of Technology on June 17-19, 1952, it was pointed out that:

> The best machine we have at the present moment can do the same as only 100 translators, and it costs you four hundred to five hundred thousand dollars a year. You've bought twenty translators for one hundred thousand dollars.

Not quite 15 years later, we saw the raw output of a Russian-to-English machine translator produce the following, totally automatic product:

> Contemporary experience/experiment of native and foreign machine building shows that decision/solution of complicated technical problems connected with search of new materials, is attained by combining of polymers in combination with different fillers, plasticizers and stabilizers.

Human editing of this mechanical product, resulted in:

Recent experience in domestic and foreign machine construction shows that the solution to complex technical problems connected with the search for new materials is attained by combining polymers in conjunction with various fillers, plasticizers, and stabilizers.

The initial product is certainly not too badly misleading, particularly to the subject matter specialist, whose "sixth sense' permits identification of misleading passages and straightening out of poorly designed sentences. Even such a machine product as:

Own polymers—this still is not material useful for manufacture of that or other machine-building component/part: it is necessary to give him/it/them optimum from the point of view of their official properties micro- and macro-structure.

seems capable of rationalization by the specialist. It is perhaps instructive to see the comments made by subject specialists who examined the machine product.

a. Estimate we can get about ¾ of the sense out of this. . . .
b. It can in many cases determine if a complete good translation is desired. . . .
c. The idea of *prompt* approximate translation is a fine one.
d. If costs are anywhere near costs of a good translation—will take the good translation very time.

One of the simplest approaches to mechanical translation involves the creation of an automatic dictionary, which lists, for given foreign language words, the English translations. It is possible to simulate the operation of such an automatic dictionary, as follows:

a. Start with a Russian sentence such as:

ОТМЕНЯТЬ право для кары убииства

b. Write each Russian word on a separate index card:

	Page Number <u>310</u>
	Line Number <u>07</u>
	Word Number <u>1</u>
ОТМвНЯТЬ	

   c. Alphabetize index cards to destroy context, and consult Russian-English dictionary.

   d. Copy the English definition(s) for each Russian word on the appropriate index card:

```
┌─────────────────────────────────────────────────────────┐
│                                                         │
│                              Page  Number  310          │
│                              Line  Number   07          │
│         ОТМеНЯТь             Word  Number    1          │
│                                                         │
│            English Definitions                          │
│            ───────────────────                          │
│            (1)   To  Abrogate                           │
│            (2)   To  Abolish                            │
│            (3)   To  Repeal                             │
│                                                         │
└─────────────────────────────────────────────────────────┘
```

   e. Rearrange index cards into original Russian word order (consulting the page, line, and word order numbers on each card).

   f. Copy the English definitions:

TO ABROGATE LAW

                              PENALTY   OF ASSASSINATION
TO ABOLISH   ORDER FOR

                              PUNISHMENT OF MANSLAUGHTER
TO REPEAL   RIGHT

   g. Edit the resulting material, by selecting the appropriate definitions, adding definite and indefinite articles, and stylize:

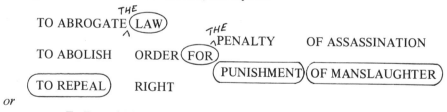

or

To Repeal The Law For The Punishment of Manslaughter

   Although this is an extremely naive approach to translation, the resulting product is probably good enough so that a subject specialist who does not know the foreign language can understand the contents well enough to index, abstract, and perhaps even produce a literary translation.

   Perhaps there is a lesson to be learned in the automatic processing area from these reactions. The success of automatic analysis should not be judged on the basis of a comparison with some theoretical criterion of perfection, but rather upon what is attainable in an economical and otherwise feasible manner.

SUPPLEMENTARY READING

1. Rynin, D., Ed., *Alexander Bryan Johnson's Treatise on Language,* University of California Press, Berkeley, 1959.
2. Wittgenstein, Ludwig, "The Uses of Language," in M. White, Ed., *The Age of Analysis,* Mentor Books, New York, 1955.
3. Reichenbach, Hans, *Experience and Prediction,* The University of Chicago Press, Chicago, 1938.
4. Ross, Ralph, *Symbols and Civilization*, Harcourt, Brace & World, New York, 1962.
5. Malmberg, Bertil, *Structural Linguistics and Human Communication,* Academic Press, New York, 1963.
6. Garvin, P. I., Ed., *Natural Language and the Computer,* McGraw-Hill Book Company, New York, 1963.
7. Bar-Hillel, Y., *Language and Information,* Addison-Wesley, Reading, Mass., 1964.
8. Morris Jack C., "The Duality Concept in Subject Analysis," *American Documentation,* 5. 117-146 (1954); See also *Journal of Cataloging and Classification,* 10, 119-121 (1954).
9. Vickery, B. C., *Classification and Indexing in Science,* 2nd ed., Academic Press, New York, 1959.
10. de Grolier, Eric, *A Study of General Categories Applicable to Classification and Coding in Documentation,* Unesco, Paris, 1962.

Six

Principles of Searching

I. INTRODUCTION

The lawyer, the chemist, the physician, the historian, the typical scholar in almost every field—all have at one time or another faced a common problem and come to a common decision. Each decides that his literature problem has assumed crucial proportions, and each demands new methods for searching and correlating the literature of his discipline. Each has felt that his is a unique problem for which a unique solution must be developed. In many of these cases, the spokesmen are correct in their estimation of the situation. The proportions of the information-retrieval problem are indeed burdensome. And it is true that each branch of knowledge has, for various reasons, developed certain literature problems that are peculiar to itself, which must be met by skillful custom redesign of any standard system of retrieval.

Certain basic principles of searching, however, have proved to be common to all subject fields. Accordingly a number of searching devices can be used effectively regardless of the subject field involved. These devices operate on the basis of certain common logical procedures. Thus the basic steps that must be taken, in conducting any searching operations are as follows:

1. A question or problem must exist and be recognized, and it must be verbalized or recorded for communication to the search system.

2. The question must be analyzed in order to select analytics (or clues) that will be useful in formulating a strategy of search.

3. The analytics selected must be transformed into a language and into a strategy configuration that conforms to those of the system used for analysis and storage of the records of the file.

4. The analytics and search strategy selected must be formalized in terms of a language and program that will conform to those of the device used for searching.

5. The searching machinery must be set into motion.

6. A response must be obtained.

To ensure understanding, it may be useful to work through these steps in terms of a search that might be conducted in a library (a search system), using the card catalog as the searching device.

1. A patron of a library might communicate a question to the reference librarian.

2. After dialog with the patron, the reference librarian would determine what the key concepts (analytics) of the patron's question might be.

3. The reference librarian would translate these concepts:

    a. Into standard subject headings.

    b. Into a strategy of search, for example, to consult each heading successively until sufficient material of interest is identified.

4. The desired subject headings would be arranged in alphabetical sequence to match the arrangement of the catalog.

5. The catalog would be consulted for each heading successively by selecting the appropriate card trays and riffling through the cards until the appropriate heading was located.

6. A response would be obtained by copying the call numbers of the source materials identified.

Were a computer to be used, the steps to be taken would be the same in kind, if not in detail. The first three steps, not really involving a machine or device, are quite in common, regardless of the retrieval system, since they are performed by people.

In this chapter are discussed the principles involved in the first three of the steps listed above, the nonmechanized steps. Chapter 7 will be devoted to the last three steps, those involving the use of searching equipment of one type or another.

In considering the subject of this chapter, it may be useful to restate the utopian objective of any information-retrieval system:

To provide on demand, with maximum usefulness, precision, and at minimum expense, pertinent information in response to any reasonable question—a reasonable question being defined as any serious question of obvious or potential significance, posed by a person who has a socially important reason for desiring the answer to the question.

It is obvious that the terms of this objective cannot be applied with formalistic precision to every search. For one reason, it would surely be a utopian society that provided clear and unambiguous patterns of "usefulness," "precision," or "expense." Common sense must once more be called into service as the final test. One can imagine a question whose positive answer is worth an unlimited amount of money:

IS THERE A CURE FOR CANCER?

An accurate response would have to be obtained, at whatever sacrifice of "principle" or ideal objective of information searching.

Still, there are a number of principles that can helpfully be applied to the systematization of the searching process.

First, let us hypothesize an ideal information-retrieval system, consisting of three operational areas:

1. Input (processing of records to be searched).
2. Output (searching, identifying, and delivery operations).
3. Auxiliary conjunction (maintaining consistency between input and output).

Each of these areas may be considered separately in more detail:

1. The input operations include the activities of analysis, vocabulary control, recording, and storage. In the course of the input operations, decisions must be made regarding each of the following:

   a. Choice of those characteristics of the subject matter (e.g., index entries) that will be made available for future retrieval operations.
   b. Choice of the form in which the selected characteristics are recorded.
   c. Choice of the location and form in which source materials are stored.

2. The output operations (of which searching is one) comprise the retrieval activity. During these operations, an attempt is made to identify analytics used during input which relate to the analytics of a given question.

3. Auxiliary conjunction may be imagined as the function of an ideal observer who, knowing both input and output, furnishes such information as is needed to maintain consistency between the input and output operations. In a real information-retrieval situation, the auxiliary conjunction is accomplished by one or more techniques, each of which contributes to the task of maintaining consistency. The more familiar of these devices and operations are as follows:

a. *Subject authority list.* A tabulation of standard subjects used in information systems for the purpose of achieving consistency in the analysis of information and used in recording the results of such analysis.

b. *Cross reference.* A notation that makes explicit a relationship between two or more terms used to designate the subject contents of graphic records, or between two or more portions of a classification system. Two forms of cross reference are as follows:

"See" references, for terms that are said to be functionally synonymous for a particular information-retrieval system.

"See also" references, for terms that are said to be related closely enough to warrant the recording of a potentially relevant subject that the searcher might find it rewarding to consult.

c. *Duplicate entry.* One of several similar subject headings under which a reference to a document may be recorded redundantly. The purpose of this redundancy is to counteract uncertainty on the part of the analyst, by permitting him to enter a reference in more than one place so that the searcher may approach any one of the entries and still be led to the desired material.

d. *Thesaurus.* A book of words that shows explicitly the relationships among the words it contains. These relationships may be those of

* synonymy
* specific to generic (often called *Broader* term)
* generic to specific (often called *Narrower* term)
* general nonspecific relationship (often called *Related* term)

II. RECORDING OF A QUESTION

We may now return to the first of the six basic steps listed at the beginning of this chapter: the recognition of a question and its recording as the basis of a search. In order to formulate a question that is to be the subject of a search of a file of graphic records, it is necessary to verbalize or otherwise record the subject of the search for communication to the operator of an information system. It is not difficult to accomplish this task if the questioner is familiar with: (1) the subject contents of the file that is to be searched, (2) the policy for analyzing the contents of the records, and (3) the vocabulary control tools used. However, it should be remembered that the person who formulates a question may never have seen or read any of the pertinent records that he hopes to locate. Therefore, it is necessary for the questioner to:

1. Predict the way in which authors, possibly unknown to him, have written about the concepts, ideas, or subjects that are of interest;

2. Predict the way in which information-center personnel, possibly unknown to him, have analyzed these records;

3. Predict the way in which analytics have been recorded.

Since it is quite difficult for the questioner to make those three predictions accurately, he must formulate his question at a sufficiently high level of generality, or in sufficiently numerous variations of expression, so that he can have reasonable assurance of being able to locate most of the records that contain information pertinent to his question (see Figure 6-1).

Generic Question
I am interested in books on space exploration (when I am really interested in the flight of Apollo 11).

Question with Variations of Expression
I wish to have materials on metal jewelry, men's accessories, and precious metals (when I am really interested in gold cuff links).

Figure 6-1.

III. SELECTION OF CLUES FROM A QUESTION

Since we are dealing with systems for mechanized retrieval of information, we can expect that these systems have been designed to conveniently provide a multidimensional approach to the retrieval of records. Such design implies that source records will have been characterized from more than one point of view. Therefore, it will be convenient to retrieve records of interest by specifying in a search question more than one aspect of subject matter. Thus, hopefully, a narrower focus and a higher degree of pertinence can be expected in the products of the search.

In traditional systems, which may be monodimensional in nature, searches would generally be directed to a single topic, or aspect. When a traditional, alphabetic index is consulted, for example, that of the *Technical Abstract Bulletin,* of the Defense Documentation Center, it is convenient to refer to a single main entry, and to read the references identified under it. Accordingly, if one were interested in locating all documents on, for example,

gunners' aiming errors in antitank weapons

it would be necesary to refer to one of the two entries provided in the alphabetic index:

Gunnery, performance (human)

or

Antitank guns, gunnery

Then, if desired, the other entry could be consulted.

In nonconventional systems which permit a multidimensional approach to searching, it would be possible to specify that

> gunnery, performance (human)
> *and*
> antitank guns

both be available as aspects in a given source document in order for that document to be identified

Once a question has been formulated, how can one select appropriate clues to serve as a basis for the searching activity? The solution to this problem is dependent on the analysis system that has been applied to the file (Figure 6-2).

Question: What reactions take place during the reduction of metal powders from their respective oxides?

(a)	(b)	(c)
Metal powdered oxides, reduction, reactions	Metal powders Powder metallurgy Deoxidation	The reaction mechanism for the reduction of metal powder oxides is . . .
Powders, metal oxides, reduction, reactions		
Aluminum powder oxides, reduction, reactions		When metal powder oxides are reduced the following reactions occur
Magnesium powder oxides, reduction, reactions		The deoxidation of metal powder oxides is associated with the following reactions
. . . . .		Aluminum powder is reduced from its oxide and is accompanied by the following reactions
Reduction, of metal powder oxides, reactions		. .
Deoxidation, of metal powder oxides, reactions		. . .

Figure 6-2. Clues selected from a question in a form to correspond with the searching system used: (*a*) hypothetical indexing system; (*b*) hypothetical classification system; (*c*) hypothetical natural-language system.

If an indexing approach has been used, then it behooves the questioner to provide clues in terms of ideas that are likely to have been indexed. If a classification approach has been used, then the questioner must select the category or class that he believes is most likely to have been used to characterize information of interest to him. If an entire text in natural language has been recorded in searchable form, then it is necessary for the questioner to predict the various ways in which the clues may be expressed in natural language, despite the fact that he may not have seen that context before.

The analysis of questions to identify analytics as reference points in searches is analogous to the analysis of source materials. As an example, a question such as:

Do you have any documents that discuss the use of natural fibers (such as abaca) and synthetic fibers (such as Dacron) in textiles?

might have such clues identified as: natural fibers, abaca, synthetic fibers, Dacron, and textiles.

In selecting the words that will be used to express analytics directed toward desired information, a number of aids are available, centering in general on a thesaurus, when an index-based, or natural-text retrieval system is involved, or on an index, when a classification-based system is involved.

For example, in the Thesaurus of ASTIA Descriptors (May 1960), the term abaca fibers is listed together with a scope note.

Abaca Fibers (Fibers, Textiles, and Dyes)

Include: Manila

The scope note is intended to indicate the usage of the term in the index.

In the *ASTIA Thesaurus,* there is provided under the heading

93 Fibers, Textiles, and Dyes

a descriptor group, as follows:

Abaca fibers	Dyes	Glass textiles	Rayon thread
Artificial leather	Elastic webbing	Leather	Silk
Asbestos fiber	Esparto fibers	Metallic textiles	Sulphur dyes
Ceramic fibers	Feathers	Nylon	Synthetic fibers
Cordage	Fibers	Nylon rope	Textile screens
Cotton cellulose	Fire resistant	Nylon thread	Textiles
Cotton mats	textiles	Orlon	Threads
Cotton textiles	Fluorescent dyes	Parachute fabrics	Woolen textiles
Dacron	Fluorescent textiles	Plastic thread	Yucca fibers
	Fur	Ramie fiber	

This list of terms are considered to be thesaurally related to *abaca fibers.* Accordingly, when "abaca" is being considered as a reference point for a search, the terms in the descriptor group are also made available for consideration as additional or alternative search reference points.

In another type of thesaurus, a semantic code dictionary, used for one type of mechanized information retrieval system,[1] the term "abaca" is listed together with its code, as follows:

Term	Code
ABACA	FABR·TUTL·OO1

The code elements (FABR and TUTL) serve, in a way, the same purpose as scope notes. For example, the code element FABR means "member of the class *fabrics;*" and TUTL means "used in *textiles."* When each of these code elements is consulted in the code dictionary, a set of terms, all having the same code element in common, are listed.

Thus under FABR (Fiber) are found the following terms:

> FIBER
> FIBRE
> FIBROUS
> FLAX
> HENEQUEN
> JUTE
> HEMP
> SISAL
> FIBERGLAS
> *ABACA*
> RAMIE
> RAYON

These terms may be considered to be thesaurally related, and available for consideration as additional or alternative search reference points. Similarly, under TUTL (Textile) are found the following terms:

> TEXTILE
> ABSORBENT COTTON
> KAPOK
> VAT DYES
> *ABACA*
> BOBBIN
> MERCERIZATION
> MOSQUITO NET

which are available for consideration in a similar manner.

---

[1] J. W. Perry and A. Kent, *Tools for Machine Literature Searching,* Interscience, New York, 1958.

In another type of thesaurus, the entry *ABACA FIBERS* might have listed under it:

> *SYNONYM(S)*
> MANILA
> MANILA HEMP
> *BROADER TERM(S)*
> FIBER
> TEXTILE FIBER
> *NARROWER TERM(S)*
> ABACA (from Musa Textilis)
> *RELATED TERM(S)*
> MARINE CORDAGE

A search directed to *abaca fibers* might yield additional materials if *manila* and *manila hemp* were used as alternative reference points, since these latter terms are used synonymously with *abaca fiber* by many. The search could be broadened or narrowed as considered appropriate, by using the terms listed above as desired.

When a classification system is the basis of a retrieval system, an index may serve as an entree to the system. Let us consider a question such as:

Do you have any materials on hydraulic turbines?

The clue selected as a search reference point might be *hydraulic turbines*. But if the question analyst did not appreciate the organization of the classification system of source materials in which appropriate responses might be located, the analyst might not be able to locate the appropriate heading in the following section of the system:

Portion of Classification System

62	Engineering
621	Mechanical engineering
621.2	Hydraulic power, Hydraulic machines
621.24	Hydraulic turbines

The alphabetic index to the system would provide convenient entrée, as follows:

> *Index to Portion of Classification System*
> Engineering, *class 62*
>   mechanical, *class 621*
> Hydraulic machines, *class 621.2*
> Hydraulic power, *class 621.2*
> Hydraulic turbines, *class 621.24*

Mechanical engineering, *class 621*
Power, hydraulic, *class 621.2*
Turbines, hydraulic, *class 621.24*

Location of the index entry "Hydraulic turbines" would identify the appropriate class "621.24."

IV. ORGANIZATION OF SEARCHING CLUES

A. Introduction

When a question has been analyzed, and clues presumed to be useful in searching have been selected, it is necessary to transform these clues into the "language" of the system that has been used to organize the file of records to be searched.

Is the process of transforming clues inherently different in mechanized systems than in conventional systems? In general it is not, but it is important to recall that in operating mechanized information-retrieval systems, there are three dimensions of extension that may be achieved over conventional searching systems (Figure 6-3).

Title of Document: "Development of Die Lubricants for Forging and Extruding Ferrous and Nonferrous Materials"
Question: Select documents on all aspects of the forging of magnesium.

(a) "Conventional" subject headings	(b) Characteristics of documents chosen for a machine system	(c) Characteristics relating to question
Metals–Extrusion	Die	
Dies–Lubrication	Lubricant	
Lubricants–Development	Forging	Forging
	Extruding	
	Ferrous material	
	Nonferrous material	
	Aluminum	
	Titanium	
	Magnesium	Magnesium
	Steel	

Figure 6-3. Characteristics (or clues) to subject content of a record are usually selected in greater number for a machine system (*b*) than for a "conventional" system (*a*); when a question is formulated it is considered to be more convenient to direct a search to a combination (or coordination) of characteristics (*c*).

1. Searches may more conveniently be based on the "coordination" of several aspects (or clues) of the source records. This type of search can be performed more effectively with machine systems because of the convenience of independently recording characteristics (or clues) of records that are considered important.

2. It is generally economical to record a greater number of characteristics (clues) of the records because of the lower unit cost for such operations. Obviously, this makes available for search and correlation a greater number of characteristics of the records.

3. It is generally convenient to search more effectively in a case where a search prescription (specification of clues) is not identical to the clues expressed as a result of analysis of records. In most traditional searching systems, it is convenient only to require that the characteristics of a record identified either *apply* or *do not apply* to the search prescription. In mechanized systems it is possible to base selections on the fact that the characteristics *partially apply* to the search prescriptions. Characteristics *partially apply* to the search prescription when:

    a. There is *partial synonymity* between characteristics.

    b. There is *partial overlap* in the scale of *generality-specificity* between characteristics.

    c. There is *partial overlap* between the characteristics sought and those available.

    d. There is information available in two or more records which, taken together, would satisfy a search prescription.

As an example of each of these situations, let us consider the following problem:

Select all documents on all aspects of the forming of light metals and vanadium.

The clues, or key words, identified as search reference points are

> Forming
> Light metals
> Vanadium

Now, let us consider the document discussed as an illustration in Figure 6-3 which is relevant to the problem, whose title is

> "Development of Die Lubricants for Forging and
> Extruding Ferrous and Nonferrous Materials"

Let us assume that the analyst who indexed this document for inclusion in an information-retrieval system selected the following entries;

1. Die
2. Lubricant
3. Forging
4. Extruding
5. Ferrous material
6. Nonferrous material
7. Aluminum
8. Titanium
9. Magnesium
10. Steel

It will be noted that none of the clues selected as search reference points (forming; light metals; vanadium) for the question are listed as index entries. And yet *forging* is really a *forming* operation. Accordingly, a system which made explicit the thesaural relationship between the two terms would permit identification of one of the aspects of the relevant document. This is an example of partial synonymity between characteristics being made explicit for search purposes.

The question clue *light metals* could be satisfied by the specific document aspect *magnesium* (which may be characterized generically as a "light metal") if the retrieval system would make explicit the specific-to-generic relationship between the two terms. This is an example of *partial overlap in the scale of generality-specificity* between characteristics.

The final question clue *Vanadium* still remains unmatched with any of the available aspects of the relevant document and regardless of how a thesaurus or other reference aid might be designed, there just is no information on that clue in the one document. In this case let us assume that *information is available in two or more documents which, taken together, would satisfy a search prescription.* It is then only necessary to suppose that a second document is available in the file, perhaps with a title such as "Forging of Vanadium." This document would provide the remaining characteristics, *vanadium* (related to *forging*), which would then provide complete satisfaction of all the aspects of the question. However, two documents would be used, each providing partial satisfaction.

B. Transformation of Clues into Language of Searching System

The clues selected from a question are usually words, terms (one or more closely "bound" words), phrases, and the relationships among them. Usually these are expressed initially in natural language, and their transformation into the language of a searching system is dependent upon the peculiarities of the particular system, and upon its coding system, if any.

1. Word Indexes. In word indexes the clues selected from graphic records during analysis are *words,* and therefore words must similarly be chosen as clues from questions in the hope that these later will find matching words in the index. Help in choosing word clues may be obtained by using a thesaurus that may suggest words as search clues that may not appear in the question.

Examples of word indexes follow:

a. CONCORDANCES. Since a concordance is an alphabetical index of *words* in a book, listed in exact context, any question directed to this type of index must have its clues made up of words.

Consider the example of a search through a full text (by computer) for all words that relate to

ADVERTISING

To ensure that an exhaustive search would be performed, it could well be appropriate to list the alternative spelling

ADVERTIZING

as well as other forms of the term, for example,

ADVERTISE	and	ADVERTIZE
ADVERTISING	and	ADVERTIZING
ADVERTISER	and	ADVERTIZER
ADVERTISERS	and	ADVERTIZERS
ADVERTISEMENT	and	ADVERTIZEMENT
ADVERTISEMENTS	and	ADVERTIZEMENTS
ADVERTISABLE	and	ADVERTIZABLE

If such a search were to be performed by computer, then it might be expeditious to conduct the search for all words starting with the characters

ADVERTI

regardless of what the word endings might be. In other words, all characters following the "i" are arbitrarily *truncated.* This has been called *right* or *rear-end truncation.*

But truncating at this point would fail to identify the word ADVERT, which is often used by the British instead of ADVERTISEMENT. So the decision might then be made to search for:

ADVERT

truncated earlier in the word.

This begins to give difficulty, since truncating at that point would bring to the searcher's attention such words as:

ADVERTORIAL

whose meaning shades off a bit from the original intent. But this is perhaps not too serious a problem, until we remember that the most common shortening for ADVERTISEMENT is

AD

Now if we were to truncate all that follows "AD" we would have a tremendous number of inappropriate words brought to our attention (along with the desired ones):

ADamite
ADaptation
ADdict
ADding machine
ADenoid
ADhere
ADjuster

and hundreds more. Now we must reconsider whether the truncation search was helpful,[2] and whether it might not have been better to specify that the search should consider each of the specific words of interest (including variant forms and spellings) as independent reference points of search.

The truncation issue can become even more interesting when we consider the possibility of *left* or *front* as well as *rear*-end truncation.[3] An example might involve a search for everything on:

MOBILIZATION

Where a rear-end truncation to:

MOBILIZ—

would take into account variant forms such as:

MOBILIZING
MOBILIZER
MOBILIZERS
MOBILIZATIONS
MOBILIZE
MOBILIZES
MOBILIZABLE
and so on

Should there be a desire to take into account as well such words as *demobilization* and *remobilization,* and all of their variant forms, then both front- and rear-end truncation searches might be performed on the set of characters:

—MOBILIZ—

---

[2] A search should not only retrieve all that is wanted, but also withhold all (or much) that is not wanted.
[3] See *Truncation Guide* (A collection of recommended term fragments for right-hand truncations used in search profiles), IIT Research Institute, Chicago, Illinois, May 1970.

wherever they may appear with a word. The shorter the set of characters (for example, —MOB— to take care of the term DEMOBBED— a shortened form of demobilized) the more unwanted words are likely to appear from the least expected places, such as

autoMOBile

b. KEY-WORD-IN-CONTEXT (KWIC) INDEX (OR PERMUTATION INDEX). As was pointed out in Chapter 5, the KWIC index is based on the cyclic permutation of words in which each "substantive" term is brought to a predetermined position and alphabetized. Since KWIC indexes are generally based on author titles, the use of words is difficult to predict. With an index of this type, the analysis of questions to yield searching clues must result in the selection of words. The discussion above, under *concordances* is therefore relevant here.

c. UNITERM INDEX. This system is another type of word index which involves the selection of key words from graphic records (Chapter 5). When a question is analyzed these key words must be predicted to provide searching clues. Unless some type of control had been exercised during analysis of source materials, to ensure that variant forms of a given word are not used, the discussion under *Concordance* above, would be relevant here.

d. NATURAL-LANGUAGE-BASED SYSTEMS. In this type of system the total text has been recorded in machine-searchable form. If a search is directed to clues based on words, all the conditions pertaining to word indexes hold true here (Figure 6-4).

2. Controlled Indexes and Classifications

a. UNCODED. In controlled indexes the clues selected from graphic records during analysis are recorded as words (or terms), which are chosen so as to regularize the manner in which the results of analysis are expressed (see Chapter 5).

If this regularization is achieved through use of a subject authority list or classification system, the clues selected from a question must be expressed in terms of the accepted language of the authority list or classification (see Figure 6-5).

b. CODED. If a code is used to express the accepted terms in the authority list or a classification system, the clues selected must be expressed in terms of the same codes (Figure 6-6).

It is necessary to record the relationships between clues (analytics) and codes in a dictionary in which the clues are represented in some orderly arrangement, for example, alphabetically or in numeric sequence.

Summaries are presented of projects on: (1) axial stress fatigue,
creep, and rupture properties of notched and unnotched specimens of heat-resistant materials; Inconel X-550, and 3% Mo-
Waspalloy; (2) effects of surface preparation methods of fatigue
and other properties of specimens; (3) grain-size effects in
fatigue and creep and their relationship to notch geometry, stress
gradient, and size of specimen; (4) damping properties of materials under various combinations of alternating and mean stress
below the cyclic stress sensitivity limit; (5) compilation of a
bibliography of damping properties of structural materials; (6) rota-
ting, bending, damping, elasticity, and fatigue properties of
notched and unnotched specimens of S-816 alloy . . .

Figure 6-4. Sample of natural-language text which is to be searched for several word
clues derived from the question: "Select all documents that discuss the mechanical
properties of nickel alloys." One selection of clues might be *mechanical properties* and
nickel alloys. These clues would not match *A* and *B* above. Another set of clues might
be derived as mechanical properties (for example, *rupture*) and *nickel alloys.* Here only
rupture would find a match with *A* in the text above. A third set of clues might be
derived as mechanical properties (for example, *rupture*) and nickel alloys (for example,
Inconel X-550). Here both characteristics of the question would find matches with *A*
and *B.*

Clues from question	Portion of subject-authority list	Portion of classification	
(a) Coordinate indexes	Coordinate indexes. See *Aspect system*	2	Machine searching systems
		21	Document systems
		22	Aspect systems
(b) Aspect system	Aspect system		
	_____ definition		
	_____ relationships		
	_____ storage organization		

Figure 6-5. In controlled indexes or in classifications, clues must be expressed in
carefully regulated terminology as given in a subject-authority list or in the classification. Clue (*a*) was not provided in the authority list as an accepted heading.
Instead, a cross reference was provided to supply the accepted heading. Clue (*b*)
was found in the authority list exactly as expressed in the question. Both clues (*a*) and
(*b*) refer to specified portions of a classification system, as determined by reference to
an index to the classification, or from knowledge of the precise scope of each heading.
If the precise scope is not known, then alternative headings must be searched.

Clues from question	Portion of subject-authority list	Codes (arbitrary) for headings in subject-authority list
Coordinate indexes	Coordinate indexes. See Aspect System	Coordinate system = 32 · 58 · 29
Aspect system	Aspect system. *See from* Coordinate indexes	Aspect System = 32 · 58 · 29

Figure 6-6. When codes are used to express accepted headings in an authority list, identical codes (32 · 58 · 29) are assigned to all synonyms or other "see from" references.

For example, should there be interest in locating information on the clue *dynamite*, an "English-to-code" dictionary would be consulted. Here a segment such as the following might be found:

English	Code
DYE	C-8
DYNAMIC	G-17
DYNAMIC ISOMERISM	P-93
DYNAMITE	E-5
EAR	A-42
EARTH	S-3

Reference to the "code-to-English" dictionary could reveal a segment such as the following under "E" (for Explosives):

Code	English
E-1	AMATOL
E-2	BLACK POWDER
E-3	CRESYLITE
E-4	CYCLONITE
E-4	RDX
E-5	DYNAMITE
E-6	GUANIDINE PICRATE
E-7	GUN POWDER
E-8	LYDDITE
E-8	MELINITE
E-9	NITROGLYCERINE
E-10	PENTAERYTHRITOL TETRANITRATE
E-10	PETN
E-11	SMOKELESS POWDER

E-12	TETRALITE
E-13	TETRYL
E-13	TRINITROPHENYLMETHYLNITRAMINE
E-14	TRINITROTOLUENE
E-14	TNT

The value of the English-to-code dictionary is to permit ready identification of a code for a given clue (in this case, *dynamite*). The "code-to-English" dictionary can serve to bring together those terms that are related in some way. In the example given above, the clue "dynamite" could lead to a listing of all explosives covered in the file.

The code-to-English dictionary is particularly useful when new terms are to be added to a system. Thus, if the new term "trimethylenetrinitramine" should be encountered and the assignment of a code to it required, reference to the "E" section of the code would permit determination that two synonyms of the new term had already been coded:

Code	English
E-4	CYCLONITE
E-4	RDX

Thus the new term would be assigned the code "E-4."

If a clue is not found in a code dictionary, the following alternatives are possible:

1. To locate another clue which is synonymous or nearly so;

2. To assume that a particular idea has not appeared in the code dictionary and therefore has not been encountered in the file to be searched; or

3. To assume that an error has been made in recording the clue in the dictionary.

C. Strategies of Search

Once the clues of a question have been transformed into the language or codes of a particular searching system, then it is necessary to select a search strategy (or search prescription)[4] which it is felt will best exploit the contents of a particular file of records in response to a particular question.

---

[4] Also called *profile, search profile,* or *user profile.*

Before considering formally the specific types of search strategies, it would be well to step back to examine what is intended to be accomplished.

If we consider a diagram such as the following:

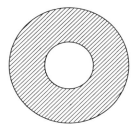

where the *outer circle* represents all of the source materials included in an information-retrieval system and the *inner circle* represents those source materials that were "retrieved" by the system, then the operation of a *perfect* system would require that *all* of the materials retrieved were of pertinent interest, and that none of the nonretrieved materials (shaded portion above) were of pertinent interest (in other words, nothing of interest was missed).

It is difficult to imagine any system behaving perfectly, so let us look at less than perfect results of searches.

In the following diagram

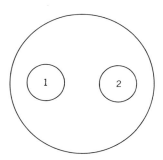

the outer circle again represents all of the materials in the system and circle 1 represents those source materials that were "retrieved" by the system. On inspection, none of these materials were found to be of pertinent interest. Rather, on inspection of the materials *not* retrieved by the system, it was found that another set of materials (circle 2) was of pertinent interest. This represents the worst case of system operation, where pertinent material did exist in the system, but the search did not locate *any* of it.

Let us turn now to another case

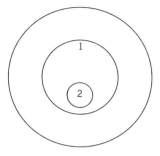

where again the *outer circle* represents all of the source materials in the system and *circle 1* represents those source materials that were "retrieved."

On inspection, only a portion of these materials were found to be of pertinent interest (circle 2). Also, no materials of interest failed to be retrieved. This type of result can provide the user of the system with confidence that nothing is being missed. On the other hand, if the quantity of materials retrieved is very large and must all be examined to discover only a few that are of interest, then dissatisfaction is likely to result.

The general case is shown in the following:

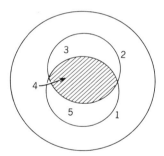

where the *outer circle* again represents all of the source materials in the system:

Circle 1 represents those source materials that were retrieved.

Circle 2 represents those source materials found to be of pertinent interest.

Crescent 3 represents those of interest *not* identified by the search system.

Shaded area 4 represents those of interest that were identified by the search system.

Crescent 5 represents those retrieved but not of interest.

The trick is to regulate the system so that 3 and 5 are as small as possible. If both cannot be minimized simultaneously, the nature of the search requirement should suggest which criterion should have priority.

One major way to regulate the information system is through the proper choice of search strategy.

The various types of search strategy are given below. In all of the following discussions, we will assume, unless otherwise stated, that the capital letters of the alphabet, A, B, C, . . . Z, are clues selected from a question, sought in a file of records. For purposes of this part of the discussion, it will not matter whether the clues are expressed as words or codes.

1. Single Aspect (or Single Clue) Search. In this case we are interested in identifying all records in a file that have a single clue in common: for example, all records that have clue A.

An example of such a question is

I wish to have all records in the file that have been authored by John. R. Meredith.

In this question, the single clue is the author's name, *John R. Meredith* (A).

Alternatively, we may wish to identify all records that have one subject in common:

I wish to have all records in the file that deal with lunar landings.

In this question, the single clue is the subject, *lunar landings* (A).

Single aspect searches are characteristic of those conducted with conventional indexing systems. Since the index entries are generally listed in alphabetical order, access to the index is attained most conveniently by specifying a single subject or author and finding it in its proper alphabetic order.

2. Strategy of the Logical Sum. In this case, we are specifying two or more aspects or clues as reference points in a search, and we are interested in identifying all records in a file that are characterized by any of these aspects or clues.

This search strategy may be represented symbolically as:

$$A + B + C + D \ldots + Z$$

which means that a record is desired if it has present

Clue A *and/or* Clue B *and/or* Clue C
and/or Clue D . . . *and/or* Clue Z

An example of such a question is

I wish to have all records in the file that have been authored by John R. Meredith or John S. Meredith or John R. Merredith or John S. Merredith.

In this question, the four clues are alternative spellings of the author's name (or authors' names):

John R. Meredith	(A)
John S. Meredith	(B)
John R. Merredith	(C)
John S. Merredith	(D)

Such a question would be asked when there was uncertainty as to the middle initial of the author (it was remembered as being either "R" or "S") and as to the spelling of the last name (either one or two "R" 's). The search strategy would be represented symbolically as:

$$A + B + C + D$$

There are other reasons why this type of search strategy might be used. For example, if a search is to be conducted for all records on *mercury*, the search strategy might call for all records that have the clues:

mercury *or* quicksilver

since the two clues are synonymous, and it may not be possible to predict which clue might be available for any particular record. In this case, if *mercury* is represented by A, and *quicksilver* by B, then the search strategy could be expressed as:

$$A + B$$

Sometimes the logical sum is used as a means of overcoming uncertainty as to the extent to which a particular information retrieval system has provided generic aspects or headings as reference points for searches. For example, an indexer may have encountered the aspect "dog" in a document which was considered sufficiently significant to select as a searchable entry. But how would questions be phrased? Would most searchers be interested generically in "animals" or more specifically in individual animals, for example, dogs, cats, horses?

If only the aspect "dog" is used, then a questioner interested in "animals" would be required to enumerate all of the specific animals that would be of interest. The resulting expression would be:

Provide me with all documents on *dogs* and/or *cats* and/or *horses* and/or . . . etc.

The symbolic statement of the expression would be representative of the strategy of the logical sum:

$$A + B + C + \ldots$$

3. Strategy of the Logical Product. Here we are interested in identifying all records in a file that have two or more clues in common: for example, all records that have clues

A and B.

This search strategy may be represented symbolically as:

A × B

which means that a record is desired if, and only if, it has present both

A *and* B

An example of such a question is

I wish to have all records in the file that have been authored by John R. Meredith in 1961.

In this question the two clues are the author's name (John R. Meredith—A) and the year of publication (1961—B).

Another example of such a question strategy is

I wish to have all records in the file that deal with lunar landings by Americans in 1970.

Here the three clues are

Lunar landings	(A)
Americans	(B)
1970	(C)

The search strategy requires that a single record must contain all three clues before it is to be considered of interest. The symbolic representation of the search strategy is

A × B × C

It is this strategy that perhaps is least familiar in terms of normal experience. In conventional catalogs, classifications, and indexes, only mono-dimensional, or single aspect searches, are conducted normally. This is the case because it is convenient to conduct only single aspect searches—that is, to specify a single area of interest, unrestricted in any way.

It is not surprising that only monodimensional, single aspect searches are performed with alphabetic indexes. Let us consider the steps that would have to be taken to conduct a three-aspect, logical product search:

   a. The entries for each of the three aspects would have to be consulted.
   b. The references to source material listed for each aspect would have to be copied, setting the references for each index entry alongside one another.
   c. The references would have to be compared visually to determine which were common to all three entries.

In traditional alphabetic indexes, the conventional single aspect search may often provide too large a response, containing too many references which are only peripherally related to current interests, if at all. In order to restrict responses selectively, conventional indexes often list modifications to the main entries, so that visual scanning may permit effective limitation of references identified.

For example, the subject index to the first edition of this text, contained the following entries:

Index(es)
    alphabetic, manipulation, 130-133
    citation, 129
    codes used, principle involved, 170-171
    controlled, 90-97
        expression of searching clues, 119-123
        role of words, language, and meaning, 157-158
    coordinate. See Aspect System; Aspect Cards; and Inverted file
    deep, exercise, 228-229
    definition, 84-85
    entries, limitation on quantity, 94-96
        modification, 97
    etc.

The indented modifications serve to specify, or limit, the meaning of the main entry (*Index*). In a way, then, the strategy of the logical product is involved when it is specified, for example, that documents are desired on *indexes*:

        If, and only if, *Citation Indexes* are described.

If "Index," the main entry, is assigned the symbol A, and "citation," the modification, is assigned the symbol B, then only those documents containing information on both topics, or:

$$A \times B$$

are desired.

4. Strategy of Logical Product of Logical Sums. In this case we wish to identify those records in a file that have one or more of several sets of clues in common: for example, all records that have clues A or B *and* C or D. This search strategy may be represented as:

$$(A + B) \times (C + D)$$

which means that a record is desired if any of the following combinations of clues is present:

1. A and C	6. A, B, and D
2. A and D	7. B, C, and D
3. B and C	8. A, C, and D
4. B and D	9. A, B, C, and D
5. A, B, and C	

An example of such a question is

I wish to have all records in a file that have been authored by either John R. Meredith (A) or John S. Meredith (B) and that were published either in 1960 (C) or 1961 (D).

$$(A + B) \times (C + D)$$

In this question, only alternative combinations (1-4) would make sense, for the alternative initials in the author's name were provided as clues because of uncertainty as to the correct ones; the same is true of the alternative publication dates provided as clues. However, it is conceivable that alternative combinations (5-9) might represent valid criteria for successful searches if either of the following two conditions were true.

a. At least one record in the file has been coauthored by two individuals, named John R. Meredith and John S. Meredith, respectively.

b. At least one record represents a two-volume work, the first of which was published in 1960 and the second in 1961.

Another example of such a question strategy is

I wish to have all paintings on file which are oils (A) or watercolors (B) which show animals (C) such as horses (D) or cows (E) and mountains (F) or trees (G).

This symbolic representation of the search strategy is

$$(A + B) \times (C + D + E) \times (F + G)$$

Here, a painting would be considered pertinent to the question if any of the following combinations of clues is present:

A and C and F	B and D and G
A and D and F	B and E and G
A and E and F	A and B and C and F
A and C and G	A and B and D and F
A and D and G	A and B and E and F
A and E and G	A and B and C and G
B and C and F	A and B and D and G
B and D and F	A and B and E and G
B and E and F	:
B and C and G	A and B and C and D and E and F and G

Of course the interpretation suggested by the symbolic representation above is not the only one that may be valid for the question statement. Another interpretation, although not seemingly reasonable, might be:

$$A + [B \times (C + D + E) \times (F + G)]$$

The strategy of the logical product of logical sums is perhaps the most useful one from a practical point of view. The resolving power of the logical product strategy is based on its ability quickly to identify specifically relevant material by requiring that two or more somewhat generic aspects are present in the source material. However, that strategy is effective only if there is

- a. Certainty that the aspects involved have been used with real consistency by analysts of source materials.
- b. No uncertainty on the part of the information seeker with regard to which aspects are really of interest.

Of course, in practice, there is very often uncertainty on both scores. Accordingly, the strategy of the logical product of logical sums is used to overcome, as much as possible, the effects of these uncertainties.

Retrieval systems based on uncontrolled indexing require extensive use of this strategy, as will be clear from the following example.

One of the search strategies (profiles) developed for the current awareness searching of a file which has been indexed using a KWAC[5] approach, relates to an interest in:

ELECTROCHEMICAL ANALYSIS OF AIR POLLUTION

Since this file depends, for searching, on an uncontrolled index, it was necessary for a search strategy to be developed which took into account:

- a. Synonyms of the desired terms
- b. Partial synonyms of the desired terms
- c. Variant forms of the terms to be searched

Accordingly, a strategy of search (profile) was written which called for:

	Parameter 1		Parameter 2
A	*polarog*	K	carbon dioxide
B	spectro*	L	carbon monoxide
C	amperomet*	M	dinitrogen pentoxide
D	sampl*	N	nitrous oxide
E	potentiomet*	O	nitric oxide
F	gas chromatog*	P	nitrogen dioxide
G	electro*	Q	sulphur oxide
H	anal*	R	sulphur trioxide
I	determination	S	sulphur dioxide
J	detection	T	exhaust
		U	air pollut*

[5] Keyword, augmented in context. This is the Chemical Abstracts Service Condensates file, which provides keywords from titles, augmented in an uncontrolled way, with one or more entries.

The asterisks indicate truncation: if the asterick appears at the beginning of a word, it is front-end (or *left*) truncation; if at the end, it is rear-end (or *right*) truncation. Each "parameter" lists a number of alternative terms (truncated or not as indicated) which form the logical sum elements of the strategy. The "parameters" are coordinated through the logical product strategy. Thus the strategy for the above question is

$$(A+B+C+D+E+F+G+H+I+J) \times (K+L+M+N+O+P+Q+R+S+T+U)$$

    5. Strategy of the Logical Difference. Here we wish to identify records in a file that are characterized by the presence of one or more clues and the *absence* of one or more specified clues; for example, all records which have clue A but where clue B is absent. This search strategy is represented as:

$$A - B$$

An example of a question illustrating this type of strategy is

    Select all records that were authored by John R. Meredith (A) unless they were coauthored by James Smith (B).

Another example is

    Provide all records on the use of aspirin (A) except when overdoses (B) were taken.

    Although this strategy can be very helpful, it is also quite dangerous to use in many situations.

    Let us assume that in relation to the example question above, one of the source materials included in the system had information on normal doses of aspirin and overdoses of phenobarbitol. Let us further assume that index entries had been provided for: *aspirin, normal doses, phenobarbitol,* and *overdoses;* without indication of how the *normal doses* and *overdoses* were linked to *aspirin* and *phenobarbitol,* respectively. A search strategy of the logical difference variety

$$A \text{ (aspirin)} - B \text{ (overdose)}$$

would cause the document discussed not to be selected as an appropriate document, whereas it is indeed relevant.

    6. Strategy of Sequence. Again we wish to identify two or more clues, but this time the clues must be found in the record in an exact sequence; for example, clues A and B must be present, but A must always precede B. This may be represented as:

$$< A \times B >$$

    An example of this strategy is a search of natural-language English text, with the object being to identify all sentences that contain the clues

Venetian and *blind* in that order. Any sentences containing the same clues but in reverse order (*blind Venetian*) would lead to a different meaning and therefore unacceptable references.

7. *Strategy of Searches Between Barriers.* In this case we wish to identify two or more clues in a record, but the clues must be found within a specified subunit of the record. This may be represented as:

<Barrier (e.g., period) X (A X B) X Barrier (e.g., period)>

An example of such strategy is

Select any record that provides the *birthdate* (A) of any American *Army general* (B); this information must appear in a single sentence of the record.

The reason why such a specification might be made is that a record may have information on the birthday of an *Army captain* in one sentence, and on the date of *death* of an *Army general* in another sentence. If the barrier specification were not made, the record would be selected based on the first clue (birthdate, but of an Army captain) and the second clue (Army general, but date of death given) and lead to the identification of a record that is not of interest as a response to the question.

In Chapter Five, this problem was discussed in terms of the usefulness of providing roles and links to reduce the amount of ambiguity that might result during searches. Every role is linked to an index entry, while several role-index entry combinations may themselves be linked together. The strategy of search between barriers may be thought of as being useful specifically to exploit the roles and links that may have been provided during the analysis operation.

8. *Strategy of Greater Than and Less Than.* In this case, we wish to identify records that contain, usually, numerical data, which lie between certain specified limits.

A question of this type might specify:

All records are desired that were published between 1950 and 1960.

The strategy would involve a search for publication years *greater than* 1949 but *less than* 1961. Or:

> 1949
< 1961

9. *Other Strategies in Current Use.* When a logical sum strategy is used alone, or as part of a more complex strategy, the question may arise as to whether each of the alternatives prescribed are of equal interest or usefulness, for example,

Although I am particularly interested in China platters (A), I will accept materials regarding China cups (B), bowls (C), pitchers (D), saucers (E), or utensils (F).

If I were now to weight my interests, I might give a value of 10 to China platter (A) since it would satisfy my interests as nothing else would. Then I would assign a value of 1 each to the other China items (B through F). Now, it would be necessary to provide a weighting element to the strategy. Thus, for each one of the items present in the strategy, the assigned weighting value would be accumulated, leading to a total "weight" for each document identified as responsive to the requirement.

A minimum value would be given for the threshold weight of a document before it would be identified as pertinent.

The weighting algorithm could be calculated in a more sophisticated manner if weights had been assigned to index entries during the original analysis of a source material, as an indication of importance of the topic in a given document. The weighting algorithm could then take into account the significance of an index entry to both the indexer and searcher, in any manner desired.

Some weighting schemes do not eliminate documents from a response to a question, but rather rank orders them by the weighting value.

V. FUNCTIONS OF SEARCH STRATEGIES

A. Introduction

Let us now attempt to picture the function that each search strategy performs in terms of the purposes of information-retrieval systems, that is, to identify relevant and to withhold irrelevant information when searches are conducted.

In the following illustrations the square:

will represent the information available in an entire system; the circles,

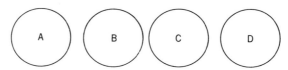

will represent that information within the entire system which is relevant to the aspect, or index entry, which is represented symbolically by the letters A, B, C, D, ...

The following

would then mean that aspect A represents a considerable fraction of the total information available in the system; while

would mean that aspect A represents only a small fraction of the total information.

Thus an information-retrieval system on *government expenditures,* which contained an entry, or aspect, on *federal and state expenditures* would be representative of the first case. A system on *foods* which listed an aspect on *dry roasted peanuts* might be an example of the second case.

B. Single-Aspect Search

A single aspect strategy would be feasible under one or more of several conditions:

1. The fraction of the total information selected, or rather the absolute amount of information thus identified, is not greater than that which the information seeker wishes to examine.
2. The aspect available for search matches sufficiently closely in generality or specificity the subject of interest, so that
   a. Too much material of peripheral interest may not be identified; or
   b. Not all the material of interest available in the system may be identified.
3. The aspect available for search has been used with sufficient precision and consistency so ᵗhat there would not be too much uncertainty that alternative aspects would have to be searched in addition (that is, using a logical sum strategy).

C. Strategy of the Logical Sum

This strategy might be represented as:

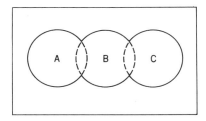

This would mean that there are three alternative aspects (A, B, and C) which might provide equally relevant responses to a question. In other words, the solid line in the diagram represents the totality of information presumed to be of interest. In a way this strategy may be considered to be quite analogous to the single aspect search, but where there is uncertainty as to (1) what is really wanted; or (2) how the wanted information may have been labeled by the analyst(s) of the source materials in the system. These alternatives are expressed logically as the logical sum.

D. Strategy of the Logical Product

This strategy might be represented as:

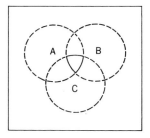

This would mean that only those materials which have three aspects in common (A, B, and C) are to be identified as relevant (the area outlined by the solid lines is representative of the materials which satisfy that condition).

Thus, an inquiry on all *federal expenditures* (A) for *road building* (B) during *1960* (C) might be representative of the logical product strategy, which attempts to provide the resolving power needed to narrow searches down by specifying the requirement for several coincident aspects.

E. Strategy of Logical Product of Logical Sums

But, just as before, when specifying any aspects as reference points in a search, there is often some uncertainty as to whether they will indeed identify what is wanted. Accordingly, alternatives may be provided for one or more of the aspects given in a logical product strategy. For A, three alternatives are given, A_1, A_2, and A_3:

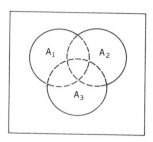

For B, two alternatives are given, B_1, and B_2:

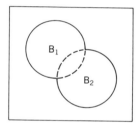

For C, two alternatives are given, C_1 and C_2:

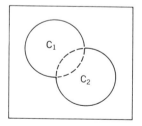

When these are all superimposed, or "coordinated" in a logical product strategy as shown

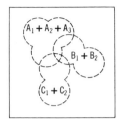

then the area of overlap (solid lines) represents the information identified as relevant according to the strategy:

$$(A_1 + A_2 + A_3) \times (B_1 + B_2) \times (C_1 + C_2)$$

F. Strategy of the Logical Difference

This strategy may be represented as:

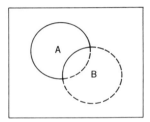

Only those documents on aspect A are identified which do *not* have aspect B in common. An inquiry illustrating this strategy is one on all publications on *federal expenditures* (A), except those for *road building* (B).

G. Other Strategies

The strategies of sequence, search between barriers, and greater than and less than, are merely special cases of the logical product strategy, and will not be pictured functionally here.

SUPPLEMENTARY READING

1. Cassirer, Ernst, "The Philosophy of Symbolic Forms," Vol. I, *Language,* Yale University Press, New Haven, 1953, pp. 198-215.
2. Berkeley, E. C., *Symbolic Logic and Intelligent Machines,* Reinhold, New York, 1959.
3. Becker, J., and R. M. Hayes, *Information Storage and Retrieval,* John Wiley & Sons, Inc., New York, 1963, pp. 335-343.

4. Taulbee, O. E., "New Mathematics for a New Problem," in A. Kent and O. E. Taulbee, Eds., *Electronic Information Handling,* Spartan Books, Washington, D.C., 1965, pp. 151-160.

5. Fairthorne, R. A., *Towards Information Retrieval,* Butterworths, London, 1961, Chapters 1, 8, and 14.

Seven

Manipulation of Searching Devices

I. INTRODUCTION

Once a question has been verbalized and analyzed, clues have been selected, and a strategy of search has been formulated, then it is time to operate the searching device. This chapter is devoted to a description of the techniques used to operate searching devices in terms of whatever searching strategy may be formulated. These descriptions use as their starting points the presentation of the physical tools (see Chapters 2 to 4).

We may consider searching systems as divided into two general classes. The first type, which can be called a search-ready system, is ready for direct use by a human operator, essentially without further use of mechanical or other tools. The second type (the machine-searchable system) requires further manipulation or operation in order that a search may be conducted.

II. SEARCH-READY SYSTEMS

In a search-ready system, those clues have been selected that seem likely to be reference points in future searches. These clues are then arranged in such a way that searching by human beings will be facilitated to the extent that, it is hoped, the time and expense of arrangement will be justified.

A. Alphabetic Index

An example of such a special-purpose array is the alphabetic index. In this type of index, all clues selected as potential reference points of searches are expressed in language, code, or other symbolism in a sequence that is generally understood, for example, that of the Roman alphabet.

Table 1 illustrates the way in which the various strategies of search discussed in Chapter 6 may be handled as routines by a human being searching an alphabetic file on questions relating to *semiprecious stones*.

The first two strategies listed on Table 1 (single aspect and logical sum) are those most familiar to users of conventional alphabetic indexes. Normally, a question would be analyzed to determine which single index entry, or aspect, would most probably refer to relevant references. Thus a search might be directed to the entry:

Semiprecious stones

Any references listed under this entry would be the total response. This is an example of the single aspect strategy.

If there were to be uncertainty as to which single entry would be most suitable, two or more alternative entries may be searched, with all of the references of each of the entries being considered as the search result. Following the example above, a search might be directed to the entries:

1. Semiprecious stones
2. Gems

in order that references listed under either of these two "near" synonyms be identified. This is an example of the logical sum strategy.

When a question is somewhat more specific in nature, the strategy can be narrowed by restricting the references identified through use of modifications of the main entry. An entry under "Gems," with a number of modifiers, such as:

Gems
        Composition, 37, 92, 258
        Hardness testing 79, 342
        Index of refraction, 6, 10, 42, 78, 312
        Quality, 15, 92, 103, 260

could be consulted to locate references on "hardness testing of gems." This may be considered as a way in which a logical product strategy may be employed using an alphabetic index. However, if use of this strategy is attempted when two or more main entries are involved in the search, then it becomes somewhat more cumbersome to handle. Thus for the same question on hardness testing of gems, reference to hypothetical main entries, such as:

Table 1

	Representation		
Type of Search	Symbolic	Examples of Values for Symbols	Search Instructions
1. Single aspect	A	A = Semiprecious stones	Search for "Semiprecious stones" under the S in the alphabetic index.
2. Logical sum	A + B + C + ⋯	A = Aquamarine B = Amethyst C = Tourmaline	Search for "Aquamarine" and "Amethyst" under the A's and for "Tourmaline" under the T's. The search is satisfied if any one of the aspects is located.
3. Logical product	A × B	A = Gems B = Index of refraction over 2.40	Search for "Gems" under the G's and for "Index of refraction" under the I's (alternatively, one of the "modifications" under "Gems" may provide a reference to Index of refraction). If the same record is identified under both headings, the search may be satisfied.
4. Logical product of logical sums	(A + B) × (C + D)	A = Bloodstone B = Aquamarine C = Opal D = Tourmaline	Search for "Bloodstone" under the B's and, if not found, for "Aquamarine" under the A's; if either is found, search for "Opal" under the O's and, if not found, for "Tourmaline" under the T's. If either of these is found, and if the same record was identified under either A or B, then the search is satisfied.

5. Logical difference	A − B	A = Semiprecious gemstones B = Amethyst	Search for "Semiprecious gemstones" under the S's and, if found, search for "Amethyst" under the A's. If any record is listed under the former heading but not the latter, then the search is satisfied.
6. Sequence	$\langle A \times B \rangle$	A = Blood B = Stone	Search for single heading under B which consists of the words "Blood" and "Stone" in that sequence.
7. Between barriers	$\langle$ Barrier $\times$ (A $\times$ B) $\times$ Barrier$\rangle$	Barrier = Beginning of main index heading A = Gems B = Index of refraction over 2.40 Barrier = Beginning of next main index heading	Search for "Gems" under the G's; then, under the modification to this index heading, search for "Index of refraction" under the I's. This modification must be located under the "Gem" heading; if it is found under another following main heading in the index, it is not deemed applicable to this search requirement.
8. Greater than, less than	Statement of question: "Locate all gems with an index of refraction exceeding 2.40."		Conduct search as for 7 above; then, if modifications list indices of refraction and numerical values for them, select only those that exceed 2.40.

Gems, 42, 79, 103, 342
.
.
.

Hardness testing, 7, 9, 62, 79, 101, 342

would be required. The page references to each of the entries would then have to be listed side by side:

42	7
79	9
103	62
342	79
	101
	342

to permit visual identification of those page references in common to both entries (79 and 342).

If a search were to be conducted for all references to gems except those on hardness testing the logical difference strategy would require the visual identification of those page references under "Gems" which are *not* given under "Hardness testing" (42 and 103).

Alphabetic indexes are amenable to searches involving *right* (rear-end) truncation (see Chapter 6). A search for all entries starting with "ADVERTI—" can be conducted readily by consulting an alphabetically arranged list of entries, such as:

ADVERTISABLE
ADVERTISE
ADVERTISER
ADVERTISERS
ADVERTISES
ADVERTIZABLE
ADVERTIZE
etc.

However a search involving *left* (front-end) truncation cannot be performed conveniently. It is perhaps obvious that a search for

—MOBIL—

when it does not occur at the beginning of an entry, would require scanning of every entry in an alphabetic index.

It may also be obvious that as searching of an alphabetic index using the remaining strategies shown in Table 1 is attempted, the process becomes more and more cumbersome. But this should not be particularly surprising, since the

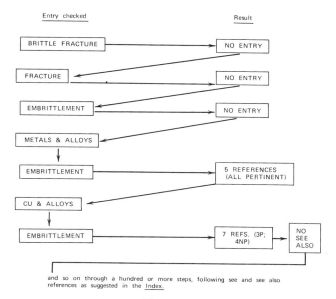

Entry checked   Result

BRITTLE FRACTURE → NO ENTRY

FRACTURE ← NO ENTRY

EMBRITTLEMENT ← NO ENTRY

METALS & ALLOYS ←

EMBRITTLEMENT → 5 REFERENCES (ALL PERTINENT)

CU & ALLOYS ←

EMBRITTLEMENT → 7 REFS. (3P; 4NP) → NO SEE ALSO

and so on through a hundred or more steps, following see and see also references as suggested in the Index.

Figure 7-1

conventional index is designed to handle conveniently only the single aspect search.

As an illustration of the difficulties involved in conducting a comprehensive literature search manually using an alphabetic index, a question related to:

BRITTLE FRACTURE

was selected and searched [1] against the 1960 Engineering Index. From consultation with the questioner, it was determined that this topic included tests related to fracture; cracking and embrittlement; and application of concepts in this area to materials or alloys. The attempt was made to carry this search through, by following up on every *See* and *See also* reference that seemed at all worthy of further investigation. Each reference was checked and judged as Pertinent (P) or Nonpertinent (NP).

The schema and results are shown in Figure 7-1. The result of the effort was 113 relevant items and 336 nonrelevant items, and an expenditure of more than a hundred manhours—another rationale for introducing nontraditional tools into the search process.

---

[1] M. A. Valvoda, "A Comparison of Manual and Machine Searching Techniques," in A. Kent, Ed., *Information Retrieval in Action*, The Press of Western Reserve University, 1963, pp. 51-71.

B. Permuted or KWIC Index

The physical form of this index is given in Chapter 5, Figures 5-3 to 5-8. It will be noted that the key words to be searched are arranged alphabetically down the central line of a printed column. This arrangement is to this extent similar to that of the alphabetical index. The implementation of searching strategies for the permuted index is mechanically similar to that discussed in the previous section.

Certain practical differences in the use of the permuted index result from the philosophy of its construction. It will be recalled that in the preparation of this type of index, key words appearing in natural language (e.g., titles) are used as the basis for the "indexing" operation. Key words are rearranged in a way that displays them in alphabetical order. Effort has not been expended in predicting relations between words as used in natural language and clues as verbalized in a question. Accordingly, in order to exploit the permuted index as well as possible, the developer of a search strategy must identify the alternative natural-language words that might relate to the clues in a question. The strategy of the logical sum is thus an important one.

For example, a search for "semiprecious gemstones" might require a search strategy such as:

> *Search for*
> Semiprecious gemstones
> *and/or*
> Garnet
> *and/or*
> Amethyst
> *and/or*
> Bloodstone
> *and/or*
> Aquamarine
> *and/or*
> Opal
> *and/or*
> Tourmaline
> *and/or*
> Topaz
> *and/or*
> Zircon
> *and/or*
> Turquoise

The search strategy must be developed in such a way that variant forms of "keywords" are also taken into account.

C. Other Pregroupings

Another example of the physical arrangement of a file of records (or of clues to contents of records) in such a way as to facilitate human, nonmechanical use, was typified by the operation of the now defunct Chemical-Biological Coordination Center. Here, codes for chemical compounds contain notations for various functional chemical groups, which are represented in this section as:

A, B, C, D, . . . , Z

When a code for a compound was written, it was recorded in a punched card (Figure 7-2). The notation for each function group was punched in a "fixed" field.

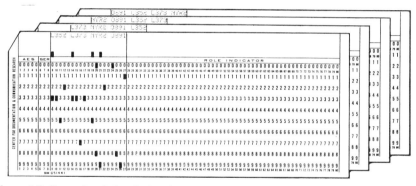

Figure 7-2. Example of chemical code recorded on card with notation for each functional group recorded in a fixed field. Alternative arrangements on separate cards provide for "alphabetization" under each of the individual groups.

Let us assume that functional groups A, B, C, and D are recorded for a certain compound. Separate punched cards are now prepared so that each functional group can appear first. Thus from a single punched card containing A, B, C, and D, three additional cards are prepared. On these cards the functional groups are "rotated" (or permuted) as follows:

B, C, D, and A
C, D, A, and B
D, A, B, and C

The cards are arranged in alphabetical order, according to the functional group that is listed first in each case. The file is now ready for use as a traditional alphabetical index as described earlier in this chapter.

D. Citation Index

As will be recalled from Chapter 5, the citation index, which may be produced by computer, nevertheless presents an alphabetical listing (e.g., of authors cited) for human consultation.

In order to conduct a search (e.g., of the author citation index), the index is entered by knowing one author who has published work of interest in connection with the question in mind. Then the references cited by that author are found listed; after these references are consulted, the authors of the cited references may then be traced in the index to discover which papers they cite; and so on.

The strategies of search that may be appropriate for use with this index are functionally the same as for the traditional alphabetic index discussed earlier in this chapter.

III. "MACHINE"-SEARCHABLE SYSTEMS

In all of the routines described in this section, it is assumed that each aspect, or clue, is represented by some physical notation. Examples of such notation include one or more notches in a marginal-hole punched card, one or more holes in a tabulating-type machine-punched card, one or more sets of holes in punched paper tape, one or more magnetized spots in a tape, one or more opaque or transparent spots in a film, etc. Each of these aspect notations, whether composed of one or more characters, symbols, or other physical representations, will be described with a single capital letter, for example, A, B, C, . . . Z.

A. Marginal-Hole Punched Cards

The basic techniques for manipulating the marginal-hole punched card are described in Chapter 2, Figures 2-18 to 2-21. These techniques may be applied in search routines for various strategies of search as summarized in Table 2.

The single aspect search strategy is illustrated by the insertion of a sorting needle in the appropriate hole(s) of the marginal-hole punched card, so that those cards notched at that point can be separated physically from those unnotched. If this were the only type of search strategy involved there would be

Table 2

Type of search	Symbolic representation	Search instructions
1. Single aspect	A	Insert needle(s) in appropriate hole(s). Those cards with corresponding notch(es) will be selected.
2. Logical sum	A + B + C + · · ·	Insert needle(s) in appropriate hole(s) for aspect A. The cards selected are considered to be the first fraction of references pertinent to the question. Those cards not selected are "needled" (sorted) for aspect B; the cards selected are the second fraction of the response. Those cards not selected are again sorted for aspect C; the cards selected are the third fraction of the response; etc.
3. Logical product	A × B	The cards in the file are sorted for aspect A. Those cards *selected* are "needled" for aspect B. The cards then selected represent the response to the question.
4. Logical product of logical sums	(A + B) × (C + D)	The cards are sorted for aspect A; those not selected are sorted for aspect B. Those *selected* after each sort are sorted for the presence of aspect C; those selected are the first fraction of the response. Those *not* selected are sorted for aspect D; those selected are the second fraction of the response.
5. Logical difference	A − B	The cards are sorted for aspect A. Those *selected* are sorted for aspect B; those *not* selected in this second sort represent the response.
6. Sequence	<A × B>	Not convenient to search by using marginal-hole punched cards.
7. Between barriers	<Barrier × (A × B) × Barrier>	Same as above.
8. Greater than, less than	Statement of typical question: "Locate all values for a given property between 50-60."	For *direct coding*, this type of question may be searched only if value intervals coded correspond exactly with the interval specified in the question, in which case the appropriate hole(s)

Table 2 (continued)

Type of search	Symbolic representation	Search instructions
		representing the desired interval can be "needled." For *numeric coding*, each unit value in the desired interval may be searched as a logical sum strategy, e.g., search for 50 and/or 51 and/or 52 and/or 53 and/or . . . and/or 60. This sorting can be accomplished more economically if an appropriately based numerical coding scheme had been chosen and applied to the selection and recording of clues.

no good reason for employing such cards. Rather, the use of a conventional alphabetic index would generally be more economical. The only minor, residual advantage for use of marginal-hole cards would then be the ability to file cards at random, since needle sorting permits selection of notched cards regardless of their position in file.

The advantages of these cards becomes more apparent with the logical product strategy, since successive needle sorting of a file of cards permits the ready selection of those cards (each representing a source document) which are characterized by two or more subjects, or aspects, in common. The advantages became even more apparent with the strategy of the logical product of logical sums, which would be quite unmanageable with an alphabetic index.

The left (front) and right (rear-end)–truncation searches described earlier in the chapter are not feasible using marginal-hole punched cards without introducing considerable complexity. The difficulty, of course, is that each index entry is represented in its entirety by a hole or a combination of holes, making it impossible to search for only a part of the word. Thus if the entry

Advertisement

is represented by a hole:

which is notched:

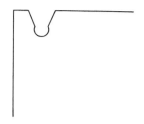

and if that entry were used to index a given document, it is searchable on an "all or none" basis. On the other hand, if it were predicted by the designer of the retrieval system that index entries would be encountered that involved variant forms, there would be at least two options available (Figure 7-3).

1. To reserve a hole for each variant form, for example, advertise, advertizes, advertisement.

2. To reserve a single hole to represent the "concept" that is common to each of the variant forms.

In the first option, a question directed to the concept common to all of the variant forms of a word would require the searching (needling) of all the holes involved to be certain that no variant form were missed.

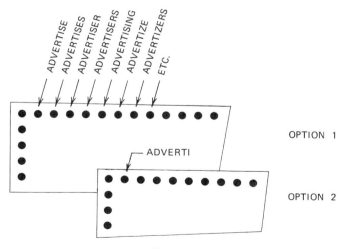

Figure 7-3

In the second option, every variant form encountered would lead to the notching of the same hole (perhaps labelled "ADVERTI. . ."), and therefore only a single "needling" would be required to locate all variant expressions of the concept.

B. Aspect Cards

1. Number Posted for Visual Comparison. The basic manipulations for this type of search are described in Chapter 2, Figures 2-10 to 2-14. The various search strategies may be handled as shown in Table 3.

As before, there would be little advantage in utilizing such a record if only single aspect search strategies were to be employed.

For the strategy of the logical sum, this approach again provides little advantage, and even becomes somewhat cumbersome in some respects. Here, the manipulation required is to select those cards which represent each of the aspects of the logical sum strategy and to copy each of the reference, or document, numbers on each card.

Table 3

Type of search	Symbolic representation	Search instructions
1. Single aspect	A	Select aspect card A from file. The record numbers posted represent the response.
2. Logical sum	$A + B + C + \cdots$	Select aspect cards A, B, C, etc. All of the record numbers posted on each card represent the response.
3. Logical product	$A \times B$	Select aspect cards A and B; compare record numbers posted on each; those numbers common to both cards represent the response.
4. Logical product of logical sums	$(A + B) \times (C + D)$	Select aspect cards A and C; compare record numbers posted on each; those numbers common to both cards represent the first fraction of the response. Compare aspect cards A and D; those numbers common to both cards represent the second fraction of the response.

Table 3 (continued)

Type of search	Symbolic representation	Search instructions
5. Logical difference	A − B	Compare aspect cards B and C; common numbers represent the third response fraction. Compare aspect cards B and D; common numbers represent the fourth fraction of the response. Select aspect cards A and B; compare numbers; all numbers posted on card A that are not common to numbers posted on card B represent the response.
6. Sequence	⟨A × B⟩	Not convenient to search with this tool.
7. Between barriers	⟨Barrier × (A × B) × Barrier⟩	Not convenient to search with this tool.
8. Greater than, less than	Typical question: "Locate all values between 50 and 60."	This type of question may be searched conveniently only if value intervals that were selected as aspects correspond exactly with the interval specified in the question (as in Table 2, item 8).

It has been for the logical product strategy that most advantage has been claimed. The cards representing each aspect in the strategy are selected and are held side by side. Comparisons are then made between the reference or document numbers on each to determine which numbers are common to each of the cards.

This advantage is negated when a search is attempted which uses the strategy of the logical product of logical sums. Let us consider the simplest such search:

$$(A + B) \times (C + D)$$

Aspect cards A and B would be selected from file. All the numbers on each would be copied onto a separate scratch sheet. The same would be done for cards C and D. Then the two sets of numbers would be compared visually to determine which are common to both lists (see Figure 7-4).

Since this is a somewhat cumbersome procedure, requiring copying of numbers each time such a search is conducted, another approach could be used to accomplish the same end, as described below.

The logical expression:

$$(A + B) \times (C + D)$$

Aspect	A	B	C	D
Doc. Nos.	10 21 12 etc.	20 31 22 etc.	10 11 62 etc.	10 11 etc.
	30 41 52	30 41 32	60 51 72	20 31 62
	70 71 82	50 81 42	61	60 51
	91 92	60 91 92		70 61 92 etc.
		80		

Sums tallied
separately

A + B				C + D		
10	21	12		10	11	62
20	31	22		20	31	72
30	41	32	etc.	60	51	
50	71	42		70	61	92
60	81	52				
70	91	82				
80		92				

Comparison of both lists to identify matches: 10, 20, 60, 70, 31, 92

Figure 7.4. Scratch Sheet.

could be converted to a series of logical product strategies:

$$A \times C$$
$$A \times D$$
$$B \times C$$
$$B \times D$$

and the logical expression rewritten as:

$$(A \times C) + (A \times D) + (B \times C) + (B \times D)$$

Then, the logical product manipulation would be conducted separately for each of the four pairs of aspect cards (A,C; A,D; B,C; and B,D). The numbers found in common for each of these four card pairs would be the search result.

It may be obvious that this procedure may prove somewhat tedious, especially as the strategies may become somewhat more complex. Thus a strategy such as:

$$(A + B + C) \times (D + E) \times (F + G + H)$$

would require conversion to:

$$(A \times D \times F) + (A \times E \times F) + (A \times D \times G) + (A \times D \times H) + (A \times E \times G) +$$
$$(A \times E \times H) + (B \times D \times F) + (B \times D \times G) + (B \times E \times G) + (B \times D \times H) +$$
$$(B \times E \times F) + (B \times E \times H) + (C \times D \times F) + (C \times D \times G) + (C \times D \times H) +$$
$$(C \times E \times F) + (C \times E \times G) + (C \times E \times H)$$

Such a search would generally not be performed because of the considerable effort involved. And yet this type of strategy may represent the general case, especially when "word" indexing has been used during analysis. It will be recalled that word indexing involves selection of words, for indexing purposes, as expressed by authors of source materials, thus permitting analysts without strong subject background to perform this chore at minimum expense. However, the price to be paid for word indexing usually is an increase in complexity of search strategy, particularly of the type being discussed. The reason for this is the uncertainty on the part of the questioner, or of the question analyst, when a search strategy is developed, as to which words were used during indexing to represent the information desired. This uncertainty is reflected in the logical sum elements of the search strategy, when alternative words of possible interest are specified as reference points in a search.

This uncertainty may be overcome partially by front and rear-end truncation procedures, as discussed earlier in this chapter, which permit more ready identification of "concepts" relating to variant forms of index entries. However, with aspect systems that involve the dedication of a unit record for each index entry, there is no way, other than by pre-input vocabulary control, to solve this problem of variant forms.

Accordingly, advantages claimed for the number-posted aspect cards using word indexing during input, become very questionable when an attempt is made to exploit the system.

2. Peek-a-Boo Principle. The basic principle of this type of search mechanism involves the superposition of aspect cards to determine which record numbers are common to the cards. The search routines for the various search strategies are shown in Table 4.

Again, this approach would not be advantageous if only the single aspect search would be involved.

However, the peek-a-boo principle is particularly attractive when logical product strategies are utilized. The basic interest in this approach apparently has resulted from the ability to superimpose aspect cards involved in such strategies one on the other, resulting in the ready visual detection of reference or document numbers common to all by noting where light can shine through.

Table 4

Type of search	Symbolic representation	Search instructions
1. Single aspect	A	Select aspect card A. The record numbers entered represent the response.
2. Logical sum	A + B + C + · · ·	Select aspect cards A, B, C, etc. All of the record numbers entered on each card represent the response.

Table 4 (continued)

Type of search	Symbolic representation	Search instructions
3. Logical product	A × B	Select aspect cards A and B. Super-impose the cards and observe those record-number positions that have common punches. Light shines through where there is a coincidence of numbers, and these numbers represent the response.
4. Logical product of logical sums	(A + B) × (C + D)	Compare, successively, the following pairs of aspect cards: A and C; A and D; B and C; B and D; those numbers identified as being in common for each of these pairs of aspect cards represent the response.
5. Logical difference	A − B	Select aspect cards A and B; compare numbers; all numbers recorded on card A that are *not* common to both cards represent the response.
6. Sequence	<A × B>	Not convenient to search with this tool.
7. Between barriers	<Barrier × (A × B) × Barrier>	Not convenient to search with this tool.
8. Greater than, less than	Typical question: "Locate all values between 50 and 60."	This type of question may be searched conveniently only if value intervals that were selected as aspects correspond exactly with the interval specified in this question (as in Table 2, item 8).

This advantage does not show up, of course, when a logical sum strategy is employed, since it is then necessary to copy all reference or document numbers recorded on each; as was described for number-posted aspect cards (Figure 7-4).

In an effort to alleviate the problem, users of such systems have exposed photographic film or have photocopied the superimposed cards, which then produces black spots where light shines through, and which provides a single permanent output record.

But when we come to the general case of the logical product of logical sums, the peek-a-boo approach becomes unusually difficult to operate economically. Thus, in the case of the strategy:

$$(A + B) \times (C + D)$$

There are two tactics that may be used:

a. The total strategy is converted to a series of logical product strategies:
$$(A \times C) + (A \times D) + (B \times C) + (B \times D)$$
so that the peek-a-boo principle may be used to best advantage. However, the more complex the strategy the less economical and attractive does this tactic become.

b. The peek-a-boo is treated as a number-posted aspect card (see earlier). In this case, of course, the disadvantages of that approach reappear.

It should be obvious that the procedure described above for accumulating photographically the document or reference numbers occurring on the cards involved in a logical sum strategy cannot be used in the strategy under discussion. A single card is created, with holes from each of the cards recorded as black spots. Obviously, once holes are recorded as black spots (rather than as holes), they are no longer amenable to peek-a-boo searching.

The left (front) and right (rear-end) truncation problems are identical with those discussed under number-posted aspect cards.

C. Tabulating-Type Punched Cards

1. Document systems

a. FIXED FIELD. In a document system (see Chapter 3), a single card is generally employed to represent a single document. All of the index information is recorded on the card. When a sorter or collator based on the fixed-field principle (see Chapter 2) is used to select cards based on criteria recorded therein, the search strategies are implemented as shown in Table 5.

Table 5

Type of search	Symbolic representation	Search instructions
1. Single aspect	A	Select fixed field to be searched, by sorter or other appropriate device, and sort file to physically isolate cards that contain the desired aspect.
2. Logical sum	$A + B + C + \cdots$	Select fixed field(s) to be searched by sorter or other appropriate device, and sort file to physically isolate cards containing each desired aspect. The combination of all these cards represents the response.

Table 5 (continued)

Type of search	Symbolic representation	Search instructions
3. Logical product	A × B	Select fixed field(s) to be searched, and sort file to physically isolate cards containing aspect A; then resort these cards for those also containing aspect B; the resulting cards represent the response.
4. Logical product of logical sums	(A + B) × (C + D)	Select fixed field(s) to be searched and sort file to physically isolate those cards containing aspect A; then those containing aspect B; these two fractions are combined, and sorted for cards containing aspect C; those selected represent a portion of the response; those not containing aspect C are sorted for the presence of aspect D; those cards selected represent the second portion of the response.
5. Logical difference	A − B	Select fixed field(s) to be searched and sort file to physically isolate those cards containing aspect A; these are then sorted for those containing aspect B. The fraction of cards *not* selected in the second sort represents the response.
6. Sequence	< A × B >	Not convenient to search with fixed-field equipment.
7. Between barriers	<Barrier × (A × B) × Barrier>	Not convenient to search with fixed-field equipment.
8. Greater than, less than	Typical question: "Locate all values between 50 and 60."	This type of question may be searched conveniently: (1) if the value intervals that have been selected as aspects correspond exactly with the interval specified in the question; (2) if the values have been coded numerically, in which case each unit value in the desired interval may be searched as a logical sum of each individual unit value represented by the range. This type of sorting can be accomplished more economically if an appropriately based numerical coding scheme has been chosen.

Again, the single-aspect strategies would provide little justification for such a system. Rather, when multiple-aspect searches are involved, then whatever economies that may be possible start to appear.

b. FREE FIELD. The search strategies for the free-field systems require little discussion. All of the strategies specified in the preceding sections may be performed in a free-field system by programming all of the desired conditions and sorting, or scanning, the file only once. Such a sort will yield only those cards that represent the response. Unlike the practice in fixed-field systems, it is not necessary to specify the field that is expected to yield relevant response. Rather since all aspects of a record are recorded on a card, one after the other, the search is conducted by scanning, in sequence, all of the information recorded in the card. This technique makes it convenient to conduct a search that specifies the sequence of clues, or that requires the recognition of "barriers" enclosing various specified combinations of aspects.

When a free-field approach is used with computer-based systems, the information to be searched may be recorded in sequential manner on, for example, magnetic tape, as follows:

1 - A, C, R, Z   2 - B, L, N, P, R   3 - B, C, Z   4 - ...

where the numerals (1, 2, 3, 4 . . .) represent document accession numbers, and the alphabetic characters (A, B, C, . . .) represent aspects of subject matters (e.g., index entries, "keywords").

A search involving aspects C and Z would proceed by having the program store these characteristics in computer memory, and then continue by having every item on the tape read and compared against the two stored aspects (C and Z).

The document number, being read first, is stored ready for printout if the search strategy is satisfied. If the strategy called for a logical product (C x Z), the number is not printed out unless both appear before the next document number is encountered on tape. If the strategy called for a logical sum (C + Z), the number is printed out if either aspect appears before the next document number is encountered; and so on for other strategies (see Table 6).

Table 6

Type of search	Symbolic representation	Search instructions
1. Single aspect	A	Program equipment to recognize aspect A, and to scan the file of records; the record numbers printed out when aspect A is recognized represent the response.
2. Logical sum	A + B + C + · · ·	Program equipment to recognize aspects A, B, and C, and to record a

Table 6 (continued)

Type of search	Symbolic representation	Search instructions
		positive response if any one of the aspects is found when the file of records is scanned; the record numbers printed out when program conditions are satisfied represent the response.
3. Logical product	A X B	Program equipment to recognize aspects A and B and to record positive response only when both aspects are present in the same record; the record numbers printed out when program conditions are satisfied represent the response.
4. Logical product of logical sums	(A + B) X (C + D)	Program equipment to recognize aspects A, B, C, and D and to record a positive response only when either aspects A or B are found in the same document with either aspects C or D; the record numbers printed out when program conditions are satisfied represent the response.
5. Logical difference	A − B	Program equipment to recognize aspects A and B and to record a positive response whenever aspect A is found in a document, except when aspect B is also present; the record numbers printed out when program conditions are satisfied represent the response.
6. Sequence	<A X B>	Program equipment to recognize aspects A and B and to record a positive response whenever both aspects are present in the same record, but only when aspect A is located earlier than aspect B; the record numbers printed out when the program conditions are satisfied represent the response.
7. Between barriers	<Barrier X (A X B) X Barrier >	Program equipment to recognize aspects A and B and to record a positive response whenever both aspects

Table 6 (continued)

Type of search	Symbolic representation	Search instructions
		are present, in the same record, but only when both are found within some specified unit; the record numbers printed out when program conditions are satisfied represent the response.
8. Greater than, less than	Typical question: "Locate all values between 50 and 60.)	This type of question may be searched conveniently: (1) if value intervals that were recorded on tape correspond exactly with the interval specified in the question; (2) if each unit value in the desired interval is searched as a logical sum of each individual unit value represented by the range. The equipment is programmed as above; record numbers printed out when program conditions are satisfied represent the response.

The truncation problem may be resolved, albeit expensively, by having each character of each aspect recorded on tape in such a way that the search program can identify each letter, one after the other, permitting left (front-end) truncation, right (rear-end) truncation, or both.

2. Aspect Systems (Inverted files)

a. COLLATOR OR SORTER-BASED. It will be recalled (Chapter 3) that when machine-sorted punched cards are used in aspect systems, an entire subfile of cards may be used to represent "postings" for a single aspect of information (Figure 7-5). The various search strategies are therefore formulated as shown in Table 7.

Searches involving the single aspect and logical sum strategies are performed without use of any sorting or collating equipment. The appropriate subfile(s), which represent the aspects involved are merely selected from storage.

When a logical product strategy is to be used, for example, A × B, the two appropriate subfiles are selected from storage and are sorted in reference, or document, number order. Thus, if the strategy involved a request for information on *hardness testing* (A) of *gems* (B), the resulting sort might appear

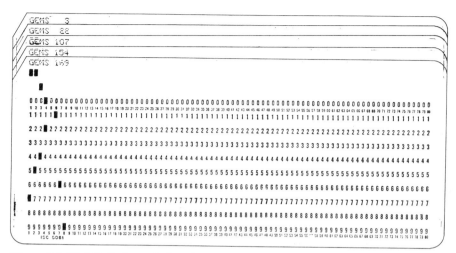

Figure 7-5. "Subfile" of punched cards on "Gems." The figures are reference or document numbers.

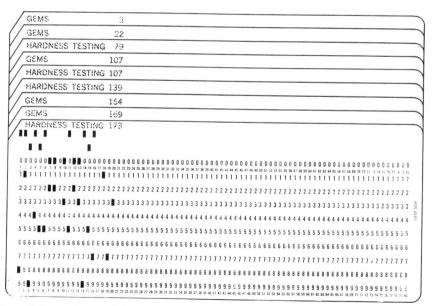

Figure 7-6. Punched cards from subfiles on "Gems" and "Hardness testing" are interfiled in ascending numerical sequence. Visual inspection of the reference or document numbers (right) reveals a common number (107).

Table 7

Type of search	Symbolic representation	Search instructions
1. Single aspect	A	Select subfile for aspect A. All record numbers recorded represent the response.
2. Logical sum	$A + B + C + \cdots$	Select subfiles for aspects A, B, C, etc. All record numbers recorded for each aspect represent the response.
3. Logical product	$A \times B$	Select subfiles for aspects A and B. Collate (or sort and visually compare) both files for coincidences of record numbers. All those record numbers that are in common between the two subfiles represent the response.
4. Logical product of logical sum	$(A + B) \times (C + D)$	Select subfiles for aspects A, B, C, and D. Collate successively the pairs of subfiles as follows: A and C; A and D; B and C; B and D; those numbers identified as common to any of these pairs represent the response.
5. Logical difference	$A - B$	Select subfiles for aspects A and B, and collate; all numbers recorded in subfile A that are *not* common to both cards represent the response.
6. Sequence	$\langle A \times B \rangle$	Not convenient to search with this tool.
7. Between barriers	$\langle Barrier \times (A \times B) \times Barrier \rangle$	Not convenient to search with this tool.
8. Greater than, less than	Typical question: "Locate all values between 50 and 60."	This type of question may be searched conveniently only if value intervals which were selected as aspects correspond exactly with the interval specified in the question (as in Table 2, item 8).

as shown in Figure 7-6. The number 107 is common to both sets of cards, as determined by visual inspection. Accordingly, the logical product strategy has been satisfied.

The same end result may be obtained using a collator. Here, the two subfiles are compared electromechanically until a matching condition is found for the reference or document numbers. Then the cards which match are caused to drop into a receptacle separate from the other cards in the subfile being compared.

The left (front) and right (rear-end) truncation problem may be resolved more easily in this situation then for any other aspect system. If each variant form of an entry is represented by a subfile (without any attempt to control variant forms during input to the system), then the subfiles for the variant forms considered to represent a "concept" may be merged, to create a larger subfile, which itself becomes an "aspect" in a search strategy. Here, rather than using a scratch pad to record all the document numbers that are involved in a logical sum element of a search, since each unit record in a subfile has recorded in it only the index entry and one document reference number, all of such records involved in each subfile of a logical sum may be merged using electro-mechanical aids (sorter or collator).

b. COMPUTER BASED. As discussed in Chapter 3, aspect card systems, when translated to computer-based systems, no longer operate on a unit record basis. Rather, the organization of information for computer search on, for example, continuous magnetic tape, is as follows:

A - 6, 15, 92, 108, 599   B - 12, 15, 80, 93, 107, 599, 632
C - 6, 42, 93, 599   D - - - -

where the letters A, B, C, D . . . represent aspects of subject matter, and the numerals represent document accession numbers. When a search is to be conducted, the appropriate lists of document accession numbers are read off tape and stored in computer memory, ready for further processing. Thus, if aspects A and C were to be involved in a strategy, the lists of accession numbers would be stored:

A	C
6	6
15	42
92	93
108	599
599	

If the strategy were a logical product, (A x C), the computer program would involve comparison of each number in one list with those of the other to discover which were common to both (i.e., 6 and 599). If the strategy were a logical sum (A + C), the program could involve intercollation of the numbers, elimination of duplicate numbers, to produce a single consolidated list (i.e., 6, 15, 42, 92, 93, 108, 599). And so on for other strategies, quite analogous to the procedures discussed in Table 6 for collator or sorter-based aspect systems. And just as with these latter systems, the truncation problem can be resolved in an analogous manner by intercollating "subfiles" (but this time on tape) representing the variant forms that are to be clustered under a single concept.

D. Film Records

The searching of film records is, strategically, analogous to the searching of other media. Therefore, this matter will not be discussed in detail.

Two approaches to film scanning have been used: continuous film and unit film. The early design of the Rapid Selector, a *continuous film* scanner, was able to conduct efficiently only the single-aspect strategy. Of the *unit film* scanners, the Filmorex is somewhat analogous to the fixed-field tabulating equipment with regard to what can be accomplished conveniently and economically. On the other hand, the Minicard equipment of Eastman Kodak resembles quite closely the free-field equipment with regard to capabilities for coping with a range of searching strategies.

IV. SEARCHING OF SEQUENTIAL VERSUS INVERTED FILES

The distinction has been made earlier between *document* and aspect systems (Chapter 3). However, a distinction that has been used more popularly by many workers in the field is between *sequential* (also scanning) and *inverted* (also collating) systems. Actually the terms *"sequential"* and *"inverted"* refer to file arrangements, and, to a first approximation, the *sequential* system is synonymous with the document system, while the *inverted* and aspect systems are synonymous.

To clarify the popular distinction that has been made, let us consider a file of five documents (numbered 1 to 5) which are characterized by one or more of five index entries (identified as A, B, C, D, and E). The index entries for each document are as follows:

> Document No. 1   A and C
> Document No. 2   B, C, and D
> Document No. 3   A and E
> Document No. 4   B and E
> Document No. 5   B and C

In the diagram on page 206 the indexing of these documents is represented by checkmarks in the appropriate boxes.

For the *sequential system,* the index entries are recorded together for each document (as shown in line I). For the *inverted system,* the document numbers are recorded together for each index entry, or aspect (as shown in column II). It is obvious that a "failsafe" conversion can be made from one system to the other without disturbing any indexing decisions, or without influencing, in the

		Document number					II (Inverted System)
		1	2	3	4	5	
Index entries	A	✓		✓			1, 3
	B		✓		✓	✓	2, 4, 5
	C	✓	✓			✓	1, 2, 5
	D		✓				2
	E			✓	✓		3, 4
I (Sequential system)		A, C	B, C, D	A, E	B, E	B, C	"Failsafe" conversion

absolute sense, the way in which the file may be exploited. Any advantages that are to be achieved may be derived from the convenience or economy with which a search may be performed using one file arrangement or another.

SUGGESTED DEMONSTRATIONS FOR CLASSROOMS

1. Illustration of searching manipulations using marginal-hole punched cards. Obtain set of approximately 25 Keysort, Needle Sort, or E-Z Sort cards, handnotcher and sorting needle. Demonstrate basic notching and sorting techniques.

2. Illustration of searching manipulations using the peek-a-boo principle. Obtain set of Remington Rand cards, Form P-1060, with appropriate hand-punch. (Local office of Remington Rand should be contacted for this material.) The same demonstration may be performed with appropriate IBM cards and a handpunch. (Local office of International Business Machines Corp., should be contacted.) Demonstrate method of punching holes to represent document numbers on an aspect card. Conduct searching operations based on principle of superimposing cards and detecting coincidence of holes.

Eight

Words, Language, and Meaning

I. GENERAL CONSIDERATIONS

A. Introduction

The fundamental problem of information retrieval is that of identifying material that has been stored earlier which may be relevant or approximately relevant to a current requirement. The significant aspect of the problem is that the relevant material must be selected from a set of possibly relevant materials. The information-retrieval system must be designed to operate for each *possible* selection, not just those which will *actually* be chosen, since this is unknown at the time of design of the system.[1]

The problem of designing an information-retrieval system would be a trivial one (a) if each event impinging on the consciousness of any human beings would result in identical streams of observations, (b) if each observer would use the identical words in identical configurations to describe each such event, and (c) if each person interested in learning of the event would phrase questions using identical terminology.

---

[1] After C. E. Shannon and W. Weaver, *The Mathematical Theory of Communication,* The University of Illinois Press, Urbana, 1949.

However, each individual has his own paradigms, or ways of perceiving nature. As an example, in Chapter 5, examples are given of four sets of index entries provided by four different student indexes for a single "document." From an analysis of these entries (Table 1), at least two observations may be made:

1. The indexers, with few exceptions, do not agree on what is important for retrieval purposes (compare, in this regard, the entries of students C and D.

C	D
Kangaroo mother's reaction	Rabbit
Observer's reaction	Zoo
Infant exchange	Carriage
Humor, mother preoccupation	Cage
Gossip	Animals, care of

Student C apparently tried to capture the essence of what the carton was about, while Student D, with one exception, merely enumerated the things visible in the cartoon).

2. In several cases, the same concepts evoked different index entries, or labels, for example,

KANGAROO and RABBIT
INFANT EXCHANGE and REVERSE SITUATION

In the first case, the concept is a physical entity (an animal). The two indexers merely disagreed on which animal it was—it was clearly a matter of mistaken identity. In the second case, the concept is not a physical entity, but rather a curious relationship among physical entities that the indexers wish to capture and express. It is so curious, in fact, that a proper label to describe it does not come to mind easily. Even when a heroic effort is made, the resulting index entries differ, but it hardly matters since neither appears to be useful for retrieval purposes.

But if there were no common paradigms among individuals, then no system of analyzing, processing, and organizing information would be useful, and a random organization of materials in an information-retrieval system would be all that would be needed.

But it is rather obvious that some paradigms are common to some groups of individuals, otherwise no communication of any kind would be possible. It is in an attempt to take advantage of common paradigms, to the maximum extent possible, that words, language, and meaning are considered in information-retrieval systems.

		Student			Frequency of use of entry
Index entry	A	B	C	D	
1. Mr. Mum	x	x			2
2. Ladies	x				1
3. Mother		x			1
4. Baby	x				1
5. Kangaroos	x	x			2
6. Rabbit				x	1
7. Zoo		x		x	2
8. Carriage				x	1
9. Cage				x	1
10. Cartoon		x			1
11. Kangaroo mother's reaction			x		1
12. Observer's reaction			x		1
13. Infant exchange			x		1
14. Reverse situation	x				1
15. Humor, mother's preoccupation			x		1
16. Gossip			x		1
17. Animals, care of				x	1

Table 1

Words, language, meaning, the topics of this chapter, are basic to all discussion of information retrieval, whether mechanized or not. We must keep in mind that the purpose of information-retrieval systems is to facilitate the communication of information. Various systems effect this communication by various "signals"—oral, visual, electronic, and so on—designed to leap the barriers of space, time, and language. But the information which is the object of searches is typically contained in graphic records, and these records are typically expressed in words.

These words are usually arranged in such a way as to produce natural language. Pictures or other graphic records which are not made up of words and language are often *described* in terms of words and natural language. Perhaps this is the reason why systems for "retrieving" graphic records have depended on language-based clues. These consist of words recorded in various ways, as in "open" language, in standardized language, or in codes. It is not surprising that words and language are used to describe or express clues selected by the exercise of recall memory or recognition memory, since the higher forms of communication among humans are indeed based on words and language.

But are the communication tools required to achieve effective *retrieval* the same as the speech and writing by means of which we conventionally communicate our thoughts? Let us remember that the basic purpose of a retrieval system is to assist in identifying desired graphic records. Communication, then, is not an end in itself, it is only a process for facilitating the identifying process. Therefore, everything true for communication systems is not necessarily true for retrieval systems.

B. Communication via Retrieval Systems

Let us start with a practical consideration. Retrieval systems, especially mechanized systems, exist only because it is impractical, inconvenient, or too expensive to use other means for finding desired records in a file. Usually the size of the file (as measured by the number of records, depth of analysis of each record, and complexity of subject matter covered) has reached the point at which an existing retrieval system is not expected to provide adequate service in response to the average inquiry.

Given a file of this size, we may assume that the number of records being incorporated into the file exceeds the ability of a potential "inquirer" to read and to remember the contents of every record that is incorporated. This assumption plays an important part in the routine of analyzing new records for the file. The analyst cannot be certain that a person who may later want to see the record will have read it previously or even have seen it before. Therefore, requests for records will be based on clues which are verbalizations of topics drawn from the requester's current interests, problems, and background and not necessarily from the text of records stored in the file.

Two questions must be answered by the analyst:

1. Which aspects of the record are of probable importance to potential users?

2. How should these aspects be expressed so that there will be a good possibility of their matching the words that potential users will choose for the expression of their requests?

The first question is discussed in Chapter Five. The second question is a particularly difficult one to resolve because an analyst reading a document is tempted to use words found in that document to record the results of his analysis. However, as we have seen, those words used in an individual document are not necessarily the same as those used in information requests. So the analyst is obliged to attempt to anticipate any way in which a searcher's point of view might be expressed.

How can anyone predict the exact words that will come to a searcher's mind when he desires information on some subject? Here are some approaches to be considered:

1. The decision may be made to operate the retrieval activity as a "closed"[2] system. This decision relieves the analyst of the responsibility of predicting which words will be used by "outsiders" in searching the file. All searches must then be performed by operating personnel of the retrieval system who are in a position to interpret requests in the familiar terms of the language used by analysts.

2. The decision may be made to operate the retrieval activity as an "open" system. This decision commits the analyst to the control of terminology in one of two ways:

a. The man feels that he is in sufficiently good intellectual contact with his potential clientele to permit his predicting which terminology will be chosen by the clientele in formulating questions. In this case, a cross-reference system or thesaurus would be developed and made available which would relate the terminology of the clientele to that of the system (where differences are predicted).

b. If he is not confident that he is in sufficient contact with the potential clientele, some experimental procedure would be needed to determine how relationships among terms are perceived by the clientele. The clientele may be required, for example, to submit to association tests, the results of which would provide some basis for choosing terminology according to its evident significance to the user of the system. One problem that must be faced here, as with any terminological prediction (vide the complaints of users of subject heading lists or of prepared thesauri), is the divergence between theoretical usage—the vocabulary that the clientele think they use, or would like to use—and actual usage.

The associations of words with other words, whether predicted by systems designers or derived from empirical or experimental data, are based partially on personal judgments of the significance of words and partially on the inherent meaning of words.

C. Relationship Between Meaning and Communication

Let us step back to examine the relationship between meaning and communication.

The principles of mechanized information-retrieval described in this book are expressions of the basic need of human beings to communicate—the need of

---

[2] In a closed system, the designer of the system also operates it, that is, he is responsible for both the input and output functions; the questioner cannot operate the system personally (the analog of the closed stacks in a library). In an open system, the designer has attempted to engineer the system so that questioners may operate it themselves (the analog of the open stacks in a library).

the writer to communicate with his contemporaries and with posterity, the need of the reader to communicate with the generators of ideas and with the reporters of fact.

Many studies of communicative behavior have used the underlying assumption that the most profitable approach to human communication begins with the *message*. From this assumption, three levels of communication may be defined:

1. Intelligibility (the identification of the phonemes and other linguistic forms which constitute a message).

2. Information (the identification of the meaning of a message).

3. Effects (the noncommunicative behavior resulting from a message).

The "communication" which is the subject of this chapter is the second of these levels: the identification of the meaning of a message, as that meaning is determined by words and language to describe the message, and as that meaning is construed by document analysts and question analysts in attempting to provide communication links between documents and readers.

Let us further examine the notion of *meaning*. For example, what does a word mean? What does a message expressed in language *mean*?

First of all, we must agree that a word is a label, and that the word is not to be equated to the "thing" that it labels. Further, as pointed out by Allen Walker Read,

A grave danger in dealing with words is to regard a word as a receptacle into which a meaning is poured. This is a false, elementalistic outlook. A word, as established in the social framework, can be regarded as having several aspects or dimensions, all of which are present at one time. A full semantic description of a word involves at least four aspects or dimensions: "phonology" (the particularization of the word-form), "syntax" (the relation of word-forms one to another), "lexicon" (the relation of the word-form to what it is used to represent or symbolize), and "pragmatics" (the relation of the word-form to the people who are communicating).

In a semantic description, the lexical component (the relation of the word-form to what it represents) may be said to be multidimensional. The word not only occupies an "area" of meaning, designating the range of situations or things to which it relates, but also it has a third dimension in the order of abstraction it represents (in the context of each particular use). Unfortunately there seems to be no way of constructing an objective scale by which the orders of verbal abstraction may be gauged. The best that can be done at present is to point out the fact in general terms, and it must be caught in the manner of a visualization or an "insight." What is important is the consciousness of the process.[3]

---

[3] Allen Walker Read, *The Lexicographer and General Semantics,* General Semantics Monographs, No. III, Institute of General Semantics, Lakeville, Connecticut, 1942.

Meaning, as displayed lexicographically, is the total experience (based on empirical investigation) of the *use* of words or language. Therefore, lexicographically speaking, there is really no meaning *inherent* in a word.

Is there, then, no fixed relationship between "word" and "meaning" upon which the documentalist can rely for his special purpose of information retrieval? Instead of depending on words and language, can he determine the way in which a word has been used and assume that this is the way in which it will be used again? Can he call this the *meaning* of the word? Unfortunately, any application of lexical structuring to information retrieval, as to any other communication activity, must take into account one of the basic characteristics of meaning—its lexicographical shift as a function of society's tendency to use words in different contexts, with different meanings, at different times.

D. Some Characteristics of Language as They May Apply to Retrieval Systems

The written form of language is a secondary system. It is dependent on the system of arbitrary, vocal symbols which provides one of the means by which human beings communicate. Language is the expression of human thinking, and, as such, is subject to continuing change. This change tends to reflect the progress of human thought toward greater and greater abstractness as seen both in mathematical and other expressions. The ability to recognize a symbolic, abstract representation of reality is essentially the basis of our culture. All scientific and mathematical achievement is built upon this foundation. The ability to transmit knowledge by means of language is the basis for education, indeed for all culture as we know it.

Every written text is made up of "minimum statements" which may or may not be formal syntactical units. These we name sentences, clauses, or phrases, according to the accepted phraseology of grammar. Every syntactical unit consists of words arranged systematically according to the structural rules of language.

The meaning of a written (or spoken) word is determined by some or all of its context. Identical words (homographs) differ in meaning when they are used in different contexts and with different referents. This difference creates possible confusion. On the other hand, functionally identical meanings may be conveyed by different words (synonyms) or expressions. In such cases, the apparent identity of the words creates another kind of confusion.

Communication that takes place through the written form of language may be inhibited when the meaning that a writer wishes to convey by a meaningful arrangement of words is not identical with the understanding of those words by a reader. The extent to which the frame of reference of the two does not coincide may be considered as a measure of the "noise" in the communication system.

We may try to counteract or neutralize this inhibition in the effectiveness of communication by using "redundancy" in our language (see Figure 8-1). Redundancy denotes the amount of information transmitted in excess of the theoretical minimum. The use of redundancy in written language may be seen as the restatement of ideas from several different points of view, or the provision of more than minimum context, so that noise in the system may be overcome, and more effective communication assured. (Compare the application of this concept to coding, as discussed in Chapter 9.)

A number of artificial languages have been developed which avoid ambiguities both in the meaning of the words listed in their vocabularies, and in the syntactical patterns used to represent relationships among those words. Such artificial languages, although the rules for their use are unambiguous, pay for this advantage by losing the expressiveness and "richness" as well as, usually, the flexibility of natural language.

THE DAREDEVIL
WAS RECKLESS

Figure 8-1. Example of a redundant expression. The word "daredevil" implies recklessness to many users of the English language, and to these users the word "daredevil" would be sufficient to communicate what has been expressed by the four words above.

II. ROLE OF WORDS, LANGUAGE, AND MEANING IN RETRIEVAL SYSTEMS

A. Introduction

From a practical point of view, *meaning* is of no consequence in an information-retrieval system except insofar as it helps a client to locate a record that he desires.

Consider the information-retrieval system that is engineered into the normal dictionary. A person who desires to learn the definition of a word that he has encountered for the first time does not need to know the meaning of the word in order to find it in a dictionary. Rather, he needs merely to know the accepted spelling of the word, and to know the rules of alphabetization that govern the usual arrangement of words in a dictionary.

The same situation may pertain when a person desires to locate books or documents on a certain subject by using a catalog in a library. Suppose that the subject of interest is *quicksilver.* Perusal of a subject catalog may be rewarding, since one or more suitable references may be listed that provide interesting information. In this case it is of no consequence whether or not the seeker of a document knows the meaning of the word *"quicksilver."* He has in any case been rewarded by the discovery of a document bearing the label "quicksilver."

Nor is it of any consequence *in this case* whether or not the document analyst, who provided the subject entry *quicksilver* in the catalog, knew what the word meant. As long as the information seeker's search for information is rewarded quickly and economically, every standard of searching efficiency has been met.

What happens when the searcher finds *no* information listed in the catalog under *quicksilver?* At this point the meaning of the word may come into play, along with its relationships to other words in language. Unless there are *no* books or documents on *quicksilver* in the library, we will assume that *quicksilver* has failed as a catalog heading for one of these reasons:

1. A document about *quicksilver* exists, but the metal is discussed in terms of a synonym, *mercury.* The document was therefore cataloged under the word "mercury," the "subject" of the document.

2. The analyst (the cataloger) did not include in the catalog a cross reference between the two terms, such as:

quicksilver. See mercury

since either he did not predict that anyone would look for the material under an alternative name, or he was not aware that such an alternative name existed.

Let us broaden our hypothetical search to include *mercury* and *mercury-containing materials.* Suppose that a file of graphic records contains information on *silver amalgam.* A danger signal flashes, to be heeded by either the analyst or the searcher, or by both: mercury is an ingredient of silver amalgam. The analyst could index this mercury-containing material under its own name. But he will serve a greater potential clientele if, at this point, he also provides a more generic index heading, such as *mercury-containing materials.* If the analyst fails to do this, then the searcher will have to draw up a list of *every* mercury-containing material, so he can look these up individually in the index.

Perhaps enough has been said to make the point that for many information-retrieval requirements, it is helpful to take the meaning of words into account in designing a retrieval system. If the words "mercury-containing material" designate or *mean* a certain substance, so, when the circumstances are right, do the words "silver amalgam" designate or *mean* the same thing.

However, how is it possible to take meaning into account in a useful way? The meaning of a word is conditioned strongly by the experiences and training of an individual. In general semantics, this characteristic of words is described as "multivalued," referring to the differences in "meaning" that a word may have in different contexts. Such differences in meaning can result from various causes. First are the *homophones,* words that sound alike but have different meanings. "Four," "for," and "fore" are homophones. Second are *homographs,* words written alike. The present and past tenses of "read" are homographs pronounced differently, one form rhyming with "weed" and the other with "wed." Then there are words that are both homophonic and homographic. "Tire," for instance, may mean to make weary, or it may designate the rubber casing on the wheel of an automobile. Last, there is the somewhat less obvious, and therefore far more dangerous, difference in meaning which is a matter not of a difference in *root,* but of a difference in evaluation. Indeed, if we think of the word "rose" from the separate viewpoints of the florist, the landscape gardener, the lover, and the child who falls into the rose bush, we will rewrite Gertrude Stein's famous line to read "A rose is *not* a rose is *not* a rose . . . ."

To a personnel manager, the "job," for instance, is an entry on a payroll or record, or the occasion for hiring or firing, an "opening" or "termination." To the individual employee, however, the same job may well mean the difference between self-respect with an adequate living standard and misery on relief. Thus "job" (personnel manager) is not "job" (employee). If association tests were conducted on persons with different backgrounds, we might find, for example, that the word "job" might suggest to executives the terms "big," "simple," "rush"; it might suggest to personnel workers the terms "analysis," "evaluation," "opening," "fill," etc., usually something related to procedure; and to the worker it might suggest the terms "pay," "word," "rent," "eat," "marry," "car," etc., and often "lose," "laid off," "fired."[4]

The moral of this discussion is that the point of view of the expected clientele must determine the meaning of every word in a retrieval system.

When this point of view is not known, the use of more clues to alternative connotations of words can increase the probability that persons with different backgrounds and experience can find the information they desire (Figure 8-2).

This approach is not an unmixed blessing, since many of the alternative routes provided may relate to tenuous connotations, and therefore may lead to the identification of not very relevant materials.

B. Specific Retrieval Systems

1. Indexing. As was pointed out in Chapter 5, indexing involves the selection of words or ideas from a graphic record on the basis of well-defined

---

[4]William Exton Jr., "Language and 'Reality'–Semantics of Industrial Relations: **II**, *Personnel,* **27**, 194-201 (November 1950).

(*a*) Pyrometers. *See also* Thermometers.
(*b*) Pyrometer. *Also see* Photoelectric pyrometers: Radiation pyrometers: Thermocouple pyrometers: Thermometers.

(*c*) Pyrometer.

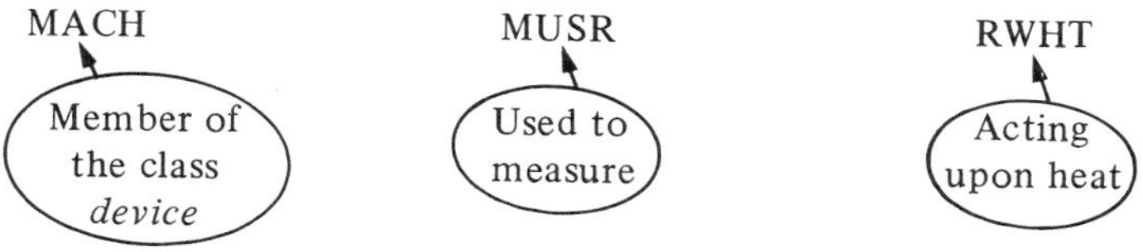

(*d*) Pyrometers.

  BT (Broader terms)

  Measuring instruments
  Temperature measuring instruments

  NT (Narrower terms)

  Optical pyrometers
  Radiation pyrometers
  Thermocouple pyrometers

  RT (Related term)

  Temperature measurement

Figure 8-2. Examples of cross references or additional clues to the meaning of *pyrometer* in information-retrieval systems: (*a*) *Chemical Abstracts* index; (*b*) Armed Services Technical Information Agency *Thesaurus of Descriptors;* (*c*) Semantic Code Dictionary; (*d*) National Aeronautics and Space Administration Thesaurus.

rules. Indexing is conducted in order to facilitate the identification or selection of desired documents after they have been stored. The two types of indexes discussed in Chapter 5, word indexes and controlled indexes, involve the use of words and language selected as clues to the subject content of records to which they refer.

a. WORD INDEXES

(1) Concordances. This type of index involves the selection of words, often without discrimination, from running text, and their display in context. No meaning is attributed to the words by the "indexer." Rather this type of index can be of aid to the lexicographer in defining by examining the various contexts of given words.

(2) Key-Word-in-Context (KWIC), or Permutation, Index. This type of index involves the use of some discrimination and value judgment with regard to the meaning of words chosen as reference points. The first level of judgment is exercised when it is decided that only words in titles of documents shall be "permuted."

The second level of judgment is exercised when certain "nonsubstantive" terms are eliminated from the permuted index. This determination is based on the assumption that conjunctions, prepositions, and similar parts of speech do not carry a heavy semantic burden in the text, and therefore should not be used as reference points in the index.

Once these judgments have been made, no meaning is attributed to the words by an indexer. As in concordance listings, the words are merely displayed in context.

(3) Uniterm Indexes. This type of index involves the selection from a record of those words that are considered important as reference points in searches.[5] When this selection is performed clerically (by persons who are not specialists in the subjects of the documents being processed), and based on more or less well-defined rules for selection of words based on frequency of occurrence or on similar nonsubstantive criteria, then no meaning is attributed to the words, or uniterms, by the indexer.

b. CONTROLLED INDEXES. The term "controlled indexing" is used here to imply the use of regularized terminology; the language of the index itself is controlled. Decisions have been made with regard to the meaning of the terminology, and with regard to the relationships among the various terms of the index.

One technique in controlled indexing is the provision of scope notes which describe the limits of subject matter embraced by each term. This limitation of subject matter defines the meaning of a term in a particular retrieval system.

Thus the term:

FATIGUE

might be used as an index entry relating to the fatigue of any materials used in any structures. A scope note might be provided:

---

[5] The Uniterm index is discussed as a word index primarily because its initial descriptions and publicity suggested that words selected without regard to their scope of meaning would serve effectively as reference points during searches. Later applications of this system of indexing have involved careful control of the scope of subject matter indexed under each word. Uniterm indexing has become an example of "controlled" indexing, involving all of the problems and advantages of such indexing applications. But once it becomes controlled indexing it is no longer "Uniterm" indexing, since the principles followed are well established in traditional subject indexing.

FATIGUE (USE only in connection with
stress of metallic materials
used in aircraft wings)

which limits the scope of "legal" use of that entry. On the other hand, the term FATIGUE is used in several fields with different referents:

1. In biology—for example, relating to human fatigue
2. In the military—for example, relating to workclothes
3. In materials—for example, relating to stress of metallic or nonmetallic materials.

The controlled index may then use a "gloss" to indicate the field to which the term is related:

FATIGUE (BIOLOGY)
FATIGUE (MILITARY)
FATIGUE (MATERIALS)

The gloss and scope note serve the same function in an information-retrieval system.

Another technique for controlled indexing is the cross reference, the "see" reference, which relates those terms or headings that are synonymous in meaning for purposes of a particular retrieval system. For example, a "see" reference such as:

Quicksilver. *See* mercury

may imply a decision that the words *"quicksilver"* and *"mercury"* are synonymous. However, an entry such as:

Canary. *See* Birds

obviously implies that *only for purposes of this index* are the words *"canary"* and *"birds"* to be considered synonymous, since in most situations the term *"birds"* is much more generic in meaning than *"canary."*

The "see also" reference is another technique used in controlled indexing to suggest that two terms or headings are closely related, or partially synonymous in meaning, *for purposes of a particular retrieval system.* For example, the cross reference:

wrist watch. *See also* alarm clock

may imply that the terms *"wrist watch"* and *"alarm clock"* have some meaning in common (both are time-measuring devices). However, an entry such as:

Milk. *See also* cows

implies that there is some subject matter of common interest between *milk* and *cows* in the particular information-retrieval system in question.

Another way in which indexing is controlled, and which involves meaning, is the use of a modification to an index entry as, for example, in

thermometer, use in measuring fever

Here, the meaning of the word *"thermometer"* has been limited (*in this retrieval system*) to designate only those thermometers that are used to measure fevers.

A similar technique in mechanized retrieval systems is the *role indicator* which limits the meaning of the word to which it is related. For example, in the role indicator-descriptor combination:

Role Indicator	*Descriptor*
starting material	milk

the meaning of milk is limited to that situation in which it is used as a starting material (possibly in the manufacture of cheese). Again, such a meaning will be valid only for this particular retrieval system.

2. Classifying. In Chapter 5 it was pointed out that classification involves the arrangement of subject matter in classes on the basis of resemblances. Classification systems are founded on predictions as to those resemblances that will be useful in connection with literature searches. A definition of each class is made on the basis of the elements that are chosen to make up that class. The individual classes in classification systems are usually described in words, whose meanings in context of the system are evident or which are specified by enumeration, by example, or by definition. Examples of these class descriptions are

> *Meaning specified by example*
> dairy products (e.g., milk, cheese, cream)
> *Meaning specified by enumeration*
> dairy products
> > milk
> > cheese
> > cream
> > butter
> *Meaning specified by definition*
> dairy products (milk products)

Rigid and multidimensional classification systems are alike in the way in which the meaning of a class must be made explicit.

3. Abstracting. The traditional abstract may be considered as like normal discursive text in its use of words and language, and in its demands on their meanings. The summary of a record is prepared in natural language. The case is similar for *extracts,* which are portions of texts written in natural language. In these cases the normal considerations with regard to words, language, and meaning require no further discussion.

However, one type of extract, the auto-abstract (Chapter 5), requires some additional discussion. Since the auto-abstract is prepared by the extraction of various sentences from a text, based on the statistical occurrence of key words in the text of a record, portions of the context of the original record are preserved in the auto-abstract. However, the selection of sentences from text without regard to continuity or logic of expression may destroy some of the context provided in normal exposition. The meaning of words in the auto-abstract is derived from the sentence unit, and it is not to be expected that all of the meaning that was implied in the original text will survive the transfer to the auto-abstract.

Another form of abstract, the telegraphic abstract (Chapter Five) is based on the construction of an artificial language which consists of the following elements:

a. Descriptors—words or phrases chosen by analysts to indicate those aspects of the subject matter of records that are considered to be important as reference points in a search.

b. Role indicators—code symbols that fit the selected descriptors into context.

c. Punctuation symbols—which group the descriptors and role indicators into units analogous to phrases, sentences, and paragraphs.

Meaning is ascribed to these elements of a telegraphic abstract in two ways:

a. Through the meaning of the words used as descriptors, alone, in the context of the role indicator-descriptor relationship, and in the context of the phrases, sentences, and other syntactical units.

b. Through the use of a "semantic" code which is applied to the words or phrases chosen as descriptors, and which serves to define the descriptors in terms of generic and functional elements of meaning.

Still another form of abstract, the "mini" abstract, is based on the recording, contiguously, of all index entries relating to a given document:[6]

STUDENTS—INTERMEDIATE ELEMENTARY SCHOOL—
LOS ANGELES COUNTY—SOCIAL STUDIES—
FILMSTRIPS—and so on

Meaning is ascribed to the mini-abstract in two ways:

a. Through the meanings of the individual index entries.

b. Through the context provided by the contiguously displayed entries.

4. Processing of Full Texts. Presumably, the only way in which the full scope of meaning inherent in words and language can be made available is by

---

[6]This is analogous to the provision of "tracings" (a record of additional entries with regard to a specific book, placed on its main entry card in the catalog).

scanning the full, original texts of records in response to each question asked. Even if it were practical to do this by computer for all but the smallest files, and even if the test of *significance* could be made effectively, the exercise would still be self-defeating because of the probable existence in a given file of many variants of expression for the same meaning. The person wishing to query the file would not be able to predict exactly which variant of expression might be available in a particular document that would be pertinent to his question (see Figure 8-3).

When full texts are processed by computer in order to provide "normalized" text suitable for facilitating retrieval operations, the aim is to regularize the expression of similar ideas so that a search will not have to deal with the full variety of expression available in natural language. These regularization procedures require that decisions be made as to the meaning of words or of syntactical patterns, so that machine operations will be based on fewer variant expressions of similar ideas.

It is to be expected that this procedure, as with indexing, classifying, and abstracting procedures, involves a "loss" of information and discriminating ability as compared to the original text found in a record. This loss occurs since each procedure involves some degree of generalization from the full text, a particularization of selected contents, or a combination of both.

III. ANALYSIS OF TERMINOLOGY

Perhaps *quicksilver* was not an entirely random selection for our example of multiple and overlapping meaning. We can choose a word and use it as we please, as a subject heading, as an aspect, as a clue in a search. We base a system on it and on the other chosen words, for eventually every system is, at some remote base, a word-based system. But at the moment that our system seems complete, firm yet flexible, workable in every foreseeable respect, we are liable to betrayal by the word itself. The quicksilver meaning runs out of our grasp.

We have discussed meaning as it affects certain specific procedures in the retrieval system: indexing, classifying, abstracting, and processing of full texts. As we consider the ambiguities of normal human discursive utterance, we have begun to see that as retrieval specialists we accept a herculean task: the imposing of order upon human thought, or, at least, upon the graphic record of that thought. Here is our hardest work, but here also is our greatest opportunity. Therefore, let us see how we may begin to approach the matter of meaning insofar as it may be made explicit and useful for retrieval purposes.

If all index terms contained a common root or stem, such as *meter*:

color*meter*

thermo*meter*

DOC M

PAGE 21
GROUP 0311

DOC M						
037 1	ABUNDANT	NUCLEAR		SPECIES		
047 1	CLOSED	SHELLS				
070 4	EVEN	ATOMIC		WEIGHT		
047 1	EVEN	NUMBER	OF	IDENTICAL	NUCLEONS	
048 1	EVEN	NUMBER	OF	IDENTICAL	NUCLEONS	
082 4	EVEN-EVEN	CORE				
111 2	EVEN-EVEN	NUCLEI				
084 2	EVEN-ODD	COMPOUND		NUCLEUS		
100 1	EXCITED	STATES	OF	EVEN-EVEN	NUCLEI	
110 4	EXCITED	STATES	OF	EVEN-EVEN	NUCLEI	
041 1	FUNCTION	OF	ATOMIC	NUMBER		
070 4	LIGHT	MIRROR		NUCLEI		
037 1	MAGIC	NUMBERS				
047 1	MAGIC	NUMBERS				
048 1	MAGIC	NUMBERS	IN	NUCLEI		
037 1	MAGNETIC	MOMENTS	OF	ODD	NUCLEI	
100 1	MAGNETIC	MOMENTS	OF	ODD-NEUTRON	NUCLEI	
100 1	MAGNETIC	MOMENTS	OF	ODD-PROTON	NUCLEI	
036 2	MASS	NUMBER				
057 1	MASS	NUMBER				
056 1	MASS	NUMBER		REGION		
057 1	MASS	NUMBER		RANGE		
057 1	MASS 5	UNITS				
050 1	MIRROR	NUCLEI		LI7	AND BE7	
101 2	MIRROR	NUCLEUS		HE5		
050 1	MIRRORED	COUNTERPART	OF	EXCITED	STATE	
041 1	NEIGHBORING	HEAVY		ELEMENTS		
057 2	NEUTRON	DEFICIENT		BISMUTH	ISOTOPES	
047 1	NEUTRONS 5					
057 1	NEUTRONS 5					
057 1	NUCLEAR	STABILITY				
057 1	NUCLEI					
036 1	NUCLEI	IN	REGION	OF	NEUTRONS 5	
037 1	OCCUPATION	NUMBERS				
082 4	ODD	NEUTRON				
037 1	ODD	NUCLEI				
047 1	ODD	NUMBER				
048 1	ODD	NUMBER	OF	IDENTICAL	PARTICLES	
100 1	ODD-EVEN	NUCLEI				
084 2	ODD-ODD	COMPOUND		NUCLEI		
047 1	ODD-ODD 5	NUCLEI				
110 4	ODD-PARITY	STATES				
047 1	PARTICULARLY	STABLE				
037 1	PERIODIC	SYSTEM	OF	ELEMENTS		
047 1	PROTONS 5					
057 1	PROTONS 5					
100 1	SINGLE	ODD		NUCLEON		
047 1	SINGLE	ODD		PARTICLE		
047 1	SPINS 5 OF	ODD		NUCLEI		
037 1	STABLE	NUCLEAR		SPECIES		

Figure 8-3. Examples of words or phrases from natural-language text that are related thesaurally to the term "magic numbers." (From D. R. Swanson, "Searching Natural Language Text by Computer," *Science,* 132, 1099-1104, October 21, 1960.)

speedo*meter*
pyro*meter*
tacho*meter*
photo*meter*
refracto*meter*

and if that root or stem had a common meaning, such as "to measure," and if, further, that common root or stem were considered useful as a reference point for all searches involving those terms, then no control of index terms would be required. If a search were to be conducted for all source materials indexed specifically for "thermometer," or for those indexed generically for "measurement" (as represented by *-meter*), then no control problems would be encountered.

Even if the index terms contained one of two common roots or stems, such as *pyr* or *therm*:

*pyr*ometer	*therm*ometer
*pyr*olysis	*therm*ograph
*pyr*ophoric	*therm*al
	*therm*odynamic

then a simple logical sum strategy directed to

pyr and/or *therm*

would select the common meaning—*heat*. Again, no input control of index terms would be required.

However, if the following list of terms is examined;

abaca	crash	mat
absorbent cotton	cloth	mercerization
animalize	decatizing	mosquito net
balloon	denier	muslin
beer	drape	nerve
boat	drill	nylon
bobbin	duck	rayon
bone	felt	sanforizing
Botany	gunny	silk
broadcloth	herringbone	synthetic fiber
carbonization	huckabuck	tissue
card	kier boil	vat dyes
chintz	knit	vinyon
cotton	lake	woolen
cottonization	linter	wool

it is noted that there are no common roots or stems, and yet there is a common thread of meaning in all, relating to textiles. Here, some control measure must be used if a search directed to *textiles* is to identify all source materials which were indexed using any one of the terms listed.

Similarly, control would be needed if each of the terms listed below were to be identifiable in terms of a common thread of meaning relating to *time:*

calendar	clock	horography
chronology	day	horology
chronometer	decade	hour
chronoscopy	eon	hour glass
chronothermometer	era	isochronon
clepsydra	gnomon	metronome

month	time bomb	time study
pendule	timeclock	time zone
periodicity	time exposure	timing
season	timekeeper	watch
sundial	time lock	year
time	time sheet	

If control for two common threads of "meaning," such as *time* and *device* were desired, the list above would shrink to:

calendar	gnomon	sundial
chronometer	hour glass	time bomb
chronothermometer	isochronon	timeclock
clepsydra	metronome	time lock
clock	pendule	watch

And if control for three common threads of meaning were desired, such as *time, device,* and *measure,* the same list would further shrink to:

chronometer	gnomon	time clock
chronothermometer	hour glass	watch
clepsydra	pendule	
clock	sun dial	

The question then may be raised as to how far such analysis may usefully be pursued. That is, since individuals who use information-retrieval systems may have differing paradigms, or ways of perceiving nature, then how "common" are the common threads of meaning that are attributed to the terms used for indexing? Obviously, as more and more of such threads are made explicit for searching purposes, they may tend to become less useful for *all* users of systems, and may become more and more special purpose.

As an example of this type of problem, the term "record" has been examined in terms of the control measures used in a variety of systems.

The dictionary definition of *record*[7] may be given as: ". . . to set down in writing; to deposit an authentic copy; to register permanently; to cause to be registered in reproducible form . . ."

The Library of Congress *Subject Headings* (6th ed., 1957) provides the following control:

RECORDS

    see also Archives.

        Libraries.

        Museums.

    also specific types of records, e.g.:

        Business records; Manuscripts; Registers of births; etc.

---

[7] Adapted from *Webster's 7th ed., New Collegiate Dictionary*, Merriam, Springfield, Mass., 1963.

The *Dewey Decimal Classification and Related Index* (16th ed., 1958) shows the following cross references:

RECORDS.

children	136.708
Christian church local	254.
domestic trade	381
farming	631.16
international commerce	382
management	
business technology	651.5
military administration	355.61
offices architecture	725.158
sales business & industry	658.817
school administration	371.2
sound manufacture	681.842
Sunday schools Christian	
religion	268.5

Here, each of the numbers at the right refers to separate headings of the classification schedule. To illustrate the diversity of control approaches implied by these headings, two of them are given:

Sales business and industry 658.817

> 658.8 Marketing (Distribution of goods)
>
> Comprehensive works on sales promotion and selling
>
> Including sales planning, sales letters, market research and analysis, marketing channel
>
> *For advertising, see 659.1; buying for the home, 647.1; marketing cooperatives, 334; securities exchanges, 332.6; marketing specific goods and services, 338.1-338.4*

Sound manufacture 681.842

> 681.8 Sound and musical instruments
>
> Manufacture of conventional, mechanical, electronic musical instruments (*all formerly 780-789*)
>
> Including sound recorders and reproducers, sound records, sound-picture recording and reproducing machines

The *Sears List of Subject Headings* shows the following vocabulary control suggestions for the same term, *record:*

RECORDS, Phonograph. *See* Phonograph records

RECORDS–Preservation. *See* Archives

RECORDS of births, etc. *See* Registers of births, etc.; Vital statistics

Some additional terms related to *record* show up when a general thesaurus is consulted (*Roget's International Thesaurus,* 3rd ed., 1962):

> record
>> *nouns* championship   36.3
>> list   88
>> chronology
>> phonograph   464.19
>> register   568.1
>> chronicle   606.4
>> OFF THE RECORD   612.16, 22
>> ON RECORD   568.17
>> *verbs* register   568.15
>> chronicle   606.14

Again, to illustrate the diversity of control implied by the references given above, two are examined in detail:

36. SUPERIORITY

3. supremacy, primacy, paramountcy, *first place*; maximum, most, *ne plus ultra* [L., the highest degree] ; headship, leadership; championship, record, new high.

. . . . .

88. LIST
NOUNS

1. list, enumeration, *tableau* [F.], scroll, screed; schedule, line-up coll.; register, registry; inventory, terrior; cadastre or cadaster, cadre; check list; tally sheet; active list, retired list, sick list.

A *Dictionary of English Synonyms* (by Richard Soule, Bantam Books, New York, 1960), shows a different configuration of terms related to *RECORD:*

> RECORD, v. t. Register, enroll, chronicle, enter, note, make an entry of, take down, make a memorandum of.
> ─────── , n. 1. Register, account, note, chronicle, archive, annals, diary, report, roll, list, entry, minute, proceedings, score, file, docket, memorandum, memorial, enrollment, registry, memoir.
> 2. Vestige, trace, memorial, relic, footprint, track, mark, trail.
> 3. Memory, remembrance.
> 4. Attestation, testimony, witness.
> 5. History, personal history, achievement, career.

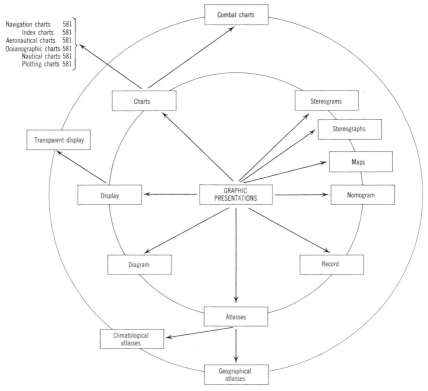

Figure 8-4. TDCK Circular Thesaurus System—one method of exhibiting graphically the generic-specific relationship among terms.

A technical thesaurus *(Thesaurus of Engineering Terms,* Engineers Joint Council, New York, 1964) provides the following related terms[8].

> Documentation
> Documents
> Drawings
> History
> Phonograph Records
> Records Management
> Records Storage

Another technical thesaurus prepared in Holland (*TDCK Circular Thesaurus System,* by J. A. Schuller, 1963) lists the following related terms:

---

[8] Related terms are described as "related in an unspecifiable manner to the term at hand. It may be a near-synoym to the term or may sometimes be synonymously or hierarchially related to the term at hand."

GRAPHIC PRESENTATIONS

Atlasses

Charts
Climatological Atlasses
Combat Charts

Diagram
Display

Geographical Atlasses
Graphic Presentations

Maps

Nomogram

Record

Stereograms
Stereographs

Transparent Display

The "circular" system is represented in Figure 8-4, where the relationships among the terms including *record* is given. The further away from the center of the diagram that a term appears, the more specific it is to the generic term of the diagram (*graphic presentations* in this case).

Another approach to control of terminology is given in a "semantic" analysis of terms (*Tools for Machine Literature Searching,* by J. W. Perry and A. Kent, Interscience, New York, 1958). The term *record* is related, in this approach, to the following terms:

INFORMATION	COMMENT
RECORD	COMMUNICATION
RECORDING	DECLARATION
DOCUMENT	DIAGRAM
ARCHIVAL	DICTIONARY
ARGAND DIAGRAM	DIPLOMA
MANUAL	DISCUSSION
AUDIT	DOCUMENTATION
BIBLIOGRAPHY	DRAFTING
BIOGRAPHY	EDIT
BIOSTATISTICS	EDITORIAL
BOOK LIST	ENCYCLOPEDIA
CARD	FOLKLORE
CARTOON	GAZETEER
CATALOG	GLOSSARY
CENSUS	GRAPH
COMMAND	GRID

HEALTH CERTIFICATE	JOURNAL
HISTORY	KNOWN
INDEX	KNOWLEDGE
INTERCOMMUNICATE	

A comparison of terms considered related in the three approaches immediately above is given in Figure 8-5.

It may be obvious that the relationships to the term *record* are thought of differently, depending upon the person who designs the thesaurus, the subject heading list, or, generically, the vocabulary control mechanism for a given information-retrieval system. Very often, the primary purpose of the vocabulary control mechanism is lost sight of, that is, to augment the ability of the information-retrieval system to produce relevant information when a question is posed.

Accordingly, instead of thinking of a thesaurus in its definitional sense, that is, a dictionary of synonyms, and antonyms, it may be more useful to think of it as a compilation which contains the terms of a given information-retrieval system's vocabulary, arranged in some meaningful form, and which provides information relating to each term that will enable the user of the information file to predict the relevance of responses to questions when this particular vocabulary control mechanism is used.

The idea for a "new" type of a thesaurus[9] arose from an existing need in an operating information-retrieval system. In the process of providing aerospace literature to industry through the National Aeronautics and Space Administration (NASA) "Technology Utilization Project," the different interpretations of the same term by industry, on the one hand, and the aerospace field, on the other, became evident; as did the fact that of 17,478 available terms for retrieval purposes listed in the "Machine Term Vocabulary," approximately 1000 terms from this listing were used to retrieve information for the clientele. For the purposes of better serving the existing and future users of the center, and for providing a tool for other existing and future centers engaged in the "Technology Utilization Project," the compilation of a thesaurus based upon a notion of "confidence level" in retrieval was begun. Unlike most "traditional" thesauri that attempt to serve as total vocabulary listings for a system for use at the time of information input, as well as an output searching device that establishes synonyms, associated terms, *see* references, hierarchies, etc., this new thesaurus approach is concerned only with those terms from the total available vocabulary that appear in the search strategies that have been developed from

---

[9] E. D. Dym, "A New Approach to Thesaurus Development," KAS Center, University of Pittsburgh, 16 pp., multilithed, 1965.

Semantic Code	Comparison of Listings	
	Term: Record(s)	
	TDCK	EJC
ATLAS	ATLAS(S)	
CHART	CHART(S)	
DIAGRAM	DIAGRAM	
DOCUMENT		DOCUMENT(S)
DOCUMENTATION		DOCUMENTATION
HISTORY		HISTORY
MAP	MAP(S)	
NOMOGRAM	NOMOGRAM	
PHONOGRAPH		PHONOGRAPH (RECORDS)
RECORD	RECORD	

Figure 8-5. Three "vocabulary-control" systems do not handle the same terms in an identical manner.

actual questions. The guiding concept of this thesaurus is based on the principle that what the user desires most is knowledge of the probability of successful retrieval. This is important from the standpoint of efficiency to the researcher and economics to the organization. If the user can be informed prior to the time of searching a query that experience has shown that for industrial purposes the probability of retrieving relevant information from the aerospace literature for certain terms in certain relationships is 50% or less, the desire to rephrase the query in terms and relationships that represent a probability of 51% or more might be created.

Since no guiding model for a thesaurus based on the idea of revealing to the user the "confidence factors of successful retrieval" existed, it was necessary to begin with the purpose desired and develop a system that would achieve this purpose. As was stated before, assuming that the user desires to know the probability of successful retrieval from a system, it would be necessary to compile the reference points from existing data derived from an operating IR system. This was done by:

(*1*) using an existing indexing system;
(*2*) using an existing "machine"-term vocabulary;
(*3*) using actual questions presented by users who are motivated to desire responses;
(*4*) using the search strategies developed, based on the operating system, to search these queries; and
(*5*) evaluating the actual results of searches performed with these strategies.

The specific procedures followed were:

(*1*) determination of the terms used in search strategies;

(*2*) Association with each term the questions in which that particular term was used in strategy;

(*3*) determination of which word in the question statement "triggered" the use

(*4*) listing of all terms associated with a particular term in all search strategies; of a particular "machine" term;

(*5*) compilation of statistical data on the number of responses identified by the computer, the number of responses deemed relevant by the analyst in answer to a query and forwarded to the user, the number of responses from the forwarded computer retrievals deemed relevant by the user, the number of responses identified manually by the analyst, and the percentage of the manual retrievals deemed relevant by the user.

To establish the terms from the total number of available terms that are used in the search strategies, reference was made to a "search strategy sheet" used to record the strategies employed for a given question.

It was next necessary to establish a relationship between term and question, as well as one term with another term. To establish the relationship of a term with a question statement, the method chosen was to determine what word and/or words in the question statement triggered the use of a particular term in the search strategy. These "question trigger terms" (QTT) are important to the formulation of the search strategy. Thus, insofar as one is interested in retrieving information concerning "low alloy steel," the term available for use for searching purposes would be "steel."

Once it has been determined what word and/or words in the question statement caused the use of a particular term in the search strategy, the next step was to list "associated terms" appearing in the search strategies with the term under consideration. These terms are listed for the convenience of the analyst, who will develop search strategies for a question presented to the system, and the user, who will formulate the question to be presented to the system. By referring to the list of associated terms, one may choose those terms reflecting a given interest, and then by referring to the list of search strategies previously presented restrict or expand the desired request.

Following the establishment of the "associated terms," the bulk of information under any given term appears. This information is divided primarily by search strategies presented to the system. The first listing, therefore, is that of search strategies (see *a* in the example following). The term under consideration is listed first and following it appear other terms arranged alphabetically as the logical expressions will allow.

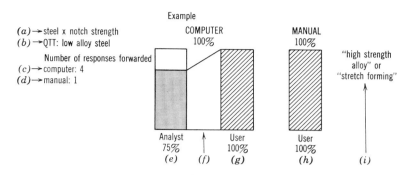

Example

(a)→steel x notch strength
(b)→QTT: low alloy steel

Number of responses forwarded
(c)→computer: 4
(d)→manual: 1

Explanation

(a) the search strategy derived from the question statement as it is presented for searching purposes:

"steel x notch strength"

(b) the question trigger term (in this case, "low alloy steel"):

"QTT: low alloy steel"

(c) the number of responses that were identified by the computer for a given search period:

"computer: 4"

(d) the number of responses identified manually by the analyst for the same period:

"manual: 1"

(e) the percentage of computer-identified responses that were deemed relevant by the analysts and were, hence, forwarded to the user (it will be noted that all evaluations of the analyst are indicated in black):

COMPUTER
100%

Analyst
75%

(f) the portion of responses forwarded for which "user evaluation" was received (in this case, all forwarded responses were considered in the 100% user evaluation):

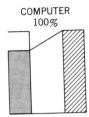

COMPUTER
100%

(g) the percentage of computer-retrieved responses (previously deemed relevant by the analyst and forwarded to the user) deemed relevant by the user for a given question (it will be noted that all user evaluations are indicated below by the stripped bar):

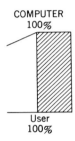

COMPUTER
100%

User
100%

(h) the percentage of manual retrievals deemed relevant by the user:

MANUAL
100%

User
100%

(i) (besides these manual-retrieval percentages) the term(s) that indicated possible index entries under which the manually retrieved could have been located:

"high strength alloy" or "stretch forming"

It is possible, by merely surveying the array of bar charts, to determine those strategies that portray the highest "confidence factor" of identifying relevant abstracts in the system.

As was previously stated, the purpose of this thesaurus is to aid the analyst and/or user by providing a means of predetermining the amount of information that will be retrieved using a particular search strategy, providing the analyst and/or user with statistical evidence as to actual, relevant information available in the system.

The above suggested a methodology for developing a thesaurus on a much more systematic basis than previously; which might lead to predictably better results than earlier thesauri.

Following current practice in developing thesauri, it should be obvious that a thesaurus may be defined as "a book of words applicable to a particular field." Specifically, a thesaurus should show explicit relationships among the words it contains. These relationships may be those of:

1. *Synonymy.* To indicate terms that may be used interchangeably to represent a single concept, e.g., *lead peroxide* and *red lead*

2. *Specific to generic relationship.* To identify terms that are part of a broader class, e.g., *ethanol* and *butanol* may both be considered to belong to the class *alcohol*

3. *Generic to specific relationship.* To identify a term that may represent a group of more specific words, e.g., *spraying equipment* includes *airless spraying equipment*

4. *General nonspecific relationships.* To indicate terms which are related to other terms but not in a totally synonymous or generic-specific manner, e.g., *Fire retardant coating* may have meaning related to *nonflammable coating*

It is perhaps obvious that none of these relationships among terms can be defined in a totally unambiguous way, since different people think of (and use) words differently in various contexts.

Two projects were undertaken, which were designed to permit the systematic development of a thesaurus and its testing.

The first was *Thesaurus of Paint and Allied Technology* (published by the Federation of Societies for Paint Technology, Philadelphia, in March 1968). More than 105,000 terms were collected from a wide sampling of the relevant literature. After elimination of duplicates and variant forms, some 30,000 terms remained, which were examined critically in order to identify only those with significance for paint technology.

Preliminary analysis was accomplished by subjecting each term to a rather unique analysis technique developed specifically for this project. This technique can be described best as that of a "road map" (see Figure 8-6) by which the areas of the field were divided into five major headings: (1) material; (2) equipment; (3) supplies; (4) process or method; and, (5) property, characteristic or condition. (For those terms that did not fall into one of the five areas, a "miscellaneous" category was established to deal with: (1) surfaces or structures

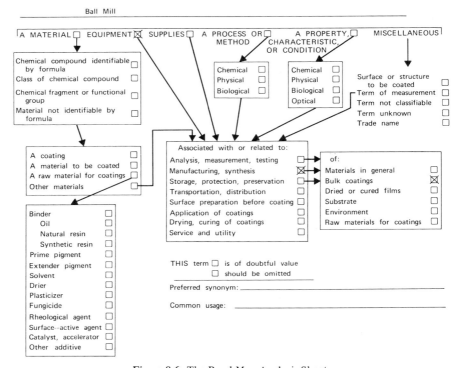

Figure 8-6. The Road Map Analysis Sheet.

to be coated; (2) terms of measurement; (3) terms not classifiable; (4) terms not known; and, (5) trade names.) After the initial placement of terms in one of the above areas, subsequent decisions were made, by following the "road map," to reduce all materials or all equipment or all supplies, etc., into more specific locations.

While this analysis procedure was being performed, technologists in Britain and Canada reviewed listings of terms obtained from indexes of British and Canadian journals and performed the "road map" analysis for those terms they considered to be significant.

From the "road maps," the terms with their analysis were recorded on punch cards and then sorted into like groupings, i.e., all oils, all prime pigments, all driers, etc. Each section was then printed out and reviewed, with terms being added or deleted to develop a comprehensive listing for each category.

This consolidation reduced the list to 4,000 terms which were again key-punched and printed out by categories. A procedure was developed for displaying relationships among these to indicate synonymy and generic-specific relationships. After these explicit relationships had been established, a rough draft of the thesaurus was prepared.

This rough draft was again reviewed by technologists. Their suggestions and criticisms were incorporated into the final draft of the first edition.

An example of a resulting entry is given below:

```
ALCOHOL    (C/30)
    BT  LACQUER SOLVENT
        OXYGENATED SOLVENT
    NT  AMYL ALCOHOL
        BUTANOL
        CARBINOL
        CYCLOHEXANOL
        ETHANOL
        HEXANOL
        METHANOL
        OCTANOL
        OXO ALCOHOL
    SEE ALSO...ANTIFREEZE
                 GLYCOL
```

No rigorous test of retrieval power of the thesaurus in an operating environment has yet been attempted.

A similar approach to thesaurus development has been taken by Price[10] in the field of special education. However, he went one step further in attempting to validate the thesaurus. He developed a validation instrument—a multiple-choice test—which investigated the relationships that potential information systems users observe between word pairs selected randomly. Surprisingly significant agreement among subjects was discerned for most pairs. The methodology seems particularly interesting as a means of calibrating a thesaurus on the basis of a particular set of users.

IV. CONCLUSION

Consideration of words, language, and meaning is obviously of importance in connection with information-retrieval systems. Control of vocabulary must be exercised in various ways. During analysis (Chapter 5), the choice of terminology to denote what is considered important for retrieval purposes, is the first time such control is exercised. Strategies that are utilized when a search is formalized (Chapter 6) provides the next element of control, but after the fact, so to speak, since the strategy often must repair the inconsistencies of analysis. Between *analysis* and *search strategy formulation* there exists the opportunity to control vocabulary by establishing relationships through cross references, thesauri, and the like, the subject of this chapter; and through codes, the subject of the chapter which follows.

---

[10] Samuel T. Price, "The Development of a Thesaurus of Descriptors for an Information Retrieval System in Special Education," doctoral dissertation, University of Pittsburgh, 1969.

SUPPLEMENTARY READING

1. M. M. Henderson, J. S. Moats, M. E. Stevens, and S. M. Newman, *Cooperation, Convertibility, and Compatibility Among Information Systems: A Literature Review.* **National Bureau of Standards Miscellaneous Publication 276, U. S. Printing Office,** Washington, D.C., June 15, 1966.

2. M. L. Manheimer, *The Applicability of the NASA Thesaurus to the File of Documents Indexed Prior to its Publication, Doctoral dissertation, University of Pittsburgh, 1969.*

3. Nagel, E., and R. B. Brandt, Eds., *Meaning and Knowledge—Systematic Readings in Epistemology,* Harcourt, Brace & World, Inc., New York, 1965.

4. Herdan, G., *Language as Choice and Chance,* P. Noordhoff N. V., Groningen, 1956, *Type-Token Mathematics,* Mouton & Co., The Hague, 1960.

5. Osgood, C. E., T. A. Sebeok, A. R. Diebold, and G. A. Miller, *Psycholinguistics,* Indiana University Press, Bloomington, 1965.

6. Brillouin, L., *Scientific Uncertainty and Information,* Academic Press, New York, 1964.

7. Bréal, M., *Semantics: Studies in the Science of Meaning* (translated by Mrs. Henry Cust), Dover Publications, New York, 1964.

8. Cassirer, Hans, "The Philosophy of Symbolic Forms," *Language,* Vol. I, Yale University Press, New Haven, 1953.

9. Morgenau, Henry, *The Nature of Physical Reality,* McGraw-Hill Book Company, New York, 1950.

10. Chase, Stuart, *The Power of Words,* Harcourt, Brace & World, Inc., New York, 1954.

11. Korzbyski, A., *Science and Sanity,* 4th ed., The Institute of General Semantics, Lakeville, Conn., 1958.

Nine

Codes and Notations

I. INTRODUCTION

A. What Is a Code?

A code is any system of symbols in the communication process, particularly a system that achieves some other desirable advantage over common language or numerical expression.[1]

The word *"code,"* in Roman times, derived from a root that designated a wax-covered wooden writing tablet. Its earliest denotation was a systematic collection, compilation, or formulation of laws, principles, rules, or regulations. However, in modern times, another sense has developed. This sense of *code* involves the existence of two languages, a source language and a target language. The "code" is then the system of rules that enables messages in the *source* language to be transformed into a *target* language (or code language).[2]

Language itself has sometimes been considered as a coding system for ideas. The alphabet provides one possible set of symbols that are combined in order to communicate in ordinary discourse and writing.

In the information-retrieval field, two other terms have often been used interchangeably with the word "code." These are *"notation"* and *"cipher."*

---

[1] Adapted from J. D. Mack and R. S. Taylor, "A System of Documentation Terminology," J. H. Shera, A. Kent, and J. W. Perry, Eds., *Documentation in Action,* Reinhold, New York, 1956, p. 19.

[2] G. W. Patterson, "What Is a Code?" *Communications of the ACM,* **3,** No. 5, 315-318 (1960).

In this book the word "notation" will be used only to designate the particular set of symbols used to represent a code. This decision implies that the notation used in a code may be changed at any time, as from numerals to alphabetic characters, without changing the system of rules for transforming messages from one language to another (Figure 9-1). In other words, the notation may be considered to be the physical representation of a code.

The word "cipher" will be reserved for those codes whose notations, whether alphabetic or composed of other symbols, are purposely scrambled in order to keep the system of rules, and thus the source language, a secret.

B. Why Establish a Code or Use a Notation?

The willful concealment of meaning—the purpose of using a cipher—will not be discussed here.

Rather, some of the obvious reasons for use of codes and notations are as follows:

1. To translate from a difficult-to-use source language to a language that is easier to use for a particular purpose, or purposes.

2. To decrease the amount of space required to record information.

3. To supplement the information available in the source language.

4. To distinguish between alternative ideas or words that are not easily distinguished in the source language.

Examples of codes and notations that characterize each of these reasons are given in the following.

(1) To Translate from a Difficult-to-Use Source Language to a Language that is Easier to Use for a Particular Purpose.

An example is the famous code:

"One if by land, two if by sea"

Paul Revere[3] and his fellow citizens did not know information theory, namely the principle of the representation of intelligence. The Paul Revere code is not quite up to modern standards, but it has the essential properties: *(1)* the

---

[3] American patriot of the revolutionary period who engaged in a midnight ride from Charlestown to Lexington on April 18-19, 1775, to give warning of the approach of British troops from Boston. The signal that he arranged with the Americans he warned was "One if by land, two if by sea." This meant that one lantern would be hung from a prearranged steeple if the British were coming by land; two lanterns if they were arriving by sea. (The author begs the indulgence of American readers for this explanation. However, a European reviewer missed the point of the example in the text and suggested inclusion of this explanation.)

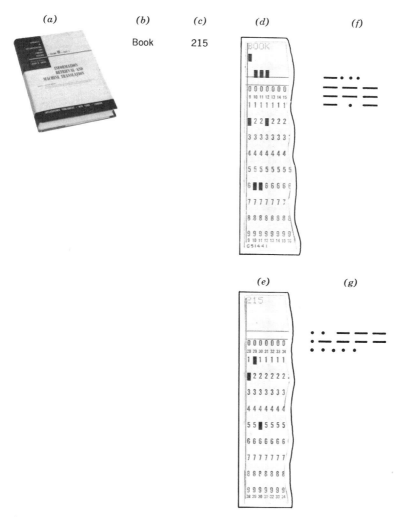

Figure 9-1. Alternative codes for a single physical object may be represented by different notations. The book pictured in (*a*) may be considered to be coded when the English language provides a system of rules to permit its representation as the notation "book" (*b*). However, another coding system may require its representation as the arbitrary notation "215" (*c*). Now, each of these notations may have alternative means of expression because other coding systems have established equivalences, such as *Hollerith code*. Thus, "book" may be represented by a notation of a series of holes in punched cards, as shown in (*d*); "215" may be represented by a notation of a series of holes in punched cards, as shown in (*e*). In *Morse code,* "book" may be represented by a notation of a series of dots and dashes, as shown in (*f*); "215" may be represented by a notation of a series of dots and dashes, as shown in (*g*).

241

news concerning the road of approach of the enemy was translated into another kind of intelligence, namely, lights hoisted on a steeple; translation is useful because it transforms a hard-to-broadcast piece of intelligence[4] into one which is easily broadcast . . . .[5]

Binary numbers are codes for arabic numbers which are easier to use with computers.

The arabic number 25 consists of a tens digit (2) and a units digit (5) when used in a decimal system. Each digit in an arabic number can be any one of ten digits chosen from: 0, 1, 2, 3, 4, 5, 6, 7, 8, or 9. When adding arabic numbers, the consequences of this limitation for each digit to ten numbers is well known: it is necessary to "carry" over to another digit when the limitation is reached. For example when adding the arabic numbers:

$$\begin{array}{r} 753 \\ + 629 \\ \hline \end{array}$$

one first adds 3 and 9, in the units position, yielding 12, which exceeds the limitation for a digit (0, 1, 2, 3, 4, 5, 6, 7, 8, 9). The sum is therefore given as 2, with a "carry" of the 1 to the tens position:

$$\begin{array}{r} 753 \\ + 629 \\ {\scriptstyle 1} \\ \hline 2 \end{array}$$

Then one turns attention to the tens position, adding 5, 2, and 1 (as carried over), yielding 8, which does not exceed the limitation:

$$\begin{array}{r} 753 \\ + 629 \\ {\scriptstyle 0\,1} \\ \hline 82 \end{array}$$

Again, one considers the hundredth position, adding 7 and 6, yielding 13, which again exceeds the limitation, so that the sum is given as 3, with 1 carried over to the thousandths position:

$$\begin{array}{r} 753 \\ + 629 \\ {\scriptstyle 1\,0\,1} \\ \hline 382 \end{array}$$

---

[4] "Intelligence" here has its military meaning, i.e., a statement about some situation. Clearly a statement about the state of illumination of two lanterns is more easily disseminated than a statement about enemy maneuvers.

[5] Henry Quastler, *A Primer of Information Theory,* Technical Memorandum 56-1, Office of Ordnance Research, U. S. Army, Durham, North Carolina, January 1956, p. 4.

Finally, one considers the thousandths position, adding 1 (as carried over) to "nothing" in the other numbers, yielding 1:

$$753$$
$$+ 629$$
$$\underline{1\;0\;1}$$
$$1382$$

and the addition is complete.

Mechanical or electromechanical adding machines for decimal systems consist of a number of wheels, each representing one digit of an arabic number. Each wheel has represented on its outer face each of the permissible arabic numbers (0, 1, 2, 3, 4, 5, 6, 7, 8, 9):

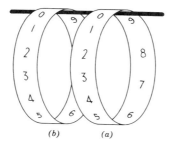

(b)   (a)

At the 9 position there is a mechanism that will engage the next wheel at its left whenever it reaches that point and clicks the next wheel one digit's worth, for example, from 0 to 1. The way in which this mechanism relates to addition is as follows:

Wheel A represents the units digit and wheel B, the tens digit. The operator of the adding machine, wishing to add two numbers (e.g., 3 and 9) first "clears" the machine (assures that every wheel is at the "zero" position). Then a key labelled 3 in the units column of the machine keyboard is depressed, causing the units wheel to move 3 places (from 0 to 3). Next a key labelled 9 in the same units column of the keyboard is depressed, causing the units wheel to move 9 places. However, when the wheel moved 7 places, it reached its limitation (one complete revolution, bringing the wheel to the zero position again) and engaged the wheel to its left (the "tens" wheel) causing it to move one place (from 0 to 1). The units wheel then continues to move the remaining places required to complete its move of 9 places, bringing it to the 2 position.

The adding machine has thus accomplished exactly what a human adder would have done, adding 3 and 9 to yield 12, "carrying" over the "1" to the tens position when the number in the units digit exceeded its limitation.

It is now possible to imagine another adding machine, in which, for convenience purposes, the "wheels" can handle only two numbers (e.g., 0 and 1) instead of ten as before. Now, the language (decimal numbers) we used before is no longer useful (since we would need wheels that can handle 10 numbers instead of the ones we do have). So we need another language that is easier to use with this new type of adding machine. Since we called the source language a *decimal-number language* because of its ability to handle 10 numbers in each digit, let us call the new language a *binary-number language* because of its ability to handle only 2 numbers in each digit.

When we add two binary numbers:

$$\begin{array}{r} 1 \\ + 1 \\ \hline \end{array}$$

We now have the sum *10*, since we have to "carry" into another column to the left every time we exceed 1 (instead of 9 as before with the decimal system). So, continuing to add:

$$\begin{array}{r} 10 \\ +\quad 1 \\ \hline 11 \\ +\quad 1 \\ \hline 100 \\ +\quad 1 \\ \hline 101 \\ +\quad 1 \\ \hline 110 \end{array}$$

and so on

The "wheels," operating as described before for decimal numbers:

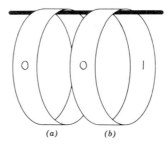

(a)   (b)

will "carry" over from one wheel to the next, as a wheel completes a full revolution.

Thus, a code is needed to translate from a difficult-to-use source language (*decimal numbers*) to a language (*binary numbers*) that is easier to use for a particular purpose (use with adding machines having wheels with only two numbers). The computer does not really have wheels as described above. Instead, information is recorded magnetically. A position on the medium on which information is recorded, such as magnetic tape, can be in only one of two states, magnetized or not. Therefore, the binary number scheme is used to deal effectively with this bistate device.

The decimal number 25 can be written as a binary number 11001. The code system which permits this translation is explained elsewhere.[6]

Other notations can be used to represent this binary number. For example, if we used photographic film, we could have a transparent (unexposed) spot to represent 1 and an opaque (exposed) spot to represent 0. So the binary number 11001 could be shown as:

2. *To Decrease the Amount of Space Required to Record Information.* An example of this need is provided by the telegraph companies. They must transmit certain ideas so often that they have chosen to use symbols that are more economical than normally spelled-out words. Such frequently occurring ideas as *Congratulations, Birthday Greetings, Greetings,* and *Best Wishes,* are more economically transmitted by means of numbers. For example, the symbols *110* might mean *Congratulations,* while *10* might mean *Best Wishes.* Thus the telegraph companies express the same ideas, but use a lesser number of characters than would be required to spell out the message in the alphabetic symbols of natural language.[7] Clearly the most commonly used phrases must be given the shortest numbers if maximum economy in transmission is to be achieved.

In mechanized information retrieval, it is often desirable to represent ideas and words in as few symbols as possible in order to assure the most efficient utilization of the search medium on which information is recorded.

3. *To Supplement the Information Available in the Source Language.* Codes are not used only to produce pure identification signals with high transmission efficiencies.

---

[6] J. Belzer, *"Binary Numbers",* in *Encyclopedia of Library and Information Science,* Marcel Dekker Inc., New York, Vol. 2, 1969.

[7] G. Herdan, *Language as Choice and Chance,* P. Noordhoff, N. V. Groningen, 1956, pp. 170-1.

An example is a geographical code for a city. The name "Pittsburgh" might be represented by the notation:

WHUSNCPAALPI

in which the following meaning might be attributed to each part of characters:

$$
\begin{aligned}
\text{WH} &= \text{Western Hemisphere} \\
\text{WHUS} &= \text{United States of America} \\
\text{WHUSNC} &= \text{North Central States} \\
\text{WHUSNCPA} &= \text{State of Pennsylvania} \\
\text{WHUSNCPAAL} &= \text{Allegheny County} \\
\text{WHUSNCPAALPI} &= \text{Pittsburgh}
\end{aligned}
$$

In this code the number of characters used is admittedly greater than that required to spell out the natural language word. But the amount of supplementary information provided with regard to Pittsburgh may be considered to justify the length.

Similarly, a code for the term CLOCK might be represented by the code:

MACI MESU TIME 01

in which the following meaning might be attributed to each set of characters:

$$
\begin{aligned}
\text{MACI} &= \text{MACHINE OR DEVICE} \\
\text{MESU} &= \text{MEASURE} \\
\text{TIME} &= \text{TIME}
\end{aligned}
$$

again the number of characters in the code exceeds that in the word *CLOCK* but supplementary information, relating to the meaning of the word is provided, and may again be considered sufficiently useful to justify the larger number of characters.

4. To Distinguish Between Alternative Ideas or Words that Are Not Easily Distinguished in the Source Language.

Natural language represented by alphabetic characters does not always distinguish between the different concepts. Numerical or symbolic notations may be used to provide unique representations.

Such limitations of natural language are exemplified by the problem of homographs. In the English language, the word "plant" may have either of two entirely different meanings, depending upon whether the context is botanical or industrial. A code can make it possible to distinguish arbitrarily between the two concepts:

$$
\begin{aligned}
\text{PLANT (biological)} &= 3205 \\
\text{PLANT (manufacturing)} &= 3206
\end{aligned}
$$

Other examples of such words are as follows:

CRASH (vehicular)
CRASH (textile)
QUACK (duck sound)
QUACK (pretender of medical skill)
RACKET (noise)
RACKET (tennis)
BUSTLE (energetic activity)
BUSTLE (padded cushion in skirt)

C. Natural Language as a Code

We mentioned earlier that, from some points of view, natural language is a code for ideas. More accurately, it should be considered to be one notation for such a code.

It has been found that the proportions of linguistic forms in a natural language remain quite constant for a given language, at a given time of its development, and for a sufficiently great number of observations. This characteristic of languages makes it a relatively effective system for the communication of thought by means of symbols. Theoretically, the coding system that may be implied by language usually enables different messages to be distinguished easily and correctly. However, language is characterized by a change in the use of vocabulary that is unpremeditated, and follows the general tendency of the changes in nature, that is, for the entropy of a system to approach a maximum.

However, it is not possible to predict whether in any particular instance a change will take place, or, if it does, what the extent of such change will be. Nor is it possible to predict the mental picture that language will create in the mind of any single human being. This fact contributes to the ineffectiveness of language as a code. Therefore, in compensation, a certain amount of redundancy is expected in language. We have defined redundancy as the quantity of information transmitted in excess of the theoretical minimum required. In language, redundancy is introduced in order to overcome the effect of noise in the communication process, by using alternative expressions to convey a single message.

Artificial languages have been used as alternatives to natural language. Examples are the shorthand systems for writing. In these notation systems, redundancy is reduced to the minimum in order to speed the recordings of dictation. Regardless of this goal, however, natural language can be abridged only to such a degree that an adequate transfer of information is still assured.

Language serves as a relatively efficient code for the transmission of ideas in terms of the purposes of a code described in the preceding section.

D. Use of Codes and Notations in Information-Retrieval Systems

Most information-retrieval systems are language-based at several stages of the communication chain, which begins at the generation of graphic records and concludes when a graphic record is provided to someone interested in some specific information. It can be said that retrieval systems, being language-based, involve the use of codes in one form or another.

Examples of the coding principles involved in various types of information-retrieval systems are given in Table 1.

II. CHARACTERISTICS OF CODES AND NOTATIONS

A. How "Good" Is a Code or Notation?

The worth of a code is based on the worth of the system behind it. A system is what the designer chooses to make it, and a "good" system can be judged only in terms of the use to which it is put. Therefore, the system behind a code must involve the isolation of a set of related activities which in some way appear to be aimed toward a common specific goal.

In information-retrieval activities, a system is hypothesized or developed in order to achieve some advance over the null system, which precludes any arrangement of records or of aspects of importance related to these records. The development of systems for information retrieval has been approached from two points of view:

1. The organization of a searching system for achieving effective and economical searches based on the information content of graphic records.

2. The organization of a searching system for achieving optimal use of a given tool or set of tools.

With the first point of view, a system may be based on one or more of the principles discussed in Table 1 in order to achieve certain desired benefits.

The second point of view implies that a predetermination has been made as to the tool, machine, or device that is to be used. The system must take these parameters into account. Predetermination as to the use of certain tools or machines in retrieval systems are often made because of the availability of certain equipment at low cost, or because of the previous commitment in money and effort, to some constant principle, requiring the reexpenditure of too much money and effort if it were abandoned.

Once these considerations have been taken into account, attention can turn to the choice of a code that will optimize the system-equipment complex that has been formulated.

How is the "worth" of a code measured? When a coding problem is relatively simple, that is, when the purposes to be served by the code are relatively easy to identify, the worth, efficiency, or effectiveness of the code can be measured readily.

For example, when considering the case of the Paul Revere code the range of all possible events was subdivided into categories of interest:

1. If the British were arriving by land, one signal light (code) would be exhibited.

2. If the British were arriving by sea, two signal lights would be exhibited.

3. If the British were not arriving, no signal lights would be exhibited.

This coding system appears efficient, but certain exigencies were not taken into account, for example:

1. What if the British attacked simultaneously by land and by sea? Should three signal lights be exhibited?

2. Would the absence of any light give positive assurance that the British were not attacking by either land or sea? Or would it perhaps mean that there was some disturbance in the communication system? Might the signal lights have been seen by the British and removed? Might Paul Revere have attempted to display signal lights but been prevented from doing so by circumstances outside of his control?

These uncertainties throw some doubt on the worth of the Paul Revere code, although it may have been an efficient one in terms of the alternative events envisaged by Revere. A more effective code might have provided for:

1. 1 signal light = British arriving by land.
2. 2 signal lights = British arriving by sea.
3. 3 signal lights = British arriving by both land and sea.
4. 4 signal lights = No sign of the British.
5. No signal lights = Disturbance in the communication system.

This code still does not take into account the possibility that one or more signal lights might accidentally or through tampering have gone out. Further coding sophistication could be added to cover this eventuality.

Redundancy could have been introduced in one of several ways. For example, the message could be repeated; that is, the signal lights required to transmit the required information could have been:

Possible event	Signal lights
1. British arriving by land	$1 + 1 = 2$
2. British arriving by sea	$2 + 2 = 4$
3. British arriving by both land and sea	$3 + 3 = 6$
4. No sign of the British	$4 + 4 = 8$

TABLE 1. Use of "Codes" in

Coding principle involved	Index-based	Classification-based
Translation from a difficult to use source language to one that is easier to use for a particular purpose.	Translation from natural (source) language to "key words" (index entries) for purpose of facilitating alphabetization of a subject index.	Translation from natural (source) language to fixed subject (classification) headings for purposes of grouping subject matter in pre-established pattern.
Decrease in amount of space required to record information.	Representation of an idea, which requires expression in natural language, by one or several key words, which are clues to enable the identification and location of that idea.	Expression of classification headings in few words, which in context of other headings, carries a considerable amount of information.
Supplement the information available in the source language.	Relating of index entries to "authority" lists which standardize the use of terminology in the index. Also provides guidance as to which terms are considered synonymous or sufficiently closely related in meaning to be grouped under a single index entry.	Same as for *Index-based* (which see). Also, by consulting other levels of the classification system, supplementary information may be obtained as to relationship among subjects expressed therein.
Distinguish between alternative ideas or words that are not distinguished in source language.	"Modification" of index entries (clues provided as to specialized meaning in a particular text) to distinguish between alternative ideas expressed by identical words.	Alternative ideas are distinguished even when these may not be discerned in the source language.

Abstract-based (auto- and telegraphic)	Natural-language-based
Telegraphic abstract provides a framework for expressing ideas which is both index (description) and classification (role indicators) based, and also artificial grammar for their expression. *Conventional* and *auto-abstracts* (*extracts*) involve selection of ideas and text from source language expressed, in turn, in natural language for purpose of decreasing time required for reading.	Usually involves "normalization" of natural language in order to facilitate searching of similar ideas expressed in alternative grammatical forms.
Selection of certain points of view from the source language generally leads to expression in less space than required for recording original text.	Usually, no more effective than source language.
Usually involves no supplementing of information from the source language.	Usually, no supplementing of source information is involved, unless "normalized" language is further encoded; then similar to telegraphic abstracts (which see).
No more effective than source text in this regard, unless special attention is provided to this point. In telegraphic abstracts, alternative ideas using identical words are differentiated when encoding is completed.	Usually no more effective than source language unless "normalized" language is further encoded.

If a single light were to go out, there would be an odd number of lights, indicating that there was a disturbance in the communication system. Therefore, if only three signal lights were visible, the viewer could deduce that possibly event (2) was taking place. But of course, if more than one signal light was disturbed, then even this redundancy would not help. However, a significant source of possible error would have been removed.

Each source of error that is removed would require more signal lights to be used, making the coding system more cumbersome and expensive. Therefore, a decision must be reached as to how much an error-removal step is worth.

Another possibility is that a fog might have come up, making the signal lights invisible. In this case, a corresponding set of toots from a fog horn might have provided a suitable alternative notation. Of course, the coding system itself must be considered independent of means used to represent or transmit the code.

Returning now to practices used by the telegraph company, we can observe that redundancy is used for error removal. A telegram that contains a message such as:

Mr. White arrives at 3 P.M. on October 12 on flight 721.

is followed by an additional message such as:

$$3 -- 12 -- 721$$

which repeats the numbers that were given in the original message. This tactic is used because the people who transmit such telegrams, under the pressure of heavy word load, often make errors involving transposition of letters of numbers, so that the original message may be transmitted as:

Mr. White arrievs at 3 p.m. on October 21 on flight 721.

The misspelling *arrievs* is not dangerous since the English language is sufficiently redundant so that most people would understand what was intended. However, there is no redundancy in the number *12,* and an error which resulted in the transmission as *21* would be extremely serious. Therefore redundancy through retransmission of the numbers is provided in order to relieve this situation.

This example has been elaborated in detail in order to make the point by analogy that it is important in evaluating or considering information-searching systems to remember that the usefulness of a notation, and the extent to which its representation is error prone, must be considered as well as the worth of the coding system behind the notation.

When considering the more complex coding problem involving the representation of the contents of a graphic record for purposes of later retrieval, it is *not* possible to predict each and every point of view that will eventually be important, as in the Paul Revere analogy.

Here it is not possible to consider the range of all possible events and to subdivide them into categories of interest (since all possible points of view cannot be predicted). In this case, the worth of the coding system must be considered from two points of view:

1. How reliably are the potential points of view of interest predicted?

2. Based on those points of view predicted, how effective or efficient is the notation used?

B. Symbolism

It is clear by now that, from the viewpoint of information-retrieval systems, any convenient symbolism (or notation) may be used to record a code. Some of the symbols commonly used to represent codes are as follows:

Letters of the alphabet	as in natural language
Numerals	as in telephone numbers
Special symbols (*, /, ?, etc.)	as in chemical codes
Dots and dashes	as in Morse telegraph code (graphic representation)
Patterns of holes in cards	as in IBM cards
Patterns of holes in tape	as in teletype tape
Patterns of opaque and transparent spots	as in film
Patterns of magnetic spots	as in magnetic tape

It should be obvious that the coding system need not change if the symbolism or notation changes (see Figure 9-2.) This does not mean that all machine systems can detect and discriminate among different symbol patterns. Therefore, the choice of symbolism is dictated by what the available machines are able to handle.

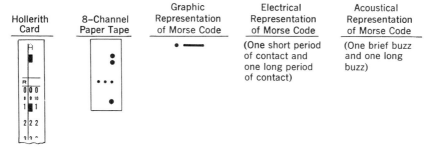

Figure 9-2. Notations for the letter "a" for several types of machines or systems.

C. Length of Notations

The "length" of a notation, or rather the number of characters in a notation, may be equal to, less than, or greater than the number of characters in the natural-language equivalent of the notation. All other things being equal, it is generally desirable to keep a notation as short as possible. Brevity means economy in recording or transmitting the notation.

However, in many mechanized information-retrieval systems, the length of a notation may only be an incidental consideration. In order to see why this should be so, let us review several of the fundamental reasons for coding and for the use of notations.

1. To Translate from a Difficult-to-Use Source Language to a Language that Is Easier to Use for a Particular Purpose, or Purposes. When the alphabet is used to record words in natural language, and it is desired to translate this alphabetic and numeric information into a language that a machine can read, it is often necessary to translate each symbol into binary digits (or "bits"). For example, the decimal number *9* is expressed in binary form as 1001. Thus, it requires four characters to write in binary what can be written by one character in the more customary decimal notation. However, the "longer" notation is more convenient to use in an electronic computer, since the higher the base[8] used, the more complex must the equipment be in order to recognize a number or symbol.

In general, therefore, unless all other considerations are equal, the counting of characters in a notation is not a valid way of measuring the worth of the notation or of the code that it represents. Character counting is just as inappropriate a way to measure worth as counting the number of coins (without considering denomination) is to measure wealth.

2. To Supplement the Information Available in the Source Language. In mechanized information retrieval, it is often advantageous for a notation to provide more than a merely unique representation of a word or idea in a source language. Often it is desired to provide related information that can be useful. Such an example is given earlier in this chapter, where the geographical notation contains a greater number of characters than the source word but, at the same time, provides added information.

Therefore, if the probable usefulness of the additional information exceeds the advantages to be gained by a more concise notation, then the longer notation should be used.

---

[8] Base, in this context, means the number of different distinct states that can be expressed by single digits in a particular system. For example, a binary system has a base of 2, since only two states can be represented by single digits (*0* or *1*); a decimal system has a base of 10, since ten states can be represented by a single digits (*0, 1, 2, 3, 4, 5, 6, 7, 8, 9*).

D. Irreversible (Nonsingular) Codes

It has been considered axiomatic that in order for a code to be useful, it must represent a *nonsingular* transformation. This means that, given a message in code language, we must be able to apply the inverse of the code transformation and decode the code-language image, recovering the original message. However, in code languages for mechanized information retrieval, nonsingularity is not necessarily a requirement.

For example, a systems designer may decide that two related words shall both be represented by the identical notation. This decision implies that the concept represented by the notation is considered to be somewhat more generic than either of the source words. Decoding the notation would not distinguish between the two nonidentical source words that it represents. As an example, the words

cheese

milk

may be provided with only a single equivalent, such as

DP (meaning *dairy products*)

Here the designer has decided that for his purposes, the more generic term will suffice. In decoding "DP" it would be impossible to determine what the specific source word has been.

This type of decision is analogous to the one that is made in a traditional indexing or cataloging system. For example, a standard entry is selected:

Dairy products

with scope notes indicating that specific *dairy products* such as *cheese* and *milk* are to be included under this entry.

In some searching systems, the uniqueness of each notation (as representing a nonsingular transformation) is considered important because the ability to discriminate among all source words or ideas is valued for some reason peculiar to a particular situation. When a unique notation system is used, it is more economical to alter the notations at some later time if some alteration should prove advantageous. Such changes can be made on the basis of a notation-for-notation substitution and can often be conducted automatically, as by computer routines.

For example, one document may have had the terms "cheese" or "milk" selected as index entries which were coded as "DP." At some later time, let us assume that there is a desire to change the notation, for one reason or another, from alphabetic to numeric characters, e.g., from "DP" to "785." A conversion dictionary would then be established which would include an item:

DP = 785

The substitution of notations could then be performed readily.

However, it is not possible to perform a substitution, or conversion, if a nonunique code language is to be transformed to a unique code language. In other words, no automatic routine can make the changes because no automatic routine can decide whether DP, in any given context, means cheese or milk.

There is another case in which it is not possible to decode a notation once it has been recorded on some search medium. This is when notations are superimposed, and the identity of each notation is destroyed (see Figure 9-3). For example, once the numbers 1-7-8 and 2-6-9 are recorded in the same "field," then it is no longer possible to reconstruct either original notation. The numbers 1-2-6-7-8-9 are recorded in a single field, with no indication as to which group of numbers form a related set.

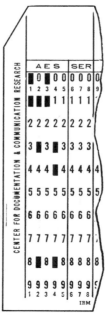

Figure 9-3. *Superposed* recording of notations in identical fields, which yields a tremendous number of "ghost" combinations. In this case, each of the notations, 08-14, 11-13, 03-08, 03-14, was recorded in columns 1-4, using the "standard" IBM punched-card code. This method is *not* what is generally referred to as random, superimposed coding.

E. Mnemonic Features of a Notation

When a notation is to be "used" only by a machine, and human beings will never be involved operationally in using it, then no thought need be devoted to mnemonic features. However, if human beings are to use a notation it is sometimes advantageous to attempt to make the notation meaningful in order to aid the human beings to use it more effectively by remembering it.

For example, the number 3416095 is the notation for a telephone in Pittsburgh. However, in order to aid humans in remembering this number, the telephone company traditionally had represented this same number as:

FIeldbrook 1-6095

The "F," when dialed, provides the same signal to the telephone exchange as if the number "3" had been dialed; similarly, the letter "I" gives the same signal as the number "4." However, it was found that persons, in attempting to remember seven numerals, would either forget parts of it, or perhaps remember the number as *3416059,* which transposes two numbers, or make other errors. It was found easier to remember a name, then a single number followed by four numbers.[9]

Similarly, in a code for a searching system, a notation that reads:

34682153

may be copied incorrectly from a code book more often than will a notation, which is pronounceable and which seems to make some sense, such as:

LECT BANL

F. Redundancy in Code Language

If, as we have said, redundancy is the amount of information transmitted in excess of the necessary minimum, there must be a computable, absolute minimum size or form of notation that will convey exactly one specific unit of information and no more.

If this is the case, then why should we "build in" redundancy? Why not provide the minimum? Every communication system is said to have a certain amount of noise. In acoustics, *"noise"* is defined as "any undesired sound." In a communication system, *"noise"* is considered to be random disturbance which is transmitted along with purposeful signals. In an information-retrieval system, *"noise"* is generally considered to be that information that is provided to an information seeker in which he has no interest. Noise, thus defined, may be caused by a number of factors:

1. The analysis of graphic records has not been sufficiently precise, and has accordingly provided retrievable references that are of little or no interest to

---

[9] The telephone company has restudied this problem and has decided that human beings may not be confused by a series of seven numerals. The telephone company, which is now able to use several combinations authorized by conventional alphabetical restrictions—HP, LS, and so on—has won an obvious advantage, providing an example where economy is weighed against possible error. In this case the telephone company chose the more economical approach.

Index entry.............*Gadgets, 15*

Text reference...........“The data handling people are very much concerned with the invention of gadgets such as character sensors and page readers which will electronically scan a page of print in any type face and record the information there on more machineable media such as magnetic tape, but I doubt very much if in the next decade or two they will be capable of doing this at a price sufficiently attractive to enable an old library, one with a hundred years of holdings, to re-record all its documents.”

Figure 9-4. Example of index entry (from M. Boaz, Ed., *Modern Trends in Documentation,* Pergamon Press, New York, 1959) which provided “noise” to the author, since to him that entry provided no substantive information on the subject of the entry. Furthermore, the entries’ “character sensors” and “page readers” might never bring to this author’s mind the entry *gadgets.*

the user of the system. Alternatively, the analysis has missed some aspect, some subject, or some document of real interest (Figure 9-4).

2. The question has been stated or analyzed in such a way that references are retrieved that are of little or no interest to the user of the system. Alternatively, records of real interest are missed.

3. The proper manipulations of the retrieval system have led to the selection of undesired documents.

It is the third of these noise-causing factors that has a direct bearing on codes and notations. The introduction of redundancy into a code language may increase the efficiency of the retrieval system by decreasing the amount of noise that may occur. The efficiency of a retrieval system may be considered as a factor of the ratio of “signal” to noise, where the *signal* is the pertinent information provided, and the *noise* is the nonpertinent. If the signal is kept constant, a decrease in noise will increase the efficiency of the system by permitting a higher ratio of meaningful information to be transmitted.

One method of introducing redundancy has as its rationale the fact that a code language may be used incorrectly and may lead to incorrect selections of materials. Thus, a notation such as *83251* may be transmitted (by telephone, telegraph, human memory, etc.) as *8251,* with one digit omitted. A way of introducing redundancy to avoid many errors of this type is to add a *check digit* at the end of each notation which represents the sum (19) of the other numbers of the notation. This would provide a warning if a digit were omitted and indicate the necessity for corrective measures.

(In actual practice, the check digit might only be the units digit (*9*) of the sum (*19*) of the other numbers (*83251*), leading to a new number *832519*.)

This type of redundancy provides the notation with a self-checking feature, but it is not a failsafe procedure. For example, if the number to be transmitted were *803251*, an error in transmission that would omit the "O" would not lead to any difference in the check digit. However, the probability of this technique being effective is sufficiently high for most applications. This probability could be increased if code numbers to be transmitted were required to be of exact numbers of digits. (The omission of the "O" would then be detected.)

Another type of redundancy involves the repetition of a notation, so that if one is garbled during transmission, the two signals will not be identical, and an attempt can be made to retransmit the notation. As mentioned earlier, the telegraph company in the United States has used this type of redundancy by providing that, whenever a message containing numerals is transmitted, such numerals are retransmitted at the end.

III. TYPES OF CODES

A. Introduction

In the earlier sections of this chapter, we have discussed the general concept of the code and its characteristics. In the present section, we shall consider some of the types of code that have actually been developed for mechanized information-retrieval systems. And paradoxically, we shall begin by discussing no code at all, under the heading "Codeless Codes."

B. "Codeless" Codes

Proposals have been made to develop mechanized retrieval systems that use no code at all in order to avoid the complexities and cost of coding. But there is no escape, since the fact remains that every machine system involves some coding, even if only on the simplest level, involving the transformation of a natural-language "descriptor" into machine language by means of one-to-one substitution of machine-readable symbols for alphabetic symbols. And even if machines were available for economically reading natural-language texts, the natural language itself is the coding system used to represent ideas in the retrieval system. The choice of the natural-language code, therefore, should be considered as a deliberate one, and with proper weighing of the advantages, disadvantages, and costs (both to store and to retrieve information) which are involved in the decision.

Therefore, the only time that *no* codes are used in a retrieval system is when records included in the system are not processed in any way, and when *all* records must be examined for pertinency whenever a search is conducted. Such a system is not a retrieval system at all, of course.

C. Tabulated (Arbitrary) Versus Algorithmic Codes

1. Tabulated (Arbitrary) Codes. The *tabulated* (or arbitrary) code is one that requires a code book or dictionary to provide code equivalents for source words and vice versa. In usual practice, this implies a considerable amount of preparation and prediction, on the part of the code makers, as to the exact letters, numbers, words, or phrases that will be routinely translated into code.

The simplest codes are transliterations (a simple form of *substitution*), that is, when each symbol in the source language has a corresponding symbol in the code language. The Morse code is an example of such a code language:

a	. —
b	— . . .
c	— . — .
d	— . .
e	.
f	. . — .
g	— — .
h	. . . .
i	. .
	etc.

Another tabulated code involves the *substitution* of sets of code symbols for words, phrases, or other meaningful units in the source language. An example of such a code is the one used by the telegraph company, where a few numerical symbols are used to describe a frequently occurring message, for example,

Message	*Code Language*
Birthday Greetings	01

In order to use a substitution code, it is necessary to have two dictionaries, one providing substitution code language for messages, and the other providing the message equivalents for the code language:

Dictionary 1 (Message-to-Code Language)

Message	*Code Language*
Birthday Greetings	01

Dictionary 2 (Code Language-to-Message)

Code Language	*Message*
01	Birthday Greetings

Another tabulated (arbitrary) code, but one which also involves an algorithm (or method for computing) is the *contraction,* which involves the application of arbitrary rules for coding. One example is a code that requires omission of all vowels, for example,

| *Source Language* | *Code Language* |
| thermometer | THRMMTR |

It is perhaps obvious that this is an irreversible code since this type of code may not provide a unique designation for every word in the source language, for instance, BRD = bread, brad, bred, bared, bored, board, beard, bard, bird, abroad, etc.

Such a singular (non-unique) code would be suitable where: (1) the subject matter to be coded is sufficiently narrow in scope, that only one or a relatively small number of alternative source-language words would ever be encountered (a file on *bakeries* might have entries on BREAD and BOARD, but not on BRAD, BEARD, etc.); or (2) the context of the coded word would provide a basis for selection from among the several alternative words (in a discussion of BAKING of BRD, most of the other possible source language words would be eliminated in favor of BREAD).

2. Algorithmic Codes. An algorithmic code is one that has rules for conversion of source words into code equivalents. (For every code, in a sense, there must exist an algorithm for coding and decoding.) However, for purposes of this discussion, the term "algorithm" will be used in its more limited, and more normal, meaning—as a method for computing.

An example of an algorithmic code is the self-checking digit described earlier. This digit is computed by summing all of the digits in the notation, and the units digit of the sum is used as the last digit of the notation.

Another algorithmic code has been described earlier. The coding, in this case the substitution of binary for arabic numerals, is performed with the aid of a formal algorithm, which provides the rules for this substitution.

Message-to-code language and code language-to-message dictionaries are not required for this type of coding system, although they may be used if the algorithm is too complex or not generally understood.

D. Direct Versus Indirect (Combination) Recording of Notations

Direct and indirect coding provide another set of criteria for distinguishing between types of codes.

In direct coding, a separate meaning is assigned to each individual part of the search medium in which a notation may be recorded. For example, in a marginal-hole punched card, each hole may be assigned a single meaning (Figure 9-5); in a machine-punched card, each individual punching position may be

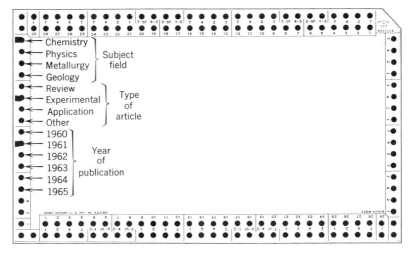

Figure 9-5. Edge-notched punched card, with direct recording of subjects (popularly called "direct coding") at left edge. Notching of appropriate holes indicated that the meaning attributed to that hole is true for the record being analyzed.

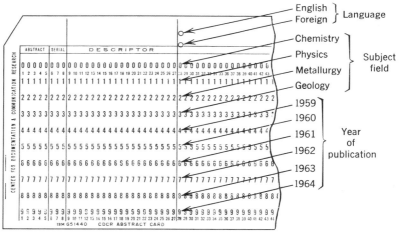

Figure 9-6. Machine-punched card, with direct recording of subjects in column 28.

assigned a single meaning (Figure 9-6); and so forth. This type of coding is relevant when dealing with unit records in a document system. Such coding is not appropriate when using computers chiefly because the use of a binary system for recording information would limit the number of direct codes possible to *two*.

Indirect (or combination) coding is used when there is a need to provide notations for more subjects, or meanings, than there are individual positions available on the search medium. Meaning is assigned to combinations of holes, or to combinations of punching positions. For example, with a marginal-hole punched card having 80 holes, indirect methods of coding must be used in order to provide room for more than 80 subjects or meanings. One such indirect recording of notations is the "selector" code illustrated in Figures 9-7 and 9-8. Indirect coding is used without exception when dealing with computers. Even when "word" indexing systems are used, and it may seem that words are being recorded "directly," without change, the characters of the word must be coded into binary form before recording.

SF	7	4	2	1	0

(a)   *(b)*

Figure 9-7. Selector code by which any one of ten subjects (or meanings) can be recorded, using two of the six holes on an edge-notched punched card. To record subject numbers 1, 2, 4, or 7, the appropriate numbered hole is notched, along with the SF (single figure) hole. Thus, for subject number 2, holes marked 2 and SF would be notched (*a*). To record subject numbers 3, 5, 6, 8, or 9, two digits are chosen which add up to the right number. Thus, for subject number 9, holes marked 7 and 2 would be notched (*b*). To record subject 0 (zero), only the zero and SF holes are notched, assuring that two holes are notched no matter what number is to be recorded. A special form of selector code is the "sequence" code, which is set up in such a way that the cards may be sorted with a minimum of effort into a predetermined sequence.

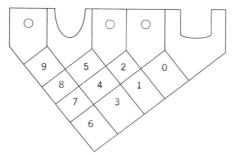

Figure 9-8. A lesser number of holes is consumed when information is recorded using a 5-hole triangle or pyramid selective code. Here, too, two notches are made for each number. In the example above the number "3" has been recorded.

The consequences of the use of direct and indirect codes are as follows:

When direct codes are used, as many subjects per document or source material as may be appropriate may be recorded. Accordingly, in Figure 9-5, if the document represented by the card shown is to be indexed for chemistry (as the subject field), experimental (as the type of article), and 1961 (as the year of publication), all of these entries may be recorded. A search may then be directed to all those cards (representing documents) that have all three entries in common, and the selection may then be accomplished without difficulty.

Similarly, when machine-punched cards (Figure 9-6) are used, a number of entries may be recorded. When a search is to be conducted using, for example, a sorter, each punching position representing an independent subject may be searched readily.

On the other hand, when indirect codes are used (Figure 9-7), only one subject of many may be recorded in a given field. Thus, if the six holes reserved for indirect codes in Figure 9-7a were labeled as shown, only one of ten subjects could be recorded. For example, we might establish a code dictionary as follows:

Subject	Code	Notching pattern
Chemistry	1	SF - 1
Biology	2	SF - 2
Metallurgy	3	1 - 2
Physics	4	SF - 4
Medicine	5	1 - 4
Electrical engineering	6	2 - 4
Civil engineering	7	SF - 7
Industrial engineering	8	1 - 7
Mechanical engineering	9	2 - 7
Petroleum engineering	0	SF - 0

If a given document were concerned only with *chemistry,* then only holes 1 and SF would be notched. However, if another document were concerned with both *chemistry* and *biology,* and if an attempt were made to record both codes 1 and 2, there would automatically be recorded the code for *metallurgy,* which is not of concern in the given document.

During design of a system, therefore, a decision must be made with regard to choice of direct or indirect codes for given segments of the card. Thus, if, as in the above example, a field of *only six holes* were available for recording the general subject field of a document, two alternatives would be available:

1. If it is predicted that documents will often be characterized by more than one subject, then the direct code would have to be used. This would force

some generalization of the "subjects" listed above to convert the ten subjects into six. The first five might be retained as chemistry, biology, metallurgy, physics, and medicine, while the last five might be generalized to one subject: *engineering.*

2. If it is predicted that documents will generally be characterized by only one subject, then the indirect code would be used. This would not require the loss in specificity for the various engineering fields as in alternative (*1*). However, the disadvantage incurred is that if a document were encountered which should be characterized by more than one subject, all but one would have to be disregarded.

E. Superimposed Versus Nonsuperimposed Recording of Notations

One type of indirect recording involves the superimposed recording of notations for more than one subject in the same field, or area of search medium.

Let us suppose that we have a field in a marginal-hole punched card, as shown in Figure 9-9*a*, and we wish to record four subjects "superimposed" in the same field. The subjects have been assigned these notations:

Subject A	8−14
Subject B	11−13
Subject C	3−8
Subject D	3−14

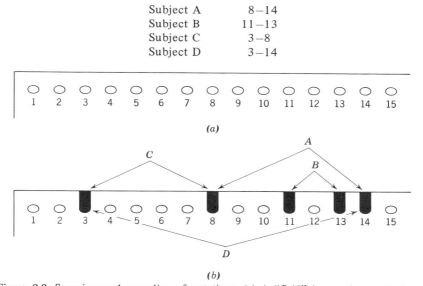

(*a*)

(*b*)

Figure 9-9. Superimposed recording of notations. (*a*) A "field" in an edge-notched card containing 15 holes. (*b*) The notations for four subjects recorded in the single field:

Subject A = 8−14
Subject B = 11−13
Subject C = 3−8
Subject D = 3−14

It will be noted that when the notations for these four subjects are notched into the field (Figure 9-9*b*), the notations for any one subject are recorded with total disregard for those notches that have already been recorded in the same field. It becomes obvious that a number that is a part of one notation may also be part of another. Thus, when the notation for subject C is to be notched, one part of it, number "8" has already been notched for subject A. When the notation for subject D is to be notched, both "3" and "14" have already been notched, and no further notching is required.

This means that if only the notations for subjects A, B, and C were pertinent to a particular record, the notation for subject D would still be recorded automatically. As a result, a search for subject D would identify this record even though it contained no pertinent information, and no notation for D had been intentionally recorded.

Because of this possibility of generating false (or "ghost") combinations by the fortuitous recording of other notations, the number of holes to be notched (or the number of notations for subjects recorded) should be limited, so that the number of false combinations generated does not exceed an acceptable minimum.

The question might be asked why should one go to the trouble of superimposing codes, when difficulties such as these may be anticipated. The only reason is to increase the capacity of a given tool, the marginal-hole punched card; that is, to increase the amount of information that can be recorded in a limited amount of space.

Let us consider the amount of space available in the example of Figure 9-9, in which a field of 15 "holes" is available. If a *direct code* were to be used, one or more of fifteen subjects could be recorded in each card. If an *indirect code* were to be used, and if the selector code illustrated in Figure 9-8 were employed, there would be three alternative approaches, all involving division of the fifteen available holes into three fields of five holes each:

1. Each field would be considered independently, permitting any one of ten subjects to be recorded in each field. Since three such fields are available, then, in a sense, it would be possible to record three of thirty subjects.

2. Two independent fields could be established, one consisting of five holes, as before; and the other consisting of two five-hole fields, one representing the "tens" digit of a number and the other representing the "units" digit of a number. This would permit one of ten subjects to be recorded in the first field; and one of 100 subjects in the second field; or, in a sense, two of 110 subjects.

3. The five-hole fields could be considered respectively, the "hundreds," "tens," and "units" digits of a number, permitting the handling of 1000 subjects, but only one of which could be recorded for each document.

In summary, the possibilities shown in Table 2 would exist for the hypothetical 15-hole field. It is evident from Table 2 that as the total number of subjects that can be encompassed in the total file *increases,* from 15 to 1000, the maximum number of subjects that can be recorded on any individual card (representing an individual document) *decreases* from 15 to 1.

Table 2

Type of code	Total number of subjects that can be handled for the total file	Largest number of subjects that can be recorded on any individual card
Direct	15	15
Indirect		
Alternative (1)	30	3
Alternative (2)	110	2
Alternative (3)	1000	1

Let us suppose then, still limited by the availability of 15 holes, that there is need to encompass a total of more than 30 subjects, but it is desired to be able to record more than three subjects on any individual card. Clearly, this is not possible using either direct or indirect codes as described earlier. Rather, an approach which permits superimposing of codes or notations in the same field is required. However, as discussed earlier in this section, this procedure produces ghost or false selections. How then to optimize the system: that is, to minimize the amount of such noise, while maximizing the number of subjects (as represented by codes and notations) that can be recorded in a given field for a given document.

In order to determine the number of notations that may be superimposed in the same field, we must determine the number of combinations that can be recorded in a field of known number of holes.[10] The mathematical equation that gives this number is

$$C = \frac{H!}{Y!(H - Y)!}$$

---

[10] As a rule of thumb, a search medium is exploited effectively with superimposed codes when, on the average, a little less than 50 per cent of the positions available for recording notations are actually used. If precision in exploiting a search medium to its absolute limits is desired, expert help of a statistician should be obtained. The discussion given here will indicate the type of statistical treatment that is needed for extracting the last drop of usefulness out of the recording of superimposed notations.

where C denotes the number of combinations of H things taken Y at a time.[11] In practice, therefore, if we wish to attach a meaning to a combination of 2 holes in a field of 15 holes (as in Figure 9-9), then we can indicate any one of 105 subjects in that field. We determine this by substituting in the above equation:[12]

$$C = \frac{15!}{2!(15-2)!} = \frac{1 \cdot 2 \cdot 3 \cdot 4 \cdot 5 \cdot 6 \cdot 7 \cdot 8 \cdot 9 \cdot 10 \cdot 11 \cdot 12 \cdot 13 \cdot 14 \cdot 15}{(1 \cdot 2)(1 \cdot 2 \cdot 3 \cdot 4 \cdot 5 \cdot 6 \cdot 7 \cdot 8 \cdot 9 \cdot 10 \cdot 11 \cdot 12 \cdot 13)} = 105$$

Similarly, for combinations of 3, 4, and more holes, the number of combinations possible are shown in Table 3.

Table 3

Number of holes in a combination	Number of combinations possible
1	15
2	105
3	455
4	1,365
5	3,003
6	5,005
7	6,435
8	6,435
9	5,005
10	3,003
11	1,365
12	455
13	105
14	15
15	1

We obtain the greatest number of combinations, i.e., distinct patterns of holes and notches, when half the sites are notched ($H = 2Y$, or $H = 2Y - 1$). For instance, there are 6435 distinct patterns in which 7 out of 15 sites are notched. Clearly, the result is the same if 8 out of 15 sites are notched, because it makes no difference if we call "holes" "notches," and "notches" "holes." (Approximately, the number of distinct patterns made by notching half of n possible sites is $(2\pi/n)^{1/2} \cdot 2n$, or roughly, $0.8 \cdot 2^n/n^{1/2}$.)

[11] The "!" sign is used in mathematics to indicate the factorial of a number, that is, the continued product of numbers from 1 upward. If $H = 3$, then $H!$ means $1 \cdot 2 \cdot 3$.

[12] C. S. Wise, "Mathematical Analysis of Coding Systems," R. S. Casey, J. W. Perry, A. Kent, and M. M. Berry, Eds., *Punched Cards,* 2nd ed., Reinhold, New York, 1958, Chapter 21.

Returning now to Table 2, use of the maximum number of combinations would increase our total number of subjects that could be handled from 1000 to 6435. However, we could still only permit *one* subject to be recorded in any individual card. And this would not satisfy our requirement that more than *three* shall be possible.

Obviously, if more than *three* subjects are to be recorded, with the notation for each subject requiring the notching of *seven* holes, the chances would be very high that all holes are notched out, giving a fantastic amount of ghost selections.

So let us return to the criteria established in our assumption; that is, the possibility of handling more than 30 possible subjects, and recording more than three per card. From Table 3 we can determine that combinations of 2, 3, 4, 5, 6, or 7 holes would meet the first criterion: more than 30 subjects possible. Now, how to determine what is optimum with regard to the second criterion: more than three subjects recorded (superimposed) per card.

If all the subjects are to be used equally often, we should contrive their notation so that, on the average, half the sites are notched after superimposition.

Suppose we have s subjects in all, and they are to be coded in superimposition m at a time. We need to find both the total number, n say, of sites required, and the number of sites, p say, notched to represent each subject. To fix our ideas, first consider two extreme, and inefficient, cases.

Suppose we use direct coding, so that each site represents a distinct subject, and p is not unity. Clearly n must be at least equal to s, else we cannot represent all subjects. Also m distinct subjects will need m distinct notches. So for maximum efficiency we must take $\frac{1}{2}n$ subjects at a time.

At the other extreme, suppose we code each subject as a distinct pattern of $\frac{1}{2}n$ notches. Now, m must be unity, because each subject occupies half the sites. On the other hand, n need not be large even for a large number of distinct subjects.

In the general case, the relation between $m, p, n,$ is approximately

$$p \cdot \ln(1 - m/n) = -\ln 2 = -0.69315$$

where ln denotes, as usual, the natural logarithm.

If m, the number of subjects taken at time, is small compared with the standard number of sites n, we have approximately

$$pm = n \ln 2 = 0.69315n$$

That is, the total number of notchings, including those superimposed, should be 69 per cent of the total number of sites, if half the sites are to be notched, on the average.

This result was first given by Mooers. It depends entirely on the patterns being assigned at random, as does the incidence of unwanted selections (false or ghost drops).

Mooers has shown that if the assignment is random, the average number of unwanted selections per search is $N/2\frac{1}{2}^n$ where N is the total number of cards in the collection.

If the assignment of notches is systematic, none of the above reasonings holds good. In particular, the number of unwanted selections may be very high.[13]

For our example, 69 per cent of the total number of sites, or holes (15), is 10.35, which means that *on the average* we can record:

$$\frac{10.35 \text{ sites (or holes) per card}}{2 \text{ sites (or holes) per subject}} = 5.175 \text{ subjects per card}$$

If the same calculation is performed for each number of sites (or holes) per subject, Table 4 could be derived.

Table 4

Number of holes in a combination	Number of combinations possible	Number of subjects per card (avg.)
2	105	5.175
3	455	3.45
4	1365	2.5875
5	3003	2.07
6	5005	1.725
7	6435	1.48

According to our criteria then either two- or three-hole combinations would meet both our criteria: more than 30 subjects possible and more than three subjects recorded per card. The choice of which one to use would depend upon "trade-off" considerations: Do we want over 105 possible combinations more than we want over 3.45 average number of subjects per card.

If *no* unwanted (or ghost) selections are to be permitted for a search system, *then superimposed systems cannot be used.*

Superimposed recording of notations may be used with machine-sorted cards (see, for example, Figure 9-10). It should be noted that the use of superimposed recording with machine-sorted cards has been misunderstood by various persons. The classic example of misunderstanding this method came when a certain company made an attempt to *superpose* numbers in identical fields of IBM cards, shown in Figure 9-11. Since too naive a superposition

---

[13] R. A. Fairthorne, private communication, 1961.

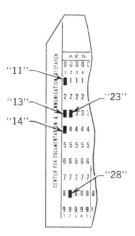

Figure 9-10. Notations superimposed on IBM card. Numbers are made up of column numbers and positions in the column. Thus, position 3 punched in column 1 represents the number 13. In the illustration above, notations 1, 13, 14, 23, and 28 are punched.

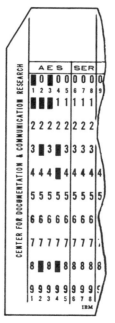

Figure 9-11. *Superposed* recording of notations in identical fields, which yields a tremendous number of "ghost" combinations. In this case, each of the notations, 08-14, 11-13, 03-08, 03-14, was recorded in columns 1-4, using the "standard" IBM punched-card code. This method is *not* what is generally referred to as random, superimposed coding.

271

principle was chosen and found wanting, the entire installation had to be changed, at considerable expense to the company involved.

An unusual means for recording of "superimposed codes" which permits considerable reduction in potential noise through overlapping characters in code elements has been discussed.[14] For example, the word "CHEST" is encoded through a "chain spelling" procedure, as:

CH
HE
ES
ST
TC

while "CHESTER" is encoded as:

CH
HE
ES
ST
TE
ER
RC

and "ROCHESTER" is encoded as:

RO
OC
CH
HE
ES
ST
TE
ER
RR

Each code element is recorded in a punched card in a position reserved for it. A search directed to, for example, CHEST, would require a logical product of CH, HE, ES, ST, and TC, which would identify CHEST to the exclusion of CHESTER and ROCHESTER even though the natural language words contain -CHEST- in common.

Another possible way in which to interpret superimposed coding is in connection with the use of marginal-hole punched cards, which have two or more rows of holes along an edge of the card, as in the following:

---

[14] R. S. Casey, et al., Eds. *Punched Cards,* 2nd ed., Reinhold, New York, 1958. p. 492 ff.

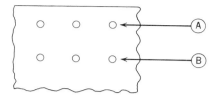

Let us assume that we wish to assign meaning independently to each of the holes (A and B). This would lead to no difficulty if only subject A were assigned to a particular document, requiring notching as follows:

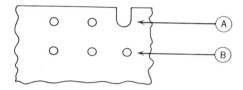

Selection for all cards notched for A could be conducted expeditiously.

If we would wish to assign both Subjects A *and* B to a particular document, both holes would be notched out:

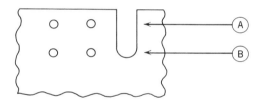

Selection for A, B, or both could again be conducted expeditiously.

However, if we would wish to assign *only* subject B to a particular document, *both* holes would again be notched out, as above. Obviously, it is impossible to notch B without simultaneously notching A, leading to the possibility of ghost selection.

The way in which this difficulty is avoided is through careful assignment of meaning to holes A and B so that, for example, a generic-specific relationship exists between the two subjects. Thus, if the following is true:

> Hole A = Primary colors
> Hole B = Red

the notching of B alone, automatically notches hole A, which is helpful rather than harmful, since a useful generic relationship is automatically recorded for later exploitation during searching.

Attention has not been paid to random superimposed coding, as computers have been used more and more for information-retrieval work. However, only recently interest has been expressed in the use of such coding to protect individuals against invasion of privacy. The hypothesis is that personal information can be recorded in this way, permitting statistical exploitation but preventing, *without question,* the reconstruction of specific information about any one individual.

F. Numeric Versus Alphabetic Notations

A numeric notation, as the name implies, uses numbers as symbols. Thus, for an edge-notched punched card, a number may be recorded as a selector notation in a "standard" field, which uses 4 holes to record any number from 0 to 9 (Figure 9-12). Numerals are recorded in machine-sorted cards (such as IBM) by keypunching a hole in a fixed position which by convention is equal to the same numeral (see Figure 9-10).

An alphabetic notation, as the name implies, uses letters of the alphabet as symbols. Examples of such a notation are given in Figure 9-13. Since 26 letters are available in the Latin alphabet as opposed to the 10 symbols available in decimal digits, the use of alphabetic symbols in codes is more economical, assuming that the same number of holes may be used to record the symbols. However, this assumption is not true (compare Figures 9-12 and 9-13).[15]

Alphabetic characters are represented in machine-sorted cards (such as IBM) by keypunching two holes in positions that are fixed by convention. In edge-notched punched cards 1, 2, 3, or 4 holes may be used (Figure 9-13).

G. Selective Versus Nonselective Codes and Notations

A *selective* code or notation is one that distinguishes in a useful manner between all meanings that are the subjects of any questions. A *nonselective* code or notation does not make such a distinction.

---

[15] Certainly large alphabets reduce the length of words, in the sense that there are more distinct words of a given length. However, this reduction is not as great as might be expected. If we use an alphabet of m characters instead of one with n characters, word length is reduced in the ratio $(\log m)/(\log n)$, at best. Thus, if we use the alphabet instead of decimal numerals, word length will be reduced at best to 70 percent of what it was before. To achieve this we would need all the cost and complications, such as larger keyboards, associated with large alphabets.

Also, the characters must be more complicated as their number increases. For each character must differ from another in at least one observable property. So n characters must use at least $(\log n)/(\log 2)$ observable properties, else you could not tell some of the characters apart.

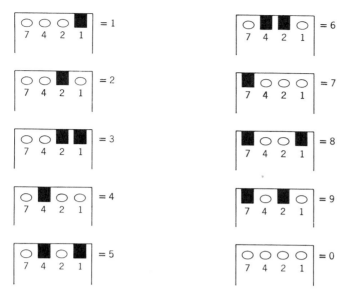

Figure 9-12. Numerical notation for edge-punched cards. This is not a selective notation, because when a search for 7 is conducted, 7, 8, and 9 will fall, and a series of additional sorts is required to identify 7 uniquely. Thus, it is often wise to label an additional hole "SF" (single figure). This is punched when only one hole is required to record a number (1, 2, 4, 7):

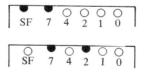

Another hole may be added for "0," so that positive notches are always involved in selection, for example, SF 74210. In this way, it is always necessary to sort twice (or use two "needles" in one sort) and no more in order to select any number.

Nonselectivity may be caused in two ways.

1. From a "systems" point of view, the meaning attributed to various notations or symbol combinations does not correspond well to the meaning of aspects of questions put to the system. This leads to the selection of unwanted material and the nonselection of wanted material more often than is considered desirable.

2. From a "coding" point of view, the notation may be recorded in such a way that unwanted material is selected. From this point of view, the direct recording of a notation is always selective; a numeric notation, such as illustrated in Figure 9-12, is nonselective for certain symbols (1, 2, 4, 7, because a single "needling"—sorting operation—produces extraneous material).

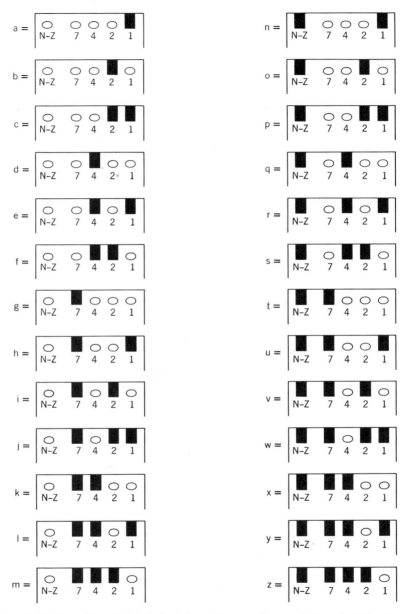

Figure 9-13. Recording of alphabetic information on edge-punched cards. This scheme is more economical with regard to number of holes used, but is more difficult to use in sorting out the desired information.

276

Absolute selectivity in the latter instance may be achieved through the use of direct recording of notations. However, in the former case, it is believed possible to achieve absolute selectivity only if those questions that do not "fit" the system developed are rejected as "unanswerable" or "unfair."

H. Fixed-Field Versus Free-Field Recording of Notations

Fixed fields are locations on a search medium that are reserved for information of a particular type, a particular form, or a particular length. *Free fields* are locations on a search medium that do not have such restrictions. Fixed-field (local) and free-field (nonlocal) notations represent information that conforms to the specifications set forth above.

Fixed-field notations generally involve a set of characters that must be of uniform length and must lend themselves to classification; that is, a certain type of notation must be recorded in a certain area of the card reserved for that purpose (see Figure 9-14).

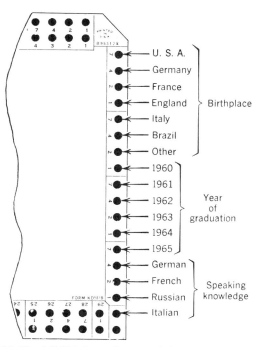

Figure 9-14. Fixed-field information recorded on an edge-punched card.

When the information to be specified on a search medium exceeds the fixed-field capacity of that medium (e.g., a tab card), a new approach to recording of notations may be considered, which involves no restriction as to the location or length of the notations (see, for example, Figure 9-15). However, in order to give the free-field approaches free reign, it has been more convenient to develop and to use magnetic tape, which has no effective limitations with regard to the amount of space to be taken in recording notations pertaining to a particular record.[16]

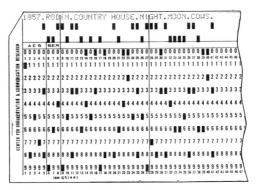

Figure 9-15. Free-field recording on IBM cards.

I. Semantic Versus Nonsemantic Codes

There has been much discussion with regard to the amount of semantic information that a code system should or should not provide. It should be realized that the notations of every coding system are, to some extent, *semantic* in nature, in that they do carry some information that is intended to be meaningful to the recipient. However, the literature has tended to enforce a distinction between semantic (meaningful) and nonsemantic codes, and for this reason a few remarks on the subject are appropriate.

Nonsemantic coding systems are those that provide no meaningful information beyond that which is inherent in the spelling of the word in the source language for which it stands as a one-to-one equivalent (Figure 9-16). Semantic codes are those with notations that do carry meaningful information in addition to that which is carried by the source word. This additional information may be generic, functional, lexicographic, or thesaural in nature (Figure 9-17).

[16] H. P. Luhn, "Superimposed Coding with the Aid of Randomizing Squares for Use in Mechanical Information Searching systems," in R. S. Casey, J. W. Perry, A. Kent, and M. M. Berry, Eds., *Punched Cards,* 2nd ed., Reinhold, New York, 1958, Chapter 23.

CAT	863984
DOG	219332
HORSE	653889

Figure 9-16. Examples of nonsemantic codes.

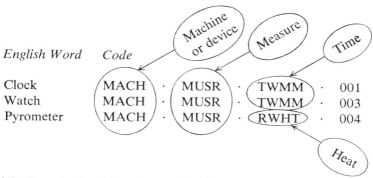

Figure 9-17. Example of notations in semantic coding system. The four-letter combinations of letters, called semantic factors, serve to show the generic relationship between the three English words, all names of measuring devices. The third factor in each case designates the thing that is being measured, and serves to distinguish between those devices that measure time (*clock* and *watch*) and that which measures head (*pyrometer*). The last numerical factor for each notation specifically designates the individual concept for which the notation stands. Thus although "clock" and "watch" share the same semantic factors, their individual identity is maintained by means of the distinctive terminal numbers.

J. Open-Ended Versus Closed Coding Systems

The quality of open-endedness of a coding system may be considered from the point of view of the particular formal notation used, or of the system that lies behind it, or of the equipment that is used in connection with it.

For example, if a decision is made to have a notation made up of four characters, recorded on the fixed field of a punched card, and it is further decided that the symbols used shall be decimal numerals, the notation is *closed* after 9999 different subjects have been handled.

Such a closed system may be partially opened, in a system based on machine-sorted cards, by the substitution of alphabetic for numeric symbols. This change increases the number of subjects that may be handled in the same amount of fixed space.

The system can be opened to an unlimited extent by adapting it to the use of more than four characters, in other words, by making available combinations beyond 9999. Of course, the equipment used to search the medium must be able to accommodate this expansion.

Open-endedness, then, implies the ability to accommodate alterations or additions to a coding system. The additions and changes may be of the type described above, or they may be of an intellectual type. These would include the addition of new subjects to the system, or the changing of those that are already there, either within the original intellectual framework, or within the framework for alterations that has been provided.

K. Postcript[17]

The terminology of code, notation, digit, and so on is still fluid. As here, we have to state our terms and stick to them. The distinctions made in these pages are important.

Perhaps they can be summed up, using the given terminology, as:

Codes are sets of rules for making symbolic expressions corresponding to various statements. Notations are methods for writing these statements down.

Clearly, many notations can be used to represent a particular code expression. Also, one notation can be used to represent expressions in various codes. (For example, the Roman alphabet serves for many languages.)

The words "language" and "translation" are sometimes used very misleadingly, especially in descriptions of data-processing equipment. We cannot tell whether a particular device really translates, e.g., French into English, or Algol into Fortran, or whether it merely transcribes or transliterates, e.g., Hollerith punched cards into 8-track magnetic tape.

The following usages have both traditional and fairly wide current practice to back them, and correspond to those in the forthcoming British Standards Institute "Glossary of Computer and Data Processing Terms."

| Translation | = | an expression in one language having the same meaning as an expression in another. |
| Transcription | = | an expression in one notation equivalent to an expression in another (the expression need have no meaning; the change is purely ortho-graphical). |

---

[17] The author is indebted to R. A. Fairthorne for this explanation.

Transliteration	=	a transcription in which each digit or letter has been transcribed independently of the others.
Script	=	notation, i.e., a method of writing, e.g., manuscript, typescript.

Often we have to distinguish between some character, in the sense of "sign design," and a physical representation having this character. For instance, we can say, "there is only one letter 'E,' " and "there are about 250 'E's' in a page of printed English." Or "there is only one sign for four, e.g., '4,' " and " '74344' contains three '4's.' " Usually the confusion can be avoided by using "character" to mean only the basic sign design ("sort") or sign character, and "sign," "symbol," and "letter" to mean either sign character or a particular physical occurrence of a sign. "Digit" has been accepted for a long time as meaning the latter when representing numbers, e.g., "74344" contains five digits, three of which are "4's." Also, "numeral" is a *character* representing an integer. Thus, in the decimal system we have ten numerals only representing zero and the integers "one' through "nine."

Unfortunately no unambiguous general terms correspond to "digit." Nevertheless, "character" should not be used when referring to particular physical representations, if only to preserve the usual meaning of the word "character."

Use of "characters per second" in advertisements for printers, etc., may be ineradicable, but should be left to those who write advertisements.

SUPPLEMENTARY READING

1. Casey, R. S., et al., Eds., *Punched Cards*, 2nd ed., Reinhold, New York, 1958: Chapter 18, pp. 391-421, J. W. Perry, "Subject Matter Analysis and Coding;" Chapter 21, pp. 438-464, C. S. Wise, 'Mathematical Analysis of Coding Systems;" Chapter 22, pp. 465-491, D. E. H. Frear, "Comprehensive Coding Schemes for Chemical Compounds;" Chapter 23, pp. 492-509, H. P. Luhn, "Superimposed Coding with the Aid of Randomizing Squares for Use in Mechanical Information Searching Systems."
2. Perry, J. W., and Allen Kent, *Tools for Machine Literature Searching,* Interscience, New York, 1958: Chapter 9, pp. 229-279, John L. Melton, "The Semantic Code;" Chapter 10, pp. 281-301, T. H. Rees, Jr., and J. W. Perry, "Special Codes;" Part 4, pp. 611-964, "A Thesaurus of Scientific and Technical Terms—The Semantic Code Dictionary."
3. Kent, Allen, Ed., *Information Retrieval and Machine Translation,* Interscience, New York, in two volumes, 1960-1961: Chapter 1, pp. 13-326, A. Kent, "Machine Literature Searching and Translation—An Analytical Review;" Chapter 49, pp. 1061-1074, N. D. Andreyev, "The Universal Code of Science and Machine Languages;" Chapter 50, pp. 1075-1090, V. V. Ivanov, "Linguistic Problems of Machine Translation

for the Information Machine;" Chapter 54, pp. 1159-1174, B. C. Vickery, "Coding for Interconvertibility;" Chapter 55, pp. 1175-1180, E. deGrolier, "Problems Involved In Coordination of Codes for Information Retrieval;" Chapter 61, pp. 1275-1280, A. Kent, "Practical Goals for Common Language Standards."

4. *Preprints of Papers for the International Conference on Scientific Information, 1958:* R. A. Fairthorne, "Algebraic Representation of Storage and Retrieval Languages;" C. N. Mooers, "A Mathematical Theory of Language Symbols in Retrieval."

Ten

Systems Design Criteria

I. INTRODUCTION

In this chapter, the word "system" will designate an organization of interacting parts intended to accomplish a particular purpose. The *performance variables* of a system are properties descriptive of the results of operations of the system, with respect to its attainment of the goals set for it. It is possible for a system to perform perfectly with regard to its stated objectives and functions, but still not be useful. Because the system designer may include or exclude as many functions as he desires, the exclusion of some functions may decrease the usefulness of the system even if the functions included are performed well. That we should preface our discussion of systems-design criteria with a reminder that the most hopefully designed systems do not always "work" well, may seem a rather negative beginning, but it is intended to serve as a note of caution, a kind of *memento mori* drawn from the experience of our predecessors in the field.

To oversimplify the case, we can say that a system is what the designer chooses to make it, and that a system can be judged as "good" only by the use to which it is put.

A system can achieve functional status in one of two ways. It can be designed, or it can "just grow," developing first in one direction and then another, in reaction to random variations of environment. If it is decided to design a system, the following factors must be considered explicitly:

1. *Objectives.* The overall purposes of the system.
2. *Functions.* Major classes of actions or performance required to achieve the objectives.

3. Performance requirements. Specific dimensions of required actions, with a statement of the standard or required level of performance for each.

4. Environment variables. Properties of the environment that affect the system and its performance.

When an information-retrieval system is to be designed, it is useful to consider the factors mentioned above, and to "engineer" a system that weights each factor in a deliberate (even though sometimes qualitative) manner. When this procedure is followed, a reasonable prediction can be made of the average performance of the system under stated conditions.

II. OBJECTIVES

It is usually difficult and often impossible to prevail upon the designer of a system to articulate the objectives that influenced his design and operational decisions.

We may list several alternative objectives, or motives, which often underlie the design of a system. The designer or operator may wish to

1. Maximize profits (or receipts).
2. Fulfill an obligation, as one made by a professional society to promote the dissemination of information among its members.
3. Enhance his own reputation.
4. Provide novel or attractive services in a competitive situation.

In some cases, he may be motivated by a combination of two or more of these incentives. Such objectives are not often verbalized because they are either subconscious or are not sufficiently altruistic. More often, purely altruistic objectives are given, and these will be the starting point for our discussions of criteria. However, we should exercise extreme care in applying such criteria if the objectives of any particular information-retrieval system that we study seem to be other than altruistic.

As stated earlier, on a very general and altruistic basis, the objective of an information-retrieval system is the provision of information or documents, in response to requests, with such quality, scope, speed, and economy that there is a scientific, economic, military, or other important justification for its establishment and maintenance. This objective is sufficiently broad that almost any practical requirement may be encompassed.

1. Quality and scope. The quality requirements range from a demand of absolute certainty that every document of potential interest is identified, to the requirement of only reasonable probability that representative or indicative subject matter is brought to the attention of an inquirer. These ranges are suggestive, respectively, of information-retrieval requirements prior to the start of an extensive research program, and requirements resulting from a casual interest in an item of minor significance.

2. Speed. The requirements for speed of response may vary from a demand for a failsafe answer in an absolute minimum amount of time to the permission for a response to be made at leisure over a period of days, weeks, or months. An example of the first requirement would arise from the need of a country to determine the spread of a pandemic in sufficient time to initiate preventive measures. The second requirement may be exemplified by a request for background information for a speech to be delivered at some time in the future.

3. Economy. Cost limitations are more or less severe, depending upon the value that inquirers place on responses to questions at various levels of quality, scope, or speed. Thus, a system for providing information on the spread of disease may command, in the United States, a development cost of considerable magnitude; while a system for retrieving the melting points of chemical compounds may be considered worth only a development cost corresponding to the annual salary of a research chemist.

In the extreme examples given above, it is relatively simple to identify objectives. However, in the general case, the system designer is hard pressed to make explicit the precise purposes of the system to be designed. This is so because often the designer has been instructed by a superior to develop and install a system that will alleviate the vaguely stated problem of "decreasing effectiveness of exploitation of recorded knowledge." Or the same instruction may be given to a system designer by a professional society made up of many members with diverse requirements.

The tasks of the designer are as follows:

1. To identify the clientele:
   a. Those who are now using an existing system.
   b. Those who might make use of an improved system.
2. To determine the scope of present and potential subject-matter interests of the clientele.
3. To determine the permissible expenditures of funds for capital and operating expenses.

A. Identification of Clientele

This group may be identified more readily in some cases than in others. If a retrieval system is to be developed for an industrial or governmental organization whose staff members are readily identified, it may be feasible to survey the entire personnel and to obtain data on their interest in the use of a new information-retrieval activity. However, after a new system has been developed, it can be expected that the provision of more effective service will attract a larger clientele than the first survey might indicate.

Some retrieval systems are developed for a more amorphous clientele, the individual members of which are not easily identified in advance. For example, a public library, in developing its subject catalog, cannot predict with confidence the percentage of its clientele who will use that tool; nor can a professional society determine in advance, when developing a new retrieval system, whether or how much of its clientele will wish to take advantage of the new facility.

The above discussion implies the sad fact that it is possible to be optimistic or pessimistic, foolhardy or cautious, aggressive or meek, in characterizing the clientele for a system. In some cases *no* clientele can be identified in advance, because no one of its potential members may be able to envision the services that a new system might provide; in other cases an apparent clientele may assume "ghost" characteristics and disappear when a new system does not provide evident advantages over an older one to which its users have become accustomed.

B. Identification of Subject-Matter Interests

A similar approach is suggested when identifying subject-matter interests. Surveys of the clientele will already have provided some guidance in this regard. However, the clientele will not always be able to predict accurately its own future subject interests, since developments which have not yet been discussed or emphasized in the literature, or which have not yet ever been initiated, may become interesting at a later time.

Therefore, the designer, in establishing the capacity of the system, must usually provide for new areas of subject matter as they develop or become important during the life of the system.

C. Determination of Permissible Expenditures

Although costs and expenditures are not "logically" to be included among the *objectives* of a system, limitation on cost is often such a strong factor in designing a retrieval system that it can become a "controlling objective."

Three types of costs that should be considered are as follows:

1. Capital costs for acquisition and analysis of records, and for purchase of a search mechanism.
2. Operational costs for conducting searches and for provision of services.
3. Costs involved in *not* providing suitable information services.

Whenever the costs of a system are to be limited by external factors, these three types of costs must be weighed and balanced off.

The first factor, capital costs, can be considered to consist of two main items: the creation of a searchable file and the acquisition of a searching mechanism.

The creation of a searchable file means, first of all, the accumulation of materials. This process is governed directly by the policy for inclusion or exclusion of records. Once this policy is established, the cost of replenishment is relatively stable regardless of which system is used.

The utilization of a searching mechanism involves the analysis of records in order to provide the clues that are to be used in the searching system. If this analysis is performed by human beings, human beings must first read and understand the contents of the record, and then record appropriate clues. (The difference in costs for varying *levels* of analysis in different systems is not as great as may be imagined. A considerable proportion of such costs are incurred in the reading and understanding of the record, a procedure that is common to all retrieval systems that involve human analysis prior to input.) When human analysis is not involved, there is still an input cost for preparing a machine-readable record; if natural language text is not to be used directly for searching, then there is an additional computer-processing cost for deriving the machine-searchable record. In all cases, when codes are to be used in the searching system, a further cost is involved in transforming the results of analysis to appropriate codes.

The cost of searching mechanism may sometimes be omitted from consideration if a mechanism is available, such as a computer, the cost of which is amortized completely over other programs, e.g., accounting or scientific calculation. However, sometimes such available or "free" tools are not ideal for use with retrieval systems, and their use may actually increase the costs of other operations in the system.

The second factor, operational costs, involves the expense of analysis of questions, of operating the searching mechanism, and of providing the results of searches to a questioner. These are expenditures both of human effort and machine time.

The third factor, the cost of not providing service, cannot be determined precisely. It involves the value of the time saved for experimentation, research, and other productive effort by the delegation of search routines to an efficient machine system.

III. FUNCTIONS

The major classes of actions or performance required for an information-retrieval system to attain its objectives are as follows:

1. Acquisition of source documents.
2. Analysis of source documents.

3. Control of terminology and subject headings.

4. Recording of results of analysis on a searchable medium.

5. Storage of source documents, extracts, abstracts, and/or bibliographic references.

6. Analysis of questions and development of search strategy.

7. Conducting of search.

8. Delivery of results of search.

9. Utilization of results of search.

Since, in general, all of these functions may be considered as "unit operations," decisions as to the design of each of them may be made independently (within limits, of course).

A. Acquisition of Source Documents

Any policy may be established for acquisition. It may be based on:

1. Purely arbitrary rules, e.g., acquisition of every tenth document that is announced as being available, or acquisition only of those documents that are not regularly accessible through another system of retrieval;

2. Subjective (artistic or editorial) decisions, e.g., acquisition of every document that one person or a group of persons believe will be of interest to a clientele or that is related to a given subject or set of subject fields;

3. Acquisition of the total document output of certain organizations, publishers, or other designated sources.

There are, of course, an infinite number of possible variations of acquisitions policy; however, it should be obvious that it is not possible to achieve completeness in acquisitions. This is so both because it becomes too expensive to acquire the last small per cent of documents, and because there is no way of knowing when everything that may have been published in a particular field has been acquired.

B. Analysis of Source Documents

As pointed out in Chapter 5, the analysis of source documents is conducted in the attempt:

1. To infer the intentions of the authors;

2. To anticipate the interests of the potential readers of documents.

Among the approaches to analysis available are as follows:

1. To use an indexing, classifying, or abstracting approach;

2. To provide greater or lesser detail of analysis for any of these approaches;

3. To avoid analysis, as such, and instead to use the entire natural-language text.

In implementing the indexing, classifying, or abstracting methods, it is customary to have humans conduct the analytical work. The analytical policy may be based on:

1. Purely arbitrary rules, e.g., only a predetermined number of index entries may be assigned for each document, or only entries relating to a given subject may be used.
2. "Subjective" decisions, e.g., the analyst is permitted to index any, and as many, subjects as he believes to be of potential interest to the clientele.

If machine routines are used in place of human analysts, the analytical policy must necessarily be limited by purely arbitrary rules.

Like acquisition, analysis presents an infinite number of possible variations. Completeness is, again, an impossible goal. This is the case because it is not possible to predict every variation of subject content that may interest some potential user.

C. Control of Terminology and Subject Headings

This "unit operation" of a retrieval system may be considered from three points of view:

1. The type of control used.
2. The extent of control.
3. The way in which control is imposed.

1. Type of Control of Terminology The first policy decision to be made, therefore, determines the language that is to be used to record the results of analysis (see Chapter 5). For example:

    a. By indexing procedures and apparatus, as:
       1. Subject authority lists.
       2. Role indicators or role directors.
       3. Modifications to index entries.
       4. Cross reference or thesaural associations.
       5. By use of codes (Chapter 9) to record the terms chosen in any of the above indexing procedures.
    b. By classifying procedures and apparatus, as:
       1. Rigid classifications.
       2. Multidimensional classification.
       3. By use of codes (Chapter 9) to record terms chosen in any of the above classifying procedures.

2. Extent of Control of Terminology. The next policy decision determines how rigidly the terminology is to be controlled. Here it is necessary to consider such factors as the number of duplicate entries to be used in an index; how "close in meaning" two index entries must be in order to warrant the use of a "see" reference rather than a "see also" reference; what the scope of meaning is for each subject heading of an index (Chapter 8), or for each class or subclass of a classification system.

3. Imposition of Control of Terminology. The last decision determines the mechanism to be used to impose terminology control. Traditionally this has been accomplished by:

a. Having analysts (indexers, catalogers, classifiers) attempt to remember the headings of classes available for the various aspects of subject matter chosen from source documents.

b. Providing analysts with authority lists, scope notes, or indexes to classification systems, to avoid placing too much reliance on human memory.

It is now possible, with modern data processing equipment, to impose control over raw indexing or classifying product of analysts by means of "dictionaries," "thesauri," or indexes which are consulted mechanically or electronically.

D. Recording Results of Analysis on Searching Medium

Once a document has been acquired and analyzed, and terminological control has been imposed, then it is possible to record on a searching medium the results of the analysis. This may be done on a medium:

1. Identical with that used to record and/or store the source document (full document, extract, abstract, and/or bibliographic reference); or

2. Separate from that used to record or store the source document.

Examples of "identical" media are those marginal-hole punched card systems which have recorded, on the same card, both the results of analysis and also the source document; another is the Minicard system, in which unit film records have recorded both the results of analysis and microimages of documents.

Examples of "separate" media are those systems (particularly aspect systems, although a number of document systems are constituted in a similar way) that record index data on some searchable medium together with a serial or accession number referring to the source documents. The source documents are then stored in appropriate order in a separate file, where they may be consulted when the operation of the retrieval system results in their identification by serial number.

The choice of searching medium is dependent upon the searching mechanisms to be used. Media suitable for various systems include:

1. Cards (such as catalog cards)
2. Marginal-hole, hand-sorted punched cards
3. Machine-sorted punched cards
4. Punched paper tape
5. Magnetic tape, cards, cores, or drums
6. Films, unit, strip, or continuous, and others

When recording results of analysis for document or aspect systems (see Chapter 3), up-dating procedures must be considered.

For a *document system,* increments to the file are added, independently so to speak, of what has already been recorded. For example, when marginal-hole punched cards are used, new material is added merely by preparing new cards, each card representing a new document that has been processed. When computer systems are used in which index data are stored on magnetic tape, new material is added to the end of the tape, without disturbing previously recorded material.

For an *aspect system,* on the other hand, increments to the file are added to one or several records. For example, when peek-a-boo cards are used, new material is added by recording (through punching) the new document accession numbers to each of the applicable cards. When computer systems with magnetic tapes are employed, the new document accession numbers must be coded at those locations where the appropriate aspects are located. This involves the "rewriting" of the tapes to include this new material.

The problem is not too severe when only a single copy of a file is involved, from which a centralized service is offered. However, if the centralized service attempts to serve a number of customers who are conducting searches locally, then the up-dating problem increases in severity, since each time the file is incremented with new material, each of the customers must be provided with a complete set of "rewritten" tapes so that their files are complete and up-to-date. Alternatively, each customer may be provided with new material, together with suitable processing instructions, which permits the rewriting of the entire file at each customer's site.

On the other hand, when a *document* is used, each customer is provided periodically with only new material, which can merely be added to the end of the file.

E. Storage of Source Documents (Full Text, Extracts, Abstracts, and/or Bibliographic References)

When the analysis of a source document has been completed, the document must then be stored in such a way that it can be located readily and used. Often, the product of analysis is an abstract, an extract, and/or a bibliographic reference to the document. These products must also be stored in such a way that they can be located readily and used.

Two decisions must be made in this connection:

1. In what physical form should the source material be stored?
2. In what arrangement should the material be stored?

1. Physical Form of Storage. The question of physical form may be resolved in a number of ways.

If the source document is extremely bulky or lengthy in relation to the bulk or length of the index card which refers to it, it is usually wise to store index data separately from the source documents. For example, in a library of books, it is considered necessary to store index data in a card catalog which is kept separate from the books. In most libraries, the books themselves are stored in a physical arrangement that corresponds to an arbitrary classification of knowledge. For that physical classification, the "index" and the "document" are stored together.

It is not possible to display one set of books to reflect a multidimensional classification system. Rather, extra sets are needed for filing according to each of the subjects selected by an analyst. If it is considered important to provide extra copies for this purpose, the cost of the extra copies must be weighed in relation to anticipated benefits.

This cost picture will improve as the size of the document decreases, for the cost of providing copies will then decrease. When we reach a document size of perhaps a page or less, as represented by an extract, abstract, or bibliographic citation, it becomes less costly to obtain extra copies for multiple storage.

But multiple storage cannot often be considered for mechanized information-retrieval systems. In general, the problem of retrieval of information has reached a point of sufficient complexity that a large number of "dimensions" or "index" entries are required to describe adequately the important subject matter of documents. It becomes quite impractical to consider a storage system that involves multiple filing corresponding to every possible access point.

In these cases, therefore, we may reconsider the two types of retrieval systems: document and aspect.

For *document* systems, it is sometimes economically feasible to store full size copies of bibliographic references, abstracts, and brief extracts together with index data. This is the case for searching devices involving the use of marginal-hole punched cards and machine-sorted punched cards, which usually have available an area for such storage. If more storage is required, additional information, and sometimes pages of documents, may be stored in these cards in microfilm (either microfilm inserts or microprint). Unit film records also provide the possibility for microstorage of documents together with index data.

In document systems, it is feasible to store a copy of the document with the index only when the unit record either displays the document, abstract, etc., upon selection, or provides an inexpensive method for printing, enlarging, or otherwise delivering a copy of the document. It becomes more and more unwieldy and expensive to store the document with the index when there is no ready way to display the document, or when the means of providing a copy involves character-by-character or line-by-line printing. Such is the case with digital computer searching devices, which would require the laborious and expensive (albeit rapid) printing of a stored document from magnetic tape, drums, etc. In cases such as these it becomes necessary, from an economic point of view, to keep the amount of such printout at an absolute minimum, e.g., a unique document serial number.

In aspect systems, the very nature of the searching principle (i.e., matching of document serial numbers) mitigates against storing a copy of a document together with the index.

2. *Arrangement of Documents.* If documents are to be stored in microfilm, a number of further decisions must be made.

a. Should the arrangement be on unit records or on a continuous record (e.g., reels of microfilm)?

This consideration is important because if access to the file of documents is to be on a random basis, and the ratio of documents needed to documents in the file is low, then a unit record is desirable. However, if the ratio is high, and there is opportunity for arranging document requests in serial number order, then a continuous microfilm would be indicated.

b. If a unit record is used, is it advantageous to attempt to prearrange in clusters those documents that have a high likelihood of being of interest?

The convenience of preparing additional reproducible copies of these unit records makes it possible to consider the maintenance of several files, each arranged in different ways.

c. If a "continuous" microfilm is used, how long should each roll of film be?

The longer the roll, the more time it takes to satisfy low-density applications, i.e., only where a few documents are desired, on a random basis. The shorter the roll, the more it approaches the unit record situation.

F. Analysis of Questions and Development of Search Strategy

The analysis of questions is conducted in order to transform the language of the inquirer into that of the information-retrieval system. The search strategy is established in order to exploit in an optimum manner the peculiar capabilities of the retrieval system used.

A question may be analyzed in greater or lesser detail to ensure that documents relevant to a question are identified without too many nonpertinent documents being included in the response.

Three levels of analysis can be considered; a question may be analyzed:

1. On the basis of words or phrases found in the question as stated.

2. On the basis of synonyms or generalizations (cross references) derived from or suggested by the wording of the question.

3. On the basis of subjective decisions, that is, interpretation of the words or phrases found in the question.

The strategy of search is the way in which the results of analysis are set up as conditions for satisfaction of a search (see Chapter 6). Basically, any strategy may be conducted using any retrieval system. However, for an identical search, some strategy may be applied more conveniently and more economically than others.

As with the analysis of documents it is customary to have human beings conduct the analysis of questions, with "artistic" or subjective considerations inevitably entering into their activity.

G. Conducting of Search

When the results of analysis of a document have been recorded on a searching medium, and a question has been analyzed and a search strategy has been selected, it is then possible to conduct a search. By this time, not many decisions remain to be made, since decisions with regard to earlier functions have predisposed the way in which a search may be conducted.

For example, if results of analysis are recorded on catalog cards, only human beings can conduct the search.[1] If marginal-hole or machine-sorted punched cards have been used, and if the results of analysis are recorded as text readable by humans as well as by machines, then searching can be conducted either by machine (according to the techniques for which the mechanisms were designed) or by humans scanning the readable text.

If machine-sorted punched cards have been used, then searching can be conducted by means of the appropriate equipment. However, faster equipment may be used after appropriate conversion of the machine record, e.g., punched cards converted to magnetic tape.

On the other hand, it is possible to conduct a search of information recorded on magnetic tape by using slower equipment. It is to be expected that

---

[1] There may be an application here of character recognition devices to make it possible for printed or typewritten text to be read automatically, but for current practical purposes, this would not be economically feasible.

appropriate high-speed equipment will be used to process magnetic tape or other magnetic or film media. But, if the machine record is converted appropriately, the search can be conducted using "slower" equipment, e.g., punched-card sorters, etc.

Some of the practical considerations which enter into decisions regarding searching procedures relate to batching of searches or searching questions one at a time, and use of a document versus an aspect system. One of the reasons given for the economy of aspect systems is that only small segments of a file are involved when a search is conducted. In other words, only those aspects appropriate to a question are involved in the search. On the other hand, the document system requires searching through the entire file for each question.

As questions are batched, however, the number of aspects involved increases, and accordingly decreases the advantage of the aspect system, since a greater portion of the file is involved in the search. Accordingly, the advantages achieved by document systems during up-dating eventually may cross over those achieved by the aspect systems at some point.

This type of "trade off" is one of the factors to be weighed in the design of a system.

H. Delivery of Results of Search

This operation is, of course, dependent on the way in which source documents are stored.

If documents are stored separately from index data, then the delivery of search results involves a three-step process.

1. The search produces serial or accession numbers of documents identified as being pertinent to a question.

2. A file of documents arranged in appropriate order is consulted in order to locate the documents identified during the search.

3. The documents may then be consulted, withdrawn, or copied.

If the documents (or extracts, abstracts, bibliographic references, etc.) are stored together with index data, then the search provides the actual source document (by physically selecting it as with a marginal-hole punched card or with a film record; or by printing out, as with a magnetic tape system).

I. Utilization of Results of Search

This function is not always considered to be a unit operation in a retrieval system. However, it deserves consideration because the manner in which each of the previously discussed functions is carried out has an important influence on the effectiveness with which the human information seeker may utilize the results of a search.

It should be remembered that every mechanized information-retrieval system involves a man-machine partnership. Even if every step of the system is mechanized, at least the final one, utilization, remains a human task. It is a temptation, in designing a retrieval system, to save money in designing the various functions involved, especially since it is so easy to measure the costs of each unit operation. Savings are sometimes illusory if the eventual human user is not served as well as he might be.

IV. PERFORMANCE REQUIREMENTS

It is not rare for a designer to be presented with the following assignment:

Develop an open-ended system that will take good care of our present retrieval needs, based on our present size of file and subject matter interests, but expandable to take care of whatever situation we will have ten years from now. Furthermore, this system must be installed at low cost; operating costs must also be very low; clerical staff should be able to operate this system, and the system should provide rapid service in response to all of the information-retrieval needs at all levels of the organization.

How does he design a system to meet all of these performance criteria? Are all of the criteria compatible? If not, what compromises need be made? Before answering such questions, and even before accepting such an assignment as this one, the designer should examine various performance requirements to be considered in the planning of an information-retrieval system.

A. Qualitative Requirements

1. Subject Coverage. This requirement is usually the first to be mentioned in designing a retrieval system: What subject or subjects are to be covered in the system? The determination may be expressed by a delineation of the sources of documents or by a specification of the subjects to be covered, with editorial criteria being laid down at the same time.

If the sources are delineated, the designer can give assurance that complete coverage can be made. However, if certain subject matter is specified, the continuing increase in number of publications and the scatter of subject references among many publications, many whose scope is without apparent relationship to the subject at hand, makes it impractical, if not impossible, to provide any assurance of complete coverage. This potential handicap must be frankly acknowledged.

For many requirements it is impractical or impossible to predict all subjects of probable interest, and it is usually specified that the system shall be open ended with regard to ability to accept new subjects, while still providing good service.

2. *Depth of Analysis of Source Documents*. Two factors must be considered in relation to depth of analysis. First, there is the specification of the point of view that should be used in analysis of documents (see Chapter 5). Second there is the problem of the degree of detail that should be used in this analysis.

Neither of these two specifications can be stated quantitatively, *nor is there any valid way of measuring how well the specifications are fulfilled.*

It may be said glibly that the point of view of analysis should be that of a chemist, a physicist, an economist, etc. However, as a practical matter, the point of view of a chemist, for example, often overlaps considerably with those of other subject specialists, so that the results of analysis often serve other disciplines. It has been established that reasonable care exercised during analysis of source documents can well result in being able to cater to many points of view. On the other hand, the perimeters of any subject-matter field are necessarily so vague that no amount of attention to a special point of view will guarantee recovery of *all* pertinent material even to the most dedicated specialist. Yesterday's astrology is today's astrophysics.

Degree of detail of analysis of documents has often been described in the literature by specifying an "average" number of descriptors, analytics, clues, or other search reference points provided for source documents. This may or may not be a valid way of measuring degree of detail of analysis, since the mere proliferation of reference points does not ensure greater or more effective penetration into the subject matter of a document.

3. *Precision of Service*. This requirement may be either qualitative or quantitave in nature. Qualitatively, it involves a specification of the acceptable ratio of pertinent to nonpertinent documents that may be supplied in response to a question. The rationale behind such a specification is that although it may not be possible to design and operate a retrieval system that will identify only documents pertinent to a question, it is reasonable to require that the density of nonpertinent material supplied not exceed some specified amount.

This requirement is perhaps the most difficult to satisfy, since it has not yet been possible to provide an operational definition of pertinency upon which both designers and users of a retrieval system agree. Indeed, it can be argued that even the designer may, in some cases, have set himself an unreasonably high goal. In such cases, however, the effect of such pessimism may be wholesome if it encourages him to improve his system.

B. Quantitative Requirements

1. Precision of Service. As just discussed, there is a quantitative aspect to the requirement for precision of service. Such a specification would involve the limitation of numbers of documents to be provided in response to a question. Similarly, it might be specified that only the first pertinent response is desired, even if further pertinent responses may be available. Such requirements for service arise from the limited time available to some questioners for reading retrieved documents, and their desire to sample the file rather than to search it exhaustively. Thus, breadth, rather than precision, becomes the operative criterion.

2. Speed. An objective of an information-retrieval system is to provide service within certain stated time limits. In considering this problem, various factors must be taken into account:

a. Time for acquisition of records to be incorporated into the system.

b. Time for analysis and other system input operations.

c. Time for analysis of questions and programming of search (by humans or by machines).

d. Time for performance of search (by humans or by machines).

e. Time for delivery of search results.

f. Time for evaluation and use of search results.

The first factor, acquisition·time, may be considered to be almost totally independent of the retrieval system used. It is to be assumed that the system will be supplied with documents acquired by the most efficient conventional methods, and that, where delays are unreasonable, preprints or other short cuts will be specified as part of the operational routine.

The second factor, analysis time, is system dependent to the extent that greater or lesser effort is devoted to analysis, to control of terminology, to encoding, and to recording of the results of analysis on some searchable medium, be it catalog cards, classification systems, punched cards, film, or tape. The time spent on this step may influence considerably the time involved in the next two system factors; an appropriate investment of time spent in the input phases may have a significant effect in decreasing the time required for question analysis and search performance.

The third factor, question analysis time, is the first in which time considerations become controlling. The first two factors involved the preparation of a file of records for search, but this third factor involves the critical time *after* a question has been asked. It is at this point that the system *user* becomes concerned with the "speed" of the system.

The fourth factor, search performance time, is also part of the critical time period after a question has been asked. The speed and efficiency of the searching mechanism is to be considered seriously at this time.

The fifth factor, time for delivery of search results, involves several time aspects. In some systems, the operation of a search mechanism produces information as to the location of a record. It is necessary then to devote time to the withdrawal of the record from storage and to its delivery as the response to a question. Critical waiting time is again involved.

The last factor, time for evaluation and use, is a function of the effectiveness of the original analysis, the effectiveness of terminology control during input, the effectiveness of question analysis, and the effectiveness of the search mechanism as a whole. This is a most critical factor, since time savings on the other operations can be destroyed by requiring evaluation time during use that might have been better invested during input or other operations.

The requirement of speed is one that is often misunderstood. We tend to forget that the elapsed time between the generation of an idea and its recording in mass-reproducible form is usually very long, often amounting to months or years. Consequently, an information-retrieval system that may operate in minutes rather than hours, days, or weeks will not decrease the access time to such an idea by a significant percentage.

There are, accordingly, two factors of speed that warrant consideration in designing a retrieval system:

a. Speed with which unit operations are conducted; acquisition, analysis, recording, storage, search, and delivery must all be considered, as units and as a whole.

b. Speed with which service is provided (or response time), regardless of the lack of speed involved in other unit operations.

C. Physical Requirements

1. Equipment. When mechanized information-retrieval systems are designed, the desired speed of searching (moderated by cost considerations) may dictate the choice of equipment. However, in many organizations, equipment already being used for other purposes may be more or less suited for information retrieval.

When such equipment is available, it is often a firm requirement that it be used for the information-searching function. The rationale for this decision usually involves consideration of the amortization of equipment costs for "primary" functions, with the information searching then being asked to bear a part—usually only a minor fraction—of the cost of the equipment. The equipment is thus made available at irregular periods, in order to permit the more frequent scheduling of primary applications.

A management decision of this sort is sometimes wise and sometimes unwise. Unfortunately, even when it is unwise there are sometimes no alternatives open.

2. Form and Type of Input. In some organizations, the design of a retrieval system must take into account stringent requirements for form and type of input to the system. Thus, if a system must provide access to a collection of magnetic tape recordings, it cannot be arbitrarily decided that documents are to be stored on microfilm, since the two storage media are not compatible without dramatic and costly intermediate steps.

Similarly, if a system will have to depend for analysis of documents on a central processing agency, it is wise to consider searching equipment that will be compatible with the form in which input is provided (e.g., punched cards and magnetic tape) rather than to stipulate some other medium that would require another step or two in its preparation.

3. Form and Type of Output. Like input, output must receive due consideration in the design of an information-retrieval system. For example, the customer may require a particular size, shape, or micro form of output. Furthermore, if the output is to undergo subsequent processing by the customer, care must be devoted to assuring that it can be processed by equipment available to him, or within his financial means.

4. Special Conditions. Physical requirements are often formulated as the result of special conditions that occur in a particular organization. Examples of such special conditions are as follows:

a. Space limitations. These may lead to a need for miniaturization of documents; they may limit the size of equipment, etc.[2]

b. Security restrictions. Government or business security requirements provide limitations on the accessibility of information which may definitely influence the design of any system designed to supply such information.

D. Special Requirements

Many special situations influence the design of a retrieval system. Examples of such influences include:

1. *Compatibility with other systems.* The design of a system may be influenced strongly by the need to coordinate with other existing systems or with older systems. The motivation for achieving compatibility is to avoid the expense of reprocessing material, or of using more than one system in conducting a search.

---

[2] The criteria for development of at least one retrieval system included portability of search equipment by truck; of another, portability of extensive files by plane.

2. *Cost limitations.* Arbitrary limits are often established with regard to the cost of developing and operating a searching system. Such "statutory" requirements impose limitations on the kind and quality of unit operations. Decisions must be made, often arbitrarily with regard to the optimum allocations of funds among the various unit operations. On the other hand, since limitations on cost of input can lead to greater costs in use of the system, some limitations may be made on the cost of *use*, thus usually providing for increased costs of input.

3. *Limitation in personnel skills.* In various areas, or under special conditions, system design may call for some minimal amount of training or intelligence on the part of personnel assigned to "run" the system.[3] In situations such as these, arbitrary limits may be established for manipulative skills and so on.

V. ENVIRONMENTAL VARIABLES

The fourth class of factors to be considered in systems design is that of *environmental variables*, those properties of the environment that impinge upon and affect the system, its design, or its performance. Such variables, as considered here, are separate from those factors—performance requirements, functions, and objectives—that the systems designer, operator, or user has more or less under his control. The environmental or, in some cases, uncontrollable variables, are typically characterized by *change:* either they result from a change, or they cause a change. We may preface our discussion of these parameters by a few general remarks on human nature.

A. Human Acceptance and Resistance to Change

In general, human beings accommodate to change with discomfort and/or pain; the suggestion of change generally brings on a reflex of resistance. This is perhaps the single, most important environmental variable that must be considered in designing and "installing" a new retrieval system. Regardless of the excellence of a retrieval system, from a technical point of view, it will be of little use if its potential or scheduled users will not patronize it because of emotional or other nontechnical reasons.

Salesmanship, then, is necessary to overcome the resistance to change.

---

[3] Such limitations may be specified in military situations where personnel with specialized training may not be readily available and where replacements necessitated by casualties must be made from a nonspecialized pool.

B. Changes in Parameters of Systems

Even after objectives, functions, and performance requirements have been established, certain parameters will have to be changed to accommodate changes in conditions or environment which, if ignored, would impede or block the effective performance of the system.

Such changes, although unexpected, occur with surprising regularity, and may be called the *entropy*[4] in the information theory. This entropy may be compensated by "overdesigning"[5] a retrieval system so that it will not fail if subjected to certain predictable overloads.

What are some of the changes that are often encountered?

1. Change in Interests of Clientele. After policy has been established with regard to subject-matter coverage, point of view, and depth of analysis, the subject interests of the clientele may undergo a gradual or sudden change, forcing the retrieval system to adjust or fail. This change may come about in a natural way, as the personal or professional interests of the clientele shift over a period of months or years. Or the change may come as a result of a change in the makeup of the clientele itself, as new members with diverse interests are added. Still another challenge comes from the changing moods of clientele; these lead, usually, to a demand for greater and greater sophistication of service from a retrieval system.

Such evolutionary changes may be predicted, and the system may be overdesigned at the start to take them into account, since it is obvious that an active clientele will gradually widen its sphere of interest. However, such overdesign brings with it increased costs which must be justified on a probability basis.

2. Change in Complexity of Subject Matter. Another evolutionary change in maturing subject fields has been the tendency for the treatment to become more and more complex, throwing an increasing burden on the retrieval system. Increase in complexity is not surprising, since continuing investigations into a subject tend to suggest more detailed problems, and to illuminate more complex interrelationships with other subject fields. Again, it is often feasible to overdesign the retrieval system to take this into account.

3. Changes in Available Tools. In a field like information retrieval, which is the target of considerable research activity, it is to be expected that newer

---

[4] Entropy, in the physical science, is a measure of that part of energy in a system which cannot be transformed into useful work. By analogy for our purposes, the term may designate a measure of the uncertainty of our knowledge.

[5] Overdesigning, as used here and later, means merely planning for future exigencies by building in a flexibility that is not otherwise dictated by the conditions which exist at the time when the designs are drawn up.

tools and developments will constantly provide increasingly effective means for exploiting recorded knowledge. Since the design of retrieval systems involves the committing of considerable capital investments, frequent overhauling or actual redesign is not easy to justify from an economic point of view. Such commitments apply especially to acquisition and analysis procedures, and to the choice of searching equipment.

The analysis and searching procedures may be overdesigned in order to provide some measure of insurance against a system's being rendered obsolete by the development of new tools, principles, and equipment.

4. Changes in File Size and File Use. The size of a file, that is, the number of records to be included, is usually established as a performance requirement. However, this factor may also become an environmental variable, since unusual and unpredictable fluctuations in file size may occur. Unforeseen acquisitions of large collections, unexpected increases in publication rates, and similar factors can change file sizes dramatically and lead to a loss of effectiveness in a retrieval system or, in extreme cases, to its collapse.

A like catastrophe may result when the use of a system dramatically exceeds the exploitation that was predicted and provided for. Again, overdesign, a built-in flexibility, will help to provide against failure in the face of such an eventuality.

5. Changes in Operating Funds. In many governmental, university, and industrial organizations, retrieval and library activities are funded on a "feast-or-famine" basis, with systems operators being forced to provide reasonable service during "lean" years and to expand explosively during periods when funds are available. Such environmental variables are cited merely as a warning; no preparation can be made that is more effective in a feast-or-famine situation than the provision of an operator and a staff with more than their share of courage, stamina, and real dedication.

VI. CONCLUSIONS

In this chapter we have followed the time-honored order of putting first things first. We have considered, in detail, the objectives that the system designer sets for himself as functions of those objectives that circumstances set for him. We have reviewed the functions, the unit operations which together make up a system of information retrieval, and we have indicated for each operation the decisions that must be made in order to make it effective not only as a self-contained unit but also, and more important, as a part of the whole. We have detailed the requirements that the designer must expect to meet if his system is to measure up, qualitatively and quantitatively, to the standards set for its performance. And finally, to round out our listing of criteria, we have enumerated the most significant of those variables which experience has indicated at once the least predictable and the most fatal of hazards.

By this time, the information scientist or librarian whose task it is to develop a system of his own will have accumulated a checklist of decisions, as it were. By pausing at each point on his list, and making his choice each time, he can, hopefully, move toward a final well-reasoned response. These, then, are the first things which we have considered first.

You may object that certain other decisions remain to be made. Recalling the detail with which we discussed the physical tools and the spectrum of codes and notations, you may ask why decisions in these areas have not been included so far in our listing of criteria. Here our answer is the corollary to the proposition submitted above: last things are to be considered last.

Information science literature has too often echoed systems designers and equipment manufacturers in overemphasizing the role of codes and machines. The plan of this chapter has been to relegate these devices to their proper place—an important one, but a place that is relatively minor among the many other aspects of concern.

Thus we come toward the end of a survey of mechanized information retrieval by seeming to neglect the machine. Our attitudes may seem especially quixotic to those who recall the brave new world of the opening chapters, where it was pointed out that the entrance of mechanized retrieval upon the world of documentation was like the arrival of the computer in data processing, implying that in an analogous series of victories mechanized information-retrieval would conquer everywhere it went.

Such a grandiose concept is not the message of this chapter. We have attempted to exhibit the materials available, and to describe the techniques. At every point, and most particularly in this chapter, we have emphasized the chain of decisions that must be made, one by one, in establishing the size, the shape, and, above all, the *purpose* of the ideal information-retrieval system. *People* must make these decisions.

In the final analysis, the machine will not dictate the system of the future. No useful system exists as a package, ready to be plugged in.

VII. EXERCISE ON DESIGN OF AN INFORMATION-RETRIEVAL SYSTEM

This chapter has covered criteria that are to be considered when designing an information-retrieval system. These criteria have been discussed in somewhat general terms; however, the student of this field is still not able to proceed with confidence in designing a system without some practical experience. Accordingly, during the teaching of graduate students it has proved useful to require that a system, albeit a small one, be designed, using a "nonconventional" approach.

In the exercise that follows, two types of systems are considered, the *document* and the *aspect*. In order to illustrate principles simply, the document system is represented by the marginal-hole punched card; the aspect system by a peek-a-boo card— one based on a tabulating card which permits handling of a file of 480 documents.[6]

The design of the system is developed in stages throughout the course, with assignments relating to it timed to correspond to the discussions of the appropriate unit operations involved.

Early in the course, at the time that discussions on "analysis" (Chapter 5) took place, an assignment was made as follows:

1. Choose a subject field that interests you.
2. Select five articles or reports from one or several periodicals that cluster in the subject field that you have chosen. List complete bibliographic citation, that is, author(s), title, journal, volume, issue, pagination, month, year.
3. Prepare two types of indexes for each article.
   (a) A "shallow" index—with three entries for each
   (b) A "deep" index—with ten entries for each article
4. Prepare two types of abstracts for each article.
   (a) A brief annotation of not more than 10-20 words.
   (b) A longer abstract of 30-50 words
5. Turn in one copy of:
   (a) citations for each article
   (b) indices for each article
   (c) abstracts for each article
6. Keep originals of all work for yourself—since your continuing assignments will be based on this material.

This material was examined from the point of view of scope of subject matter involved. This was done to provide assurance that a manageable project had been selected—not too diverse, nor too confined in coverage, as evidenced by the index entries chosen.

Slightly later in the term, after automatic analysis methods had been discussed, the five articles may be used as a basis for an exercise in KWIC indexing, as follows:

[6] The IBM D10688 card is used, which has been partially die cut in 480 punching positions, permitting the student to use a pin, a ball point pen, or other simple tool to complete the punching in any position by "poking out" appropriate holes to represent document numbers. This card is the same type used with the IBM Port-a-Punch.

For your "file" of five articles, prepare a "Key-Word-In-Context" index; simulating where necessary what would ordinarily be performed automatically.

1. Prepare a list of "nonkey" words—not to exceed 100 words.
2. Derive a KWIC index from the titles.
3. Hand in:
    a. List of titles chosen for your project,
    b. The list of nonkey words,
    c. The alphabetized KWIC index.

This exercise permits the comparison of key words selected automatically with index entries selected by humans.

Next, in order to prepare the student for thinking through what vocabulary control steps might be taken, when eventually designing the system, the following exercise might be useful:

For each of the key words in your various analyses, list:

1. One or more synonyms
2. One or more words which are more generic. (Where possible, these synonyms and more generic words should be derived from the other key words that you selected during analysis of your five articles.)

If you have difficulty in this exercise for some of your key words, you may leave blanks. This should be done, however, only when:

1. No realistic synonyms seem available.
2. Your key word is so generic that only "nonsense" words would have to be used.

Finally, the project assignment is given, approximately three or four sessions prior to the end of the term:

A. Marginal-Hole Punched Cards

During the trimester you have selected five documents to be used for developing an information-retrieval system. You have prepared: (1) bibliographic citations; (2) a KWIC index of titles; (3) shallow indexes; (4) deep indexes; (5) annotations; and (6) abstracts for these five documents.

The project assignment is: (1) to design an information-retrieval system equipped to handle a potential 1000 documents and (2) to incorporate your five documents into it by using one marginal-hole punched card for each document. You may use any, or any part, of the above analyses of your documents to design your system. You are not required to use any certain number of these analyses. The decision as to what would be appropriate and useful in our system will be yours and will be one of the elements determining your grade.

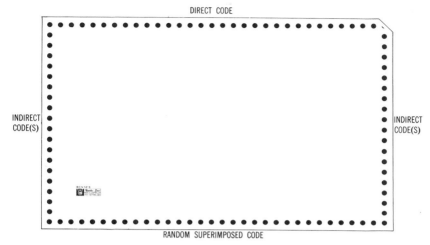

Figure 10-1. Master code card sheet.

1. Code Development and Card Layout. From the information found in your various analyses, select at least three different classes of information for use, one each at least, with a direct code, an indirect code, and a random superimposed code.

Prepare a *master code card sheet* (Figure 10-1). Trace one of the blank marginal-hole punched cards onto a sheet of paper large enough so that coding area information can be recorded beyond the traced edge of the card, i.e., in the margin. This master code card sheet should be large enough to include concise directions, where necessary, such as which of your original six analyses you are using for each type of code. No extra sheets may be used to give directions if they are not included on the master code card sheet.

a. DIRECT CODES. Indicate in the margin of the master code card sheet the meaning you are assigning to each direct code hole.

b. INDIRECT CODES. Indicate on the master code card sheet the indirect coding system selected. Prepare an English-to-code and code-to-English dictionary.

c. RANDOM SUPERIMPOSED CODES. Using the bottom row of holes of the card, number each hole consecutively, starting from left to right with 01, 02, etc. Prepare an English-to-code dictionary and a code-to-English dictionary.

d. ENCODING OF YOUR FIVE DOCUMENTS. Finally, apply the coding system you have devised to each of the five documents in your system by pencilling in (or punching out) the place where you would notch out a hole. *Do not mount* your punched cards. Hand them in loose. The accession number you have assigned to each document should appear in the upper left hand corner of its punched card followed by the document's bibliographic citation. Information you have encoded must also appear in the body of the punched card under each of three columns—I.C., D.C., or R.S.C. (Indirect Code, Direct Code, or Random Superimposed Code)—so that your punching may be proofed. Additional information on your shallow and deep index entries, annotations; and abstracts are to be recorded on the reverse side of the card.

B. Peek-a-Boo Cards

This part of your project assignment is to convert a portion of your marginal-hole punched card system to a peek-a-boo system proceeding as follows:

Select any seven aspects that you have used in your coding system. Write the aspect (subject) in the upper left part of the peek-a-boo card. Although your peek-a-boo cards permit the recording of 480 document numbers, your file consists of only five documents. Therefore, use only the first vertical column (labeled 2 at the bottom) to record the appropriate document numbers by using a pencil to poke out the appropriate hole(s). For example, if document numbers 1, 4, and 5 all have in common the aspect written on your first card, then numbers 1, 4, and 5 should be punched out in the first column (labeled 2 at the lower left-hand side of the card), etc. (Figure 10-2).

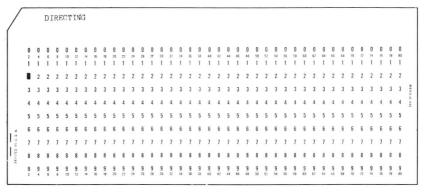

Figure 10-2. Peek-a-boo card for one aspect (directing) of the information-retrieval system developed originally for marginal-hole punched cards. Document number 2 is punched out.

C. Hand in the Following

1. Master card code sheet.

2. Those dictionaries needed to explain your indirect and random, superimposed codes.

3. One page with one short paragraph describing present subject matter in your system and visualized potential subject matter in your system; one short paragraph giving reasons for choice of material put on punched cards; one short paragraph explaining possible uses to be made of your system.

4. Five marginal-hole punched cards.

5. Seven peek-a-boo cards.

After the system has been designed it has proved instructive for the student to engage in a search strategy exercise based on the system just devised, as follows:

You have now designed a marginal-hole punched card information retrieval system in which you have included one example each, at least, of a direct code, an indirect code, and a random superimposed code.

For this assignment, prepare eight questions (and their search strategies) based on any one of all of these codes. Two each of the following types of questions and their search strategies are to be devised:

1. Logical product—with at least 3 aspects
2. Logical sum—with at least 3 aspects
3. Logical product of logical sums
4. Logical difference

One question of each set of two questions should be answerable successfully, i.e., *at least one but not all five* articles will be pertinent. The other question of each set of two questions should not be answerable successfully, i.e., either *none or all of the* articles would be pertinent.

This last exercise permits the student to attempt to operate the system, and to gain some experience with regard to determining limits of usefulness of the system.

I. LOGICAL PRODUCT (SUCCESSFUL SEARCH)

Question (Underline each aspect or clue which you consider important. Then, write above each clue a letter, e.g., A, B, C):

Record below the logical statement for the strategy to be used.

Document(s) satisfying the strategy are: _____

Search record:

Document 1 _____ contains these clues: _____ in code _____
         2 _____   _____   _____
         3 _____   _____   _____
         4 _____   _____   _____
         5 _____   _____   _____

LOGICAL PRODUCT (UNSUCCESSFUL SEARCH)

Question (Underline each aspect or clue which you consider important. Then, write above each clue a letter, e.g., A, B, C):

Record below the logical statement for the strategy to be used.

Search record:

Document 1 _____ contains these clues: _____ in code _____
           2 _____   _____   _____
           3 _____   _____   _____
           4 _____   _____   _____
           5 _____   _____   _____

Explanation for failure:

II. LOGICAL SUM (SUCCESSFUL SEARCH)

Question (Underline each aspect or clue which you consider important. Then, write above each clue a letter, e.g., A, B, C):

Record below the logical statement for the strategy to be used.

Document(s) satisfying the strategy are: _____

Search record:

Document 1 _____ contains these clues: _____ in code _____
           2 _____   _____   _____
           3 _____   _____   _____
           4 _____   _____   _____
           5 _____   _____   _____

LOGICAL SUM (UNSUCCESSFUL SEARCH)

Question (Underline each aspect or clue which you consider important. Then, write above each clue a letter, e.g., A, B, C):

Record below the logical statement for the strategy to be used.

Search record:

Document 1 _____ contains these clues: _____ in code _____
           2 _____   _____   _____
           3 _____   _____   _____
            4 _____   _____   _____
           5 _____   _____   _____

Explanation for failure:

III. LOGICAL PRODUCT OF LOGICAL SUMS (SUCCESSFUL SEARCH)

Question (Underline each aspect or clue which you consider important. Then, write above each clue a letter, e.g., A, B, C):

Record below the logical statement for the strategy to be used.

Document(s) satisfying the strategy are: _____

Search record:

Document 1 _____ contains these clues: _____ in code _____
           2 _____
           3 _____
           4 _____
           5 _____

LOGICAL PRODUCT OF LOGICAL SUMS (UNSUCCESSFUL SEARCH)

Question (Underline each aspect or clue which you consider important. Then, write above each clue a letter, e.g., A, B, C):

Record below the logical statement for the strategy to be used.

Search record:

Document 1 _____ contains these clues: _____ in code _____
           2 _____
           3 _____
           4 _____
           5 _____

Explanation for failure:

IV. LOGICAL DIFFERENCE (SUCCESSFUL SEARCH)

Question (Underline each aspect or clue which you consider important. Then, write above each clue a letter, e.g., A, B, C):

Record below the logical statement for the strategy to be used.

Document(s) satisfying the strategy are: _____

312 _Systems Design Criteria_

Search record:

Document 1 _____ contains these clues: _____ in code _____
           2 _____   _____   _____
           3 _____   _____   _____
           4 _____   _____   _____
           5 _____   _____   _____

LOGICAL DIFFERENCE (UNSUCCESSFUL SEARCH)

Question (Underline each aspect or clue which you consider important. Then, write above each clue a letter, e.g., A, B, C):

Record below the logical statement for the strategy to be used.

Search record:

Document 1 _____ contains these clues: _____ in code _____
           2 _____   _____   _____
           3 _____   _____   _____
           4 _____   _____   _____
           5 _____   _____   _____

Explanation for failure:

Which code supplied the most clues or aspects to satisfy your search strategies?
Which code supplied the least number of clues to satisfy search strategies?

Eleven

Evaluation

I. INTRODUCTION

As was made clear in Chapter 10, an information-retrieval system is not designed and developed as an end in itself. Rather, it must satisfy some requirements in order to justify its existence, and these requirements must be better satisfied or more economically satisfied than by other means if there is to be a rationale for the continuing existence (and support) of the system. So evaluation and testing is needed to establish how well the system justifies its existence.

It may be too simplistic to assert that if the primary objective of an information-retrieval system is to retrieve relevant information, then the system must be able to withstand an evaluation based on the capability of the system to do just that. But if this is not the primary criterion to be used in evaluation, then no other seems to matter. So in a sense we can say for information systems that the proof of the pudding is in the eating: in other words, we must understand the user of the system—what he wants, how much, in what form, and how fast.

In order to evaluate an information-retrieval system the proper functioning of the system must be understood, as well as the criteria users of the system employ in judging the relevance of the information retrieved. A properly functioning system will retrieve precisely that information which has been asked for. But this does not guarantee that this is the information that *should* have been asked for, or that it is really wanted. And so it becomes critical in designing, operating, and evaluating information-retrieval systems, to understand what a user of the system may mean when he says that information retrieved is relevant or not relevant, and to evaluate the user, in turn, to better understand his motivation in acquiring information.

313

II. DEFINITIONS

There are two terms that must be defined before any further discussion of evaluation is meaningful: *relevant* and *motivated user.*

Relevant may be defined simply as: bearing on the matter at hand.

Thus it should be expected that a system will retrieve information which bears on the matter at hand, but more particularly, specific information bearing on a specific matter at hand for a specific person (a *motivated user*).

Motivated user may be defined as a person requesting information which he hopes and expects will satisfy a requirement.

It has become a *sine qua non* of evaluation procedures that motivated users must be involved in judging the relevance of information retrieved from a system. Said in another way, information has no *inherent* relevance, except and unless it bears on an interest or requirement of a user. The motivation of the user for acquiring that information cannot be measured quantitatively and therefore the relevance judgments of a person other than the user cannot be assumed to be the same as that of the user, even though he may pose as a qualified substitute (or surrogate) for the user.

III. PERFORMANCE CRITERIA FOR INFORMATION-RETRIEVAL SYSTEMS

The criteria *of the user* in judging an information-retrieval system have been characterized as related to:[1]

1. *Recall.* The retrieval of relevant documents by the system.

2. *Precision.* The withholding of nonrelevant documents by the system.

3. *Effort.* The time and energy that must be expended to obtain relevant information from the system.

4. *Response time.* The interval between the formulation of a question and the receipt of a satisfactory output.

5. *Informativeness and form of search output.* The ability to predict relevance of a document identified by the system from the document surrogate (bibliographic citation, abstract, extract, etc.) provided as output.

---

[1] F. W. Lancaster, *Information Retrieval Systems: Characteristics, Testing, and Evaluation,* John Wiley & Sons, Inc., New York, 1968, pp. 54-62; and C. Cleverdon et al., *Factors Determining the Performance of Indexing Systems* Vol. 1 (Design), Vol. 2 (Test Results), Aslib–Cranfield Research Project, Cranfield College of Aeronautics, England, 1966.

6. *Document input policies.* The age, reliability, level of treatment, and language of documents processed into the system; in other words, the extent to which the system contains relevant material, whether or not retrieved.

Performance criteria are not helpful in evaluating systems quantitatively unless measures are available that can be employed with precision.

A number of measures have been developed that relate to the *recall* and *precision* criteria. Six such measures proposed in the mid-1950s[2] are resolution, elimination, pertinency, noise, recall, and omission. These measures or "factors," as they were called, are defined in terms of four quantities:

n = Number of documents embraced by a given system

m = Number of documents retrieved by the system in response to a question and therefore of possible pertinent interest.

w = Number of documents that are found to be of actual pertinent interest by personal inspection of the m documents retrieved by the system.

x = Number of documents of actual pertinent interest which are among the totality n embraced by a given system.

The factors are as follows:

Resolution factor = The fraction of total documents to which attention is directed, or

$$\frac{m}{n}$$

Elimination factor = The fraction of total documents from which attention is diverted, or

$$\frac{n-m}{n}$$

Pertinency factor = The fraction of documents to which attention is directed that are found on inspection to be pertinent, or

$$\frac{w}{m}$$

Noise factor = The fraction of documents to which attention is directed that are found on inspection not to be pertinent, or

$$\frac{m-w}{m}$$

---

[2] J. W. Perry, Allen Kent, and M. M. Berry, *Machine Literature Searching*, Interscience, New York, 1956.

Recall factor = The fraction of pertinent documents to which the system directed attention, or

$$\frac{w}{x}$$

Omission factor = The fraction of pertinent documents to which the system failed to direct attention, or

$$\frac{x - w}{x}$$

Current discussions place primary emphasis on two measures[3] for evaluating system performance: recall and precision. *Recall*, as used currently, is what was called *recall factor* earlier. *Precision* is what was earlier called *pertinency factor*. Despite nomenclature differences, it is clear that there is agreement as to the importance of these measures and the extent to which the performance of systems in terms of these measures is influenced by search strategy, depth and consistency of indexing, and quality and level of the documents in the file.

IV. RELEVANCE PREDICTABILITY

It is recognized that it is impossible, in practice, to use these measures with absolute precision since it is impossible to determine precisely how many documents are actually relevant in the entire file, without a motivated user examining the *entire* file in relation to a given question. Since motivation on the part of the user would disappear well before such a task could be completed, that critical value could not be obtained. Accordingly, sampling procedures have been proposed which would permit approximation of that value.[4]

Even when quantitative measures for evaluating the operation of information systems are introduced, uncertainty remains that only those factors easy to evaluate are being measured, and the difficult but perhaps most critical ones are being neglected. For example, it is known that information systems perform imperfectly, so much so that the output provided to the user is not the document, or original source material, since so much would not be relevant. Rather, some surrogate of the document (such as bibliographic citation, abstract, or extract) is provided instead. This surrogate is provided to the user so that a determination of the relevance of the original source material can be made on the basis of the examination of the surrogate.

---

[3] F. W. Lancaster, loc. cit., pp. 54-63.

[4] G. Salton, *Automatic Information Organization and Retrieval,* McGraw-Hill Book Company, New York, 1968, pp. 294-315.

But the user may not be willing to examine the entire output in response to a question even when document surrogates are provided. So very often a surrogate for the user screens the surrogates for the documents in an attempt to increase the *pertinency factor* (or *precision*) of that portion of the output finally offered to the user.

The questions must then be asked regarding the relevance predictability of the surrogates:

1. Does the user surrogate make the same relevance judgments as the motivated user?

2. Are the judgments regarding relevance or nonrelevance made on the basis of examination of the document surrogate the same as those that would have been made on the basis of examination of the original source material?

A methodology for exploring both questions has been suggested in an investigation of the relevance predictability of citations, abstracts, and first and last paragraphs of documents.[5]

Another phenomenon that seems of critical importance in evaluation is what might be called the time dependence of relevance judgments. When a motivated user judges the relevance of the output of a system, the documents (or their surrogates) are presented and examined in a given sequence (structured or not). Each judgment may be influenced by what has been judged before; that is, what is learned from examining the contents of one document may lead to a relevance judgment for a later document that might have been different had the later document been examined first. Therefore, it is not possible to assume that the relevance criterion is applied consistently.

In order to assure the consistent application of a relevance criterion, the evaluator would be required to judge a document based on its relevance to the question that was posed to the system. But if the motivated user, left to his own devices, would evaluate output from a system, he might judge documents on the basis of their relevance to his *interests,* regardless of whether these interests are reflected in his question, which served as the basis for the search. In some cases, the system might look better than it should, when a document which is not relevant to the question is judged relevant based on the current interests of the motivated user. In other cases the system might look worse than it should, when a document, clearly relevant to the question, is judged nonrelevant nevertheless. This judgment might be made by a motivated user whose curiosity is satisfied by earlier output and who may then judge later output as irrelevant no matter how relevant to the *subject* it may be.

---

[5] A. Kent, et al., "Relevance Predictability in Information Retrieval Systems," *Methods of Information in Medicine,* **6,** No. 2, 45-51 (April 1967).

This may seem like a fine point, but it may relate to a factor of greatest consequence in the user's perception of performance of the system. In other words, a system that produces output which is all precisely related to the subject of a search may still be considered by the user to contain a substantial amount of nonrelevant material.

This phenomenon suggests that properly designed interactive information-retrieval systems will be able to provide much more user satisfaction than batch systems, if the systems would permit adjustment in strategies by the user after each unit of output is examined and a search terminated when the curiosity of the user is satisfied.

V. THESAURUS EVALUATION

Recent attention to the development of thesauri as a means of improving system performance has suggested means for evaluating this and other vocabulary control mechanisms. It will be recalled that the thesaurus displays terms that are said to relate to a main term in the following ways:

synonyms
broader terms
narrower terms
related terms

It would seem that each of these relationships must have a functional consequence in the operation of an information-retrieval system. This consequence of a relationship displayed in a thesaurus should be rather straightforward, for example:

If two words, said to be synonyms in a thesaurus, are both used for indexing purposes, they should both produce the same relevant documents in response to a question.

Thus, if a search strategy containing a given term produces a certain quantity of relevant documents, the substitution for that term with a synonym should produce the same relevant documents in the output. Furthermore, substitution with:

a broader term	should produce a larger output, within which is included the same relevant documents
a narrower term	should produce a smaller output, none of which does not appear in the original output

The determination as to whether a thesaurus satisfies these criteria requires the isolation of a pure "strain" of relevant output, derived through the proper functioning of an information-retrieval system. This can be done in terms of a given question, with a given strategy which is searched against a given file on behalf of a given motivated user who evaluates the output at a given time.

The output considered relevant by the user can be held as a "standard," so that output of searches against the same file, with substitutions made in the strategy, can be compared with the "standard."

An indirect method of evaluating a thesaurus has been developed[6] which has the following objectives:

1. To determine whether sophisticated workers in a field (which is the subject emphasis of a thesaurus) are in substantial agreement that taxons generated in the thesaurus represent recognizable categories of meaning for that field.

2. To determine whether these workers are in substantial agreement with the hierarchical relationships that were established for the terms within each taxon.

3. To determine whether these workers were consistent in their judgments about the meanings associated with a retrieval language used in the thesaurus.

To these ends a multiple-choice test was developed and administered to actual and potential users of an information-retrieval system. The test instrument consisted of pairs of terms selected uniformly from throughout the thesaurus, with the test subjects obliged to select the appropriate thesaural relationship.

VI. SIMULATION AND EVALUATION

A model system has been developed[7] which permits the manipulation of documents and search requests, and produces responses. The system makes available several hundred different content analysis procedures, each producing somewhat different output. The model was designed to permit the testing of automatic analysis and search procedures. The facilities in the model include:[8]

1. A system for separating English words into stems and affixes which can be used to reduce incoming texts into word stem form.

2. A synonym dictionary, or thesaurus used to replace significant word stems by concept numbers, each concept representing a class of related word stems.

---

[6] S. T. Price, *The Development of a Thesaurus of Descriptors for an Information Retrieval System in Special Education,* Doctoral disseration, University of Pittsburgh, Pittsburgh, Pa., 1969.

[7] G. Salton, *Automatic Information Organization and Retrieval,* McGraw-Hill Book Company, New York, 1968, pp. 9-20.

[8] G. Salton, loc. cit. pp. 10-11.

3. A hierarchical arrangement of the concepts included in the thesaurus which makes it possible, given any concept number, to find its "parent" in the hierarchy, its "sons," its "brothers," and any of a set of possible cross references.

4. Statistical association methods used to compute similarily coefficients between words, word stems, or concepts, based on co-occurrence patterns between these entities in the sentences of a document, or in the documents of a collection, so that associated items can then serve as content identifiers in addition to the original ones.

5. Syntactic analysis methods which permit the recognition and use, as indicators of document content, of phrases consisting of several words or concepts where each element of a phrase must hold a specified syntactic relation to each other element.

6. Statistical phrase recognition methods which operate like the preceding syntactic procedures by using a preconstructed phrase dictionary, except that no test is made to ensure that the syntactic relationships between phrase components are satisfied.

7. Request-document matching procedures which make it possible to use a variety of different correlation methods to compare analyzed documents with analyzed requests, including concept weight adjustments and variations in the length of the document texts being analyzed.

VII. BEHAVIORAL STUDIES

Since the user is a part of an information-retrieval system, testing and evaluation must include study of the user.[9]

Study of the user must be approached with great care. It has been pointed out that people alter their behavior according to what they have experienced and what they expect to experience. People change with experience. They put up with what they are obliged to put up with. Any amelioration of, or even just change in what they have to put up with may give some sense of satisfaction. Thus any system involving human beings is, whether it is intended as such or not, a test of how some human beings behave when subjected to such a system. In particular, a retrieval system tests its users at least as much as they test it.[10]

Emphasis until now has been placed on performance measures, but evaluation must also consider cost benefits, or, in more modern terminology "cost effectiveness."

---

[9] D. Amick, "Information Processing in Basic and Applied Science: An Exploratory Study at the Interface of the Sociology of Science and Information Science." Doctoral dissertation, University of Pittsburgh, Pittsburgh, Pa., 1970.

[10] R. A. Fairthorne, "Implications of Test Procedures," *Information Retrieval in Action*, The Press of Western Reserve University, Cleveland, Ohio 1963, pp. 109-113.

Here it is possible to compare systems on the basis of the costs of performing various functions, or overall costs of producing given outputs. But when we consider "effectiveness" in relation to cost, we must return to fundamentals. At the start of this chapter it was stated that the primary objective of an information-retrieval system is to retrieve relevant information.

We are now prepared to quarrel with this statement, since the proof of the pudding is not only in the eating but in its proper digestion; in other words, the information provided to a user must be *used*. And here we begin to consider how to measure the assimilability (or transferability) of the output of a system. Measures of actual use of information become less precise and become related to behavioral investigations. Some user studies have been carried out to permit understanding of the satisfaction of user needs.[11]

VIII. CONCLUSION

The discussion of testing and evaluation given here has been sketchy and incomplete and has emphasized what the beginning student might find most useful. However, considerable work, not referenced here, has been done which relates to the topic of this chapter. This work has been categorized by Treu in the following way:[12]

1. *Query—file search—system response.* Involving the submission of the search request, development of a formal strategy of search, and the examination of the response of the system to the formal search strategy.

2. *Out-of-system-service context.* Involving the study of specific elements of a retrieval system (for instance, comparative evaluation of alternative system response products or study of inter-indexer consistency).

3. *Questionnaire and interview.* Involving the attempt to determine the requirements and satisfaction of users who have been served by a given system.

4. *Operating system observation.* Involving study of a system in its operational environment, including staff, facilities, and equipment, and their deployment in performing given functions.

5. *System modeling and operation simulation.* Involving the representation or approximation of the system and its operation.

The student wishing to pursue the matter further would find Treu's review useful. The bibliography which follows should then be pursued.

---

[11] See Chapters on "Evaluation" and User Studies," in *Annual Reviews of Information Science,* Encyclopedia Britannica, Inc., Chicago.

[12] S. Treu, "Testing and Evaluation: Review," in A. Kent et al. (Eds.) *Electronic Handling of Information: Testing and Evaluation,* Thompson Book Company, Washington, D.C., 1967, pp. 71-88.

BIBLIOGRAPHY

1. F. W. Lancaster, *Information Retrieval Systems: Characteristics, Testing, and Evaluation*, John Wiley and Sons, Inc., New York, 1968.
2. A. Kent, O. E. Taulbee, J. Belzer, and G. D. Goldstein, (Eds.), *Electronic Handling of Information: Testing and Evaluation,* Thompson Book Company Washington, D.C., and Academic Press, London, 1967.
3. M. M. Henderson, "Tentative Bibliography on Evaluation of Information Systems," National Bureau of Standards, Washington, D.C., February 18, 1965.
4. G. Salton, *Automatic Information Organization and Retrieval*, McGraw-Hill Book Company, New York, 1968.
5. D. R. Swanson, "The Evidence Underlying the Cranfield Results," *Library Quarterly*, **35**, 1-20 (January 1965).
6. See also, chapters on "Evaluation" in C. A. Cuadra, editor, *Annual Review of Information Science and Technology*, Encyclopedia Britannica, Chicago, Volumes starting in 1967.

Twelve

Research

I. PREAMBLE

... today those embarking on scientific research may console themselves by looking at the history of scientific research and thanking the good fortune which did not cause them to be born at the time when scientific discovery might be rewarded by death at the stake—today they have nothing worse to fear than poverty, obscurity, ridicule and frustration.

P. Freedman
The Principles of Scientific Research[1]

This preamble does not ring quite true with regard to documentation and information-retrieval research today. Most senior research investigators in this field are neither poor nor obscure, since the problems on which they are working have achieved international attention; the level of funding is increasing constantly, albeit slowly. Not too many of the research workers are ridiculed, and few show signs of enduring frustration.

Perhaps then there is enough continuing interest so that the student of the information-retrieval field may wish to consider research as a career objective. If so, what is the substance of research in this field? But first, what does research in general involve?

---

[1] P. Freedman, *The Principles of Scientific Research*, 2nd ed., Pergamon Press, New York, 1960.

II. INTRODUCTION

A. Research and the Scientific Method

1. Research. Research has been characterized simply as a systematic and refined technique of thinking, and employing specialized tools, instruments, and procedures in order to obtain a more adequate solution of a problem than would be possible using ordinary means. It starts with a problem, collects data or facts, analyzes these critically, and reaches decisions based on actual evidence. Research involves original work instead of a mere exercise of personal opinion. It evolves from a genuine desire to know, rather than a desire to prove something. (However, it may *evolve* from a desire to prove something.)

From this characterization, it is not surprising that the basic precept of research is considered to be a rejection of authority! The authority may be a previously "proven" fact, the accepted opinions of "those who should know," or even the judgment of the research administrator and of the fund grantor.[2]

2. The Scientific Method. Research has generally been carried out by using the "scientific method," which has been defined as:

The principles and procedures used in the systematic pursuit of intersubjectively accessible knowledge and involving as necessary conditions the recognition and formulation of a problem, the collection of data through observation and if possible experiment, the formulation of hypotheses, and the testing and confirmation (or rejection) of the hypotheses formulated.[3]

The application of the scientific method represents the highest research skill, and involves considerably more than a "cookbook" approach.

The *formulation of a problem* is often more essential than its solution, and it has often been said that many scientists owe their greatness not to their skill in solving problems but to their wisdom in choosing them. This wisdom is often gained by becoming a scholar in the specialties involved—an investment in time that must be made without any guarantees that something new or significant can be contributed.

Observation also requires unusual skills and rigorous discipline, lest observations be made with bias, due to some significant parameter being overlooked, and misinterpretations and incorrect inferences being drawn from them.

One of the best teachers of scientific method, Silvanus Thompson, frequently stressed the necessity for a scientist to be on guard against unjustified assumptions and baseless inferences. It is worth recalling how, in one of his

---

[2] A. Kent, "Research Is a Gamble," *Science,* **137**, No. 3534 (September 21, 1962).

[3] From *Webster's New International Dictionary,* 3rd ed. Merriam, Springfield, Mass., 1961.

lectures, after explaining this to the students, he showed them two objects—one apparently a stone, and the other apparently a large, nicely painted, horseshoe, permanent magnet—and asked which of these would attract an iron nail. All the students immediately said that the horseshoe magnet would and the stone would not. Silvanus Thompson then demonstrated that the reverse was the case; the stone was a lodestone, and the horseshoe "magnet," a painted wooden model. The students' inference had been based on characteristics of the two objects which were not, from a scientific point of view, in any way related to their magnetic properties, although the students' frequent observations had led them, through association of ideas, to infer such a relationship.[4]

The *formulation of hypotheses* again requires a high order of skill and insight, but requires very often a leap more or less in the dark. However, this leap must not be misinterpreted as reality, since a hypothesis is only a provisional interpretation of observations. Goethe has characterized this situation well when he said that hypotheses are the scaffolds which are erected in front of a building and removed when the building is completed. They are indispensable to the worker; but he must not mistake the scaffolding for the building.

Finally, the *testing and confirmation (or rejection) of the hypothesis* must be performed with great care, since often measurement is involved, which requires considerable skill in gathering and interpretation of data.

It should be recognized that errors in measurement and interpretation may creep in due to emotional bias, or a naiveté about the factors influencing them, and that a measurement whose accuracy is completely unknown has no use whatever.[5]

Most important, however, must be the realization that even a measurement whose accuracy is known may be quite insignificant unless one understands what is being measured, since an "apparatus" seldom measures the quantity it is supposed to, and more often measures something which is assumed to be related to the quality in question by a known law.

B. The Information-Retrieval Problem

It has been said that the progress of civilization is dependent upon the accretion of knowledge and experience which is then available for further development and which takes into account what has been done before. Since the invention of the printing press the dissemination of the record of civilization's progress has been assured, and has led to a continuously increasing store of

---

[4] From P. Freedman, *loc cit.*

[5] E. B. Wilson, Jr., *An Introduction to Scientific Research*, McGraw-Hill Book Company New York, 1952.

recorded knowledge available for examination. The amount of recorded knowledge available has increased so dramatically that problems have been created with regard to: (1) learning of the existence of recorded knowledge; and (2) knowing how to locate what is wanted from this recorded knowledge once its existence is known.

In attempting to alleviate these problems, the primary publication media have been augmented by secondary and tertiary publication media which purport to provide access to the original recorded knowledge in a convenient and useful manner. These secondary and tertiary media have been concerned with the digesting, indexing, and classifying of knowledge to facilitate the identification of source materials that are of potential interest. Often the reading of secondary media (digests, abstracts, or extracts) is substituted for the reading of source materials.

The very nature of the secondary and tertiary media presents problems with regard to:

1. Selection of subject matter which is considered to be of most interest, from within, or relating to, the source materials.

2. Expression and arrangement of this subject matter in a manner that coincides with the way in which readers will look for it.

These problems cannot be resolved precisely for several reasons:

1. Once a judgment is exercised in selection of subject matter from source materials, *some* subject matter will necessarily be omitted from the secondary and tertiary media and will therefore be unavailable to the users of these media.

2. In the expression and arrangement of subject matter, it is impossible to predict, *a priori*, how readers will look for subject matter, so that again, *some* material, although available, will not be located by the users of the secondary and tertiary media.

The problems of information retrieval, therefore, relate to these basic questions discussed above. However, there are other problems which relate to the specific input unit operations that must be performed in operating any information-retrieval system. These are summarized in Table 1.

These various problems should be kept in mind when reviewing research and development that has been, and continues to be, conducted in this field.

III. THE NATURE OF INFORMATION-RETRIEVAL RESEARCH

A. Introduction

Research activities are reported in many ways in various media. Only the National Science Foundation has taken the responsibility for collecting

Table 1

Unit operation	Problems
Acquisition	The shifting interests of a changing clientele, or a change of emphasis in the literature, leads to difficulties in formalizing a policy than can be followed consistently by individuals to whom the acquisition function is delegated.
Analysis (e.g., abstracting, extracting, indexing, classifying)	The requirement to predict, based on examination of source materials, which aspects are of current and lasting interest to a clientele presents difficulties of two major types: 1. Shifting interests of clientele with time are often unpredictable because new problems generate concepts which may not have been articulated when source materials were published. 2. Subject matter expertise of analyst is not often of the same depth and character as that of clientele, leading to incompatibilities between what may be recorded as a result of analysis and what may be requested by clientele.
Vocabulary control	Meaning of vocabulary used to record results of analysis may shift as a function of: 1. time 2. usage in other fields and cultures. Aids employed in establishing relationships among terms (e.g., standard headings, cross references, thesauri) are volatile and not precise in nature.
Recording of results of analysis on searchable medium	Decisions on "machine" language used are often critical, since changing technology frequently makes change of medium desirable.
Storage of source documents	Micro form appears to be an economical solution to the problem of storing, viewing, and copying of large collections; however, clienteles do not show universal acceptance of this form of storage.

statements by workers in the United States and abroad who are engaged in activities pertinent to research in this field. The publication which resulted:

"Current Research and Development in
Scientific Documentation"

has been an extremely useful handbook for workers in this field.

Statements provided have been classified as follows:

1. Information needs and uses
2. Information storage and retrieval

3. Mechanical translation
4. Equipment
5. Related research
   a. Character and pattern recognition
   b. Speech analysis and synthesis
   c. Linguistic and lexicographic research
   d. Artificial intelligence
   e. Psychological studies

B. Information Needs and Uses

Those listed as performing research in this area represent a variety of professional societies, universities, libraries, governmental agencies, industrial organizations, and others.

The reports of the efforts frequently belie that portion of the heading under which they are listed, namely, "Information Needs." Actually, the reports reveal studies of the total communication process, user habits, user attitudes, use patterns, use statistics, literature or authors citation statistics, and user desires, not all necessarily relating to "needs" of users.

The point of the matter is that the *needs* of users may not necessarily be measurable by the studies conducted. For example, if the habits of a given library user were studied, one might find that he walked up and down the aisles of the stacks in order to locate a given book. If this habit were interpreted as a need, then the tools and systems that might be developed to serve the user better might involve providing the user with a pair of roller skates to speed up user movement through the aisles.

On the other hand, a study of user desires might reveal an earnest wish to alleviate the symptoms of the problem, but without understanding of the mechanisms that might actually be utilized to solve the problem itself.

Here then might be found examples of measurements being made on that which may be insignificant.

C. Information Storage and Retrieval

This class of studies includes the following: "the design of new information systems, the comparative testing or evaluation of proposed or operating systems, the determination of the theory underlying the design and operation of information systems, and the problems involved in organizing information for storage and searching."

As before, a wide variety of organizations are represented in the studies reported.

The research and development reported may be categorized under seven topics, as discussed below.

1. New Systems Development. A number of organizations are involved in the development of "new," "more convenient," "more advanced," and "more sophisticated" systems for collecting, indexing, classifying, abstracting, or extracting the literature of specific subject fields. Some report their efforts in terms of experimental or pilot studies; others suggest that their efforts have yielded operational results in terms of newly developed specialized information centers.

There is no apparent coordination among these activities, with regard to principles used in the systems or to subject fields handled. Nevertheless, many claim successful services emerging, but few indicate the criteria used for defining success in anything but the most qualitative terms.

2. Equipment. Most of the organizations reporting research and development involving "equipment" discuss the application of specific data processing, computing, film handling, or other devices to one or more of the unit operations of information retrieval (e.g., analysis, vocabulary control, searching, delivery of search results).

Generally, these studies are not controlled research experiments which reveal the effect of the individual pieces of equipment on the efficacy of the total information system involved. In particular, the investigations usually do not provide quantitative evidence of the way in which users benefit from the application of one or another type of equipment. The lack of such evidence is not surprising, however, since criteria for such quantitative evaluation have not yet been formalized in the information-retrieval field.

Nevertheless, the economies or conveniences that may be attained in terms of the performance of one or more individual unit operations should not be overlooked.

One of the more interesting studies is with regard to the use of time-sharing computers, with remote input-output stations communicating with a central equipment complex. The ability to utilize large computers, with the investment only in relatively inexpensive input-output stations, permits attaining many of the benefits of using such equipment while contributing only that portion of the capital costs which is proportionate to actual use.

3. Content Analysis. A considerable number of organizations report experiments of content analysis by computers and human beings.

At least one organization is concerned with the recording of full texts of source materials in machine-readable form. Because of the expense of keyboarding such texts anew, the attempt is being made to use as a starting point the diverse by-products of original preparation of these texts for printing. These include punched-paper tape produced during typewriterlike composition (e.g., using Flexowriters) for offset printing, and Monotype tape and Linofilm produced as an intermediate step during composition for letterpress printing.

Another effort is producing computer programs for manipulating machine-readable text so that editing and various types of linguistic analyses may be performed.

Some linguists are studying the full texts of source materials in order to discern regularities that may be exploited by computers for information-retrieval purposes. Others are attempting to develop programs to "normalize" (or standardize) the full texts grammatically so that information-retrieval operations may be conducted more effectively.

In a sense, the problems involved in full text processing are perhaps irresolvable, since it is difficult to visualize how a computer may be programmed to recognize *significant* contents and facts for information-retrieval purposes. The fundamental question that must be resolved is what criteria human beings use to determine what may be significant to them when perusing a full text. It may be obvious that the mere presence of words or phrases in the texts of source materials does not, *ipso facto*, make it significant.

Several investigations are reported which aim to identify significant information by programming computers to abstract, index, and classify on the basis of full text processing. As discussed in Chapter 5, these efforts are examinations of the frequency of occurrence of key words (singly or in groups) in full texts, and make the assumption that frequency of occurrence of terms has semantic significance. This assumption must, of course, be questioned.

At least one group of workers despairs of full text processing by computer, and has been using, instead, abstracts prepared by skilled human beings as a basis for automatic "indexing." In this case, at least there is some basis for the assumption that significant text is being processed, since a specialist has already exercised judgment in this regard when preparing the abstract.

Many projects step back even further in automatic text processing, by using only titles of source materials for automatic indexing. Here, the key-word-in-context or KWIC program (see Chapter 5) is based on the assumption that a specialist (the author in this case) has devoted considerable attention to preparing a title which is indicative of the significant contents of the source material.

Some effort is being devoted to the comparison between indexes prepared by human beings and computers. What is being discovered is that human beings tend to index inconsistently, while computers are inexorably consistent. However, the consistency of computer processing may not always lead to significant results, while the human beings may tend to overcome the disadvantages of inconsistency by producing more significant results.

The "trade-offs" involved are considered as a function of subject background and indexing experience in an investigation of index entries chosen by human beings when they are working in a specific subject field, as well as in interdisciplinary areas.

Several investigators despair of computer retrieval and content themselves with studies of how computers may be exploited to facilitate the "self-organization" of files of information, thus leaving the task of retrieval to human beings.

A recurring argument found in a number of reports is that "information" retrieval is not the same as "document" retrieval. The thesis is that the clientele of information retrieval systems is more interested in the retrieval of data, facts, and "information" from within a document, rather than the document itself. A critique of this matter has been published elsewhere.[6]

4. Vocabulary Control. It has long been recognized that it is difficult or even impossible to define precisely most words that are to be used for retrieval purposes. This despite the recognized need for such definition in order to assure consequent precision in search results. Accordingly, a number of investigations are reported which address themselves to standardization of the "vocabulary" used for indexing purposes.

It is difficult enough to obtain agreement among a group of specialists working in a narrow field with regard to the precise meaning of their specialized vocabulary. It is well-nigh impossible to obtain such agreement among specialists in differing fields when the vocabulary of an interdisciplinary, information-retrieval system is being examined. Accordingly, two alternative thrusts may be discerned:

a. Living with unstandardized vocabularies, but developing thesauri in an attempt to overcome the ensuing difficulties by displaying relationships of words and terms (e.g., synonym, or generic to specific relationships).

b. Establishing a "standard" vocabulary code, or "language" which has not achieved acceptance, and attempting to *sell* or *dictate* its use.

The first alternative suffers in that most of the burden of coping with the vocabulary control problem is shifted from the designer or operator of the information-retrieval system to its clientele. Thus the clientele is asked to choose those related words that in his, the user's, opinion, cover his peculiar interests. However, he is not provided with guidance as to the probable consequences of his selections in terms of their influence on the system's ability to identify relevant responses to his question and withhold those responses that are not of interest.

The second alternative usually founders because of the difficulty of training individuals to use a "standard" vocabulary that may not coincide with their own paradigms, or ways of perceiving "nature."

---

[6] A. Kent, *Specialized Information Centers*, Spartan Books, Washington, D.C., 1965, pp. 22 and 36.

Despite the difficulties inherent in the two alternatives above, some thesaural developments in highly specialized subject fields may be fruitful. Of course, it is precisely in the same type of highly specialized subject field that a special classification or a standard vocabulary would have the best chance of being successful.

5. Search Strategies. Many information retrieval-system designers and operators articulate their basic objective in terms of providing more or less "noise-free" responses to questions posed of their systems—that is, a high percentage of relevant responses in terms of the total response. The strategies used for searching are, of course, influential in this regard.

In a number of projects attention is directed toward adaptation of strategies used (with a hoped-for increase in relevance of the response) in terms of previous experience. This previous experience (called *feedback*) may be exploited routinely when a continuing information-retrieval service is being provided to an individual user on a discrete topic or set of topics. Here, the user may be asked to rate each response provided him in terms of relevance or nonrelevance to his current interests. These ratings may then be interpreted in one or more of several ways; a "nonrelevance" rating means that:

1. The index entry that caused its selection should:
   a. not be used in further searches for the same user-topic; or
   b. be suspect, until enough statistical evidence builds up to support its being omitted in further searches.
2. The search strategy that was used should:
   a. be reformulated so that further searches for the same user-topic may not result in the *same* type of nonrelevant selection; or
   b. be suspect, until enough statistical evidence builds up to support its being altered for further searches.

Some projects describe research on these matters as being related to *adaptive* retrieval—in the sense that retrieval is *adapted* on the basis of *feedback* from the system user.

The analysis of many user questions results in some uncertainty as to which search strategy will yield optimal results. Accordingly, several alternative strategies may be used, with the user being presented with responses "graded" or "labeled" according to the probability of relevance as predicted by the strategy used.

The choice of strategies used for search, and the consequent usefulness of search results are, of course, related to original indexing depth and consistency, usefulness of index entries selected, and manner and degree of control exercised over vocabulary used in the system. Accordingly, some projects are concerned with the study of occurrence of, and association among, words in both full texts and in indexes, in terms of automatic cross-referencing or other automatic associating which would influence positively the relevance of responses obtained in an information-retrieval system.

So far, the development and adaptation of search strategies have been assumed to be human tasks. Nevertheless, some investigators are experimenting with means by which users may ask questions, or otherwise communicate with information-retrieval systems using a formalized language that still preserves enough of the semantic structure of natural languages so that learning its use would not be inhibited.

There are apparently several tacit assumptions buried in this work, of which the most questionable is

that free-flowing inquiries, relating to user paradigms, may be matched with free-flowing natural language text, relating to author paradigms, with consequences of acceptable ratios of relevant responses resulting.

Whether this assumption is reasonable or not will be determined on the basis of whether *significance* in natural language text may be identified automatically.

6. *Evaluation Criteria.* As may be obvious by now, the research and development efforts in the field of information storage and retrieval have not been characterized generally by careful attention to the scientific method. Accordingly, when it became obvious to observers that substantial resources were being invested in this field and that results could not be quantitatively measured, pressure developed to evaluate progress in general, as well as performance of specific systems. Also there was activity directed toward developing some standard measures for evaluation of information-retrieval systems. See Chapter 11.

7. *General Theory.* Some investigators have presented thoughts regarding general theories of information storage and retrieval. These *thoughts*, as they must be characterized rather than as *theories*, have covered such topics as non-Boolean-retrieval processes, redundancy, document categorization based on word frequency distributions, and mathematical models for information dissemination via information networks.

D. Mechanical Translation

A number of projects described under "mechanical translation" (MT) deal with research on problems of automatic translation from one natural language to another. Included are reports on work on the techniques of the actual MT process, and some studies of the characteristics of the source and target languages involved.

Although these studies are of considerable interest, they will not be discussed further in this, an introductory text in the field of mechanized information retrieval.

E. Equipment

Considerable effort is reported in the development of special purpose equipment for information handling.

Photographic (or related) storage systems (in greater or lesser image size reductions) concerned with sequential roll film, unit records, sheets, and others with scrolls, are of interest to several investigations. The desire for rapid "readout" is common to all of the film or filmlike approaches—some approaching access sequentially, others on a random basis. One project even reports an attempt to readout information stored in micro form while still employing peek-a-boo search techniques.

Further developments of peek-a-boo card systems which would facilitate replication of cards, on-line printing of responses, etc., are being attempted.

Media are being considered which permit compact storage and convenient processing and retrieval of information. Such media range from computer core storage to thermoplastic tape.

Some effort is also being made in the development of composing and printing equipment, ranging from reactive typewriters to converters from linotype and Monotype linecasting machine codes into conventional computer codes.

Associative memories for computers, which would permit rapid associations without requiring special programs, are beginning to attract attention.

F. Related Research

Most of the projects reported here are not expected to have immediate impact on operational information-retrieval systems. Nevertheless, the work on automatic recognition of characters, patterns, pictographs, and speech; linguistics and lexicography; and artificial intelligence are interesting in that breakthroughs in these areas might basically change the ways in which new information storage and retrieval systems may be designed in the future.

IV. CONCLUSION

Current research is not generally characterized by careful application of the scientific method, nor is there strong indication that there is general awareness of good research methodology.

Some research is reminiscent of the story of the man whose friend found him examining the ground directly beneath a street light. He was asked what he lost, and he replied, "My car keys." Much later he was asked whether he was certain that he had lost the keys under the street light. He replied, "No, I lost them down the street, but it's too dark to look there."

It is perhaps instructive to recall another story:

A former student, when returning to visit his old professor, said to him, "Do you know what is the most valuable thing which you ever taught me?" When the professor replied that he did not remember, the former student repeated the lesson he had memorized: "When you enter a public auditorium in this country go to the left!" For a moment, the old professor thought that the student was joking, but soon he remembered that he had been trying to point out the value of the habit of looking for irrational biases and taking advantage of them. From force of habit, people of this country go to the right; and therefore the best empty seats are almost invariably on the left.

Stated somewhat differently, the two lessons are as follows:

1. Experimental work is not significant merely because measurements are obtained. In order to be significant, the measurements must somehow be related to the solution of a problem that is of concern.

2. Just because most workers are concentrating on certain approaches does not mean that these approaches are fruitful ones or even significant.

Perhaps an analogy might be useful here: Placing a person in a stationary plane and having scenery move past him does not necessarily result in physical movement, even though the person may have had a sensation of flying. Just so in information retrieval. Just because systems may cause references, titles, abstracts, or full texts to flash past an information seeker's eyes, does not mean that useful communication has been achieved.

Perhaps one last quotation might be in order in this regard. Dr. Arthur Samuel was discussing the topic of "bird watching" in one of his papers:[7]

When man first attempted to fly he studied the birds, and the early unsuccessful flying machines were mechanical birds. It was not until man stopped studying birds and began to study aerodynamics that much progress was made. The modern jet airplane must cope with the same aerodynamical problems with which birds contend, but the mechanisms used in the solution of the problem of light are quite different.

This lesson might be heeded by those in the field of mechanized information retrieval who would engage in significant research in this field.

---

[7] A. L. Samuel, *Annals of the American Academy of Political and Social Science*, **340** (1962).

Appendix

Supplemental Material for Classroom Use

This section consists of related material for Chapters 5 and 9 which may be used selectively in graduate courses. It would be helpful for those who are using this text for self-study to apply as much of this material as possible.

Chapter 5—Principles of Analysis

Exercise 1

Select 10 titles of books or articles, and prepare (using index cards):

a. A concordance of the titles
b. A permutation index for the titles

Compare the results and discuss similarities and differences.

Exercise 2

Discuss the physical arrangement of foods in a supermarket as an example of a pigeonhole classification system. Discuss the steps that would have to be taken in the supermarket to convert it into an example of a multidimensional classification system.

Exercise 3

Discuss relative merits of word indexing versus controlled indexing versus classification for representing the contents of the catalog of a mail-order store.

Exercise 4

Index the following news item providing two or more examples of redundancy in the process.

Mrs. Emily T. Watterson acquired a stone, English-style residence at 2601 Sherbrooke Rd., SHAKER HEIGHTS, from Wilbert J. Austin Memorial Trust. Austin, before his death, was president of Austin Co., a world-wide engineering and construction company.

Mrs. Watterson is the wife of John S. Watterson, Jr., a partner with Paine, Webber, Jackson, & Curtis. Watterson is a broker and investment dealer in charge of Ohio area operations for the brokerage firm.

The $85,000 house was built in 1928. It includes four bedrooms, four baths, living room, dining room, kitchen, breakfast room, and library in addition to a third-floor room. Two bedrooms, the library and the living room have fireplaces. There is a four-car attached garage.

A stream runs alongside the two-acre, wooded and landscaped site.

Mrs. Mary Louise Curtiss negotiated the transaction for A. B. Smythe Co.

Exercise 5

In the text given in Exercise 4, provide one or more questions based on the text which could not be answered by a scanning of all words or combination of words appearing in the text.

Exercise 6

This exercise is intended to illustrate the influence of point of view in content analysis.

An article on ice cream, from *Encyclopaedia Britannica,* 1959 edition, has been reproduced in Exhibit 1. Various index policies have been used to produce the results given in Exhibits 2-16.

It is suggested that the students frame questions after perusing the text of Exhibit 1, and that they then determine whether the indexing policies provided in Exhibits 2-16 would provide this article as a response for each indexing policy.

EXHIBIT 1. Article on "Ice Cream" reprinted with permission from *Encyclopaedia Britannica,* 1959 edition.

ICE CREAM. Ice cream is a dairy food. The "liquid mix," or unfrozen ice cream, for representative, good-quality vanilla ice cream contains about 80% by weight of cream and milk products and 15% sweeteners. Almost 70% of the milk or its equivalent used in ice cream manufacture in the United States is bought during the spring and early summer months when milk production is at its peak. Because milk solids may be stored as frozen or concentrated cream or milk, for use in later periods of low milk production on farms, ice cream has been called the "balance wheel" of the dairy industry.

Cream, milk, nonfat milk solids, sugar and sometimes eggs form the basis of all ice cream. A small amount (less than 0.5%) of stabilizer is generally included by ice cream manufacturers. Several different types of stabilizers are generally in use.

Ice cream is a popular form of milk, with food values in slightly different proportions. One-third pint of vanilla ice cream is about equal to one-half cup of whole milk in calcium, protein and the B vitamins, and to a little more than one cup in vitamin A and calories.

Pasteurization in the manufacturing process, homogenization and automatically controlled freezing contribute to the quality of ice cream. Homogenization blends the fat globules with the nonfat milk solids to help form a stable emulsion. Homogenization aids development of a smooth texture by retarding churning of fat globules in the freezer.

Automatic control of the whipping process produces ice cream of uniform consistency. The incorporation of air by whipping is necessary to produce a palatable product. Ice cream without whipping would be like bread that has not risen.

The ingredients of ice cream are combined in varying proportions, but always in a way to make solids in the ice cream about 38% of its weight. Each U.S. state and many cities set minimum legal requirements for ice cream. Butterfat in ice cream may range from 8 to 14%; nonfat milk solids from 8 to 12%. The trend in the 1950s was toward the higher content of nonfat milk solids. The use of the latter is limited by the amount of lactose, or milk sugar, which is contributed by the nonfat milk solids, since excessive lactose may crystallize and cause a "sandy" ice cream.

HISTORY. The invention in 1867 of the centrifugal cream separator helped to launch a business which by the latter 1950s was selling about 2,000,000,000 qt. of ice cream a year in the U. S. alone. Water ices were known in the Roman empire, and Marco Polo is supposed to have brought a recipe for milk ices from the far east. Centuries later, chefs for the courts of Europe experimented with ice cream recipes and tried, unsuccessfully, to keep the secret for the nobility. Its production became practical after the discovery that salts mixed with ice produce a lower temperature than that of ice alone. In the late 19th century the introduction of mechanical refrigeration greatly assisted the growth of the ice cream industry.

VARIETIES. *Ice Cream.* This is fundamentally a cream and milk product which may be flavoured with such foods as vanilla, chocolate, berries, fruits, nuts and candy. More than 100 flavours of ice cream have been made.

Mousses, Parfaits. These are frozen without stirring. Mousse is a frozen dessert or sweetened and flavoured whipped cream or thin cream and gelatin. Parfait is a frozen dessert of whipped cream, eggs cooked with syrup and flavouring.

Fruit Sherbets. Sherbets are frozen dairy foods made of milk, sweeteners and fruit flavouring. There are many varieties; viz., lemon, orange, pineapple or any fruit or berry. Where the fruit juice used is only slightly coloured, a little fruit and vegetable colouring may be added.

Fruit Ices. Fruit, fruit juices, water and sweeteners are used in water ices. Many of the same flavourings used for sherbets are added, but no milk products are included.

MANUFACTURING PROCESS. The "mix" contains all of the ingredients except the fruits, nuts or other special flavouring. The mixer uses a standardized and balanced formula or recipe. In a modern plant, the mix is pasteurized and homogenized and then is cooled rapidly to below 40°F.

At least half the ice cream made in the 1950s was frozen on the continuous-type freezer, a refrigerated tube with revolving blades or beaters which is surrounded by a refrigerant. The mix moves through the freezer without stopping and comes out in less than a minute as partially frozen ice cream. Fruits, nuts and similar flavourings are added at this time. Liquid flavourings such as vanilla extract, are added to the mix just before freezing. Chocolate syrup is the exception. It is added as the mix is made for chocolate ice cream.

The partially frozen ice cream is drawn off into containers which are covered immediately and sent on conveyors to a hardening room where the temperature ranges from 0 to −20°F. Containers range in size from single paper cups to large cans containing several gallons. The ice cream is kept in the hardening room for several hours to harden evenly throughout. It is then delivered in refrigerated trucks to dealers. There it is placed in refrigerated cabinets where it is kept frozen until sold.

The ice cream mix and the frozen ice cream are tested routinely for the amount of butterfat, total solids and bacteria. A maze of sterilized pipes and automatic machinery produces and packages the ice cream, the procedures being checked by the manufacturer and by health authorities. Samples of ice cream on the market are retested to make sure the quality is protected where it is sold.

EXHIBIT 2. Index entries for article on "Ice Cream" (Exhibit 1), as published in the 1959 index to *Encyclopaedia Britannica.*

> FROZEN DISHES: see ICE CREAM
> ICE CREAM
> CREAM
>   ice cream
> MILK
>   ice cream
> HOMOGENIZATION
>   ice cream
> LACTOSE (Milk sugar)
>   ice cream
> MILK SUGAR: see LACTOSE
> REFRIGERATION AND ITS APPLICATIONS
>   ice cream

- MOUSSE (Food)
- PARFAIT (Food)
- SHERBET (Food)
- FRUIT ICES
- FREEZING MIXTURE
  - ice cream

EXHIBIT 3. Index entries for article on "Ice Cream" (Exhibit 1), as selected to illustrate a very detailed (or "deep") indexing.

- ICE CREAM
  - as dairy food
- DAIRY FOOD
  - ice cream as example
- LIQUID MIX
  - term for unfrozen ice cream
- ICE CREAM
  - composition
- CREAM
  - as component of ice cream
- MILK
  - as component of ice cream
- CREAM AND MILK PRODUCTS
  - as component of ice cream (85% by weight)
- SWEETENER
  - as component of ice cream (15% by weight)
- MILK
  - peak production season
- ICE CREAM
  - as "balance wheel" of dairy industry
- NONFAT MILK SOLIDS
  - as component of ice cream
- SUGAR
  - as component of ice cream
- EGGS
  - as component of ice cream
- STABILIZERS
  - as component of ice cream (<0.5%)
- ICE CREAM
  - food value
- CALCIUM
  - content in ice cream
- PROTEIN
  - content in ice cream
- ICE CREAM
  - legal composition requirements
- BUTTERFAT, IN ICE CREAM
  - legal requirements
- NONFAT MILK SOLIDS, IN ICE CREAM
  - legal requirements
- "SANDY" ICE CREAM
  - caused by crystallized lactose
- LACTOSE CONTENT OF NONFAT MILK SOLIDS
  - effect on ice cream
- MILK SUGAR: See LACTOSE
- CENTRIFUGAL CREAM SEPARATOR
  - in ice cream manufacture
- CREAM SEPARATOR, CENTRIFUGAL
  - in ice cream manufacture
- ICE CREAM
  - annual consumption
- WATER ICES
  - in Roman Empire
- MILK ICES
  - from Far East
- REFRIGERATION
  - with ice-salt mixture
- REFRIGERATION, MECHANICAL
  - effect on ice cream industry
- ICE CREAM
  - flavors
- MOUSSES
  - description
- PARFAITS
  - description
- FRUIT SHERBETS
  - description
- SHERBET, FRUIT
  - description

VITAMINS B
  content in ice cream
VITAMIN A
  content in ice cream
ICE CREAM
  manufacturing process
HOMOGENIZATION, OF ICE CREAM
  effect on texture
ICE CREAM
  control of consistency
ICE CREAM
  solids content (38%)

FRUIT ICES
  description
ICES, FRUIT
  description
ICE CREAM, VARIATIONS
  description
ICE CREAM
  manufacturing process
FREEZER, CONTINUOUS-TYPE
  use in ice cream manufacture
ICE CREAM
  testing procedures

EXHIBIT 4. "Uniterms" for article on "Ice Cream" (Exhibit 1) selected to represent same depth of analysis as index entries used in 1959 index to *Encyclopaedia Britannica* (Exhibit 2).

FROZEN
DISHES
ICE CREAM
MILK
HOMOGENIZATION
LACTOSE
MILK SUGAR
REFRIGERATION
APPLICATIONS
MOUSSE
FOOD
PARFAIT
SHERBET
FRUIT
ICES
FREEZING
MIXTURE

EXHIBIT 5. "Uniterms" for article on "Ice Cream" (Exhibit 1) selected to represent same depth of analysis as index entries given in Exhibit 3 to illustrate a very detailed subject analysis.

ICE CREAM	FOOD	ANNUAL
DAIRY	VALUE	CONSUMPTION
FOOD	CALCIUM	WATER ICES
LIQUID	CONTENT	ROMAN EMPIRE
MIX	PROTEIN	MILK ICES
COMPOSITION	VITAMINS B	FAR EAST
CREAM	VITAMIN A	REFRIGERATION

COMPONENT MANUFACTURING ICE-SALT
MILK PROCESS MIXTURE
PRODUCTS HOMOGENIZATION MECHANICAL
85% (EFFECT) INDUSTRY
WEIGHT TEXTURE FLAVORS
SWEETENER CONTROL MOUSSES
15% CONSISTENCY DESCRIPTION
PEAK LEGAL PARFAITS
PRODUCTION REQUIREMENTS FRUIT
SEASON BUTTERFAT SHERBET
NONEAT "SANDY" ICES
SOLIDS (or "Milk CRYSTALLIZED FREEZER
   Solids") LACTOSE CONTINUOUS-TYPE
EGGS MILK SUGAR TESTING
STABILIZERS CENTRIFUGAL PROCEDURES
< 0.5% SEPARATOR

EXHIBIT 6. "Telegraphic" abstracts for article on "Ice Cream" (Exhibit 1) at a "shallow" level of analysis. (Note that all "barriers" that would be included in an analysis of this depth are not shown here.)

Role indicator	Description
1. (Material processed) KEJ, (property given for) KOV, (product) KWJ,	2. Frozen
3. " "	4. Dairy food
5. (Material processed) KEJ, (property given for) KOV, (product) KWJ,	6. Ice cream
7. (Material processed) KEJ, (property given for) KOV, (product) KWJ,	8. Frozen dessert
9. (Material processed) KEJ, (property given for) KOV, (product) KWJ,	10. Mousse
11. (Material processed) KEJ, (property given for) KOV, (product) KWJ,	
13. (Material processed) KEJ, (property given for) KOV, (product) KWJ,	14. Fruit sherbet
15. (Material processed) KEJ, (property given for) KOV, (product) KWJ,	16. Fruit ice

Role indicator	Description
17. (Major component) KUJ,	18. Milk
19. (Major component) KUJ,	20. Cream
21. (Minor component) KIJ,	22. Butterfat (8-14%)
23. (Minor component) KIJ,	24. Nonfat
25.	26. Milk solid (8-12%)
27. (Minor component) KIJ,	28. Egg
29. (Minor component) KIJ,	30. Sugar (15%)
31. (Minor component) KIJ,	32. Fruit
33.	34. Juice
35. (Minor component) KIJ,	36. Stabilizer (0.5%)
37. (Minor component) KIJ,	38. Gelatin
39. (Property given) KWV,	40. Milk
41.	42. Food
43.	44. Value
45. (Process) KAM,	46. Pasteurization
47. (Process) KAM,	48. Homogenization
49. (Process) KAM,	50. Whipping
51. (Process) KAM,	52. Aeration
53. (Process) KAM,	54. Mixing
55. (By means of) KQJ,	56. Flavor
57.	58. Addition
59. (Major component) KUJ,	60. Fruit
61. (Major component) KUJ,	62. Nut
63. (Major component) KUJ,	64. Berry
65. (Major component) KUJ,	66. Candy
67. (Major component) KUJ,	68. Chocolate
69. (Major component) KUJ,	70. Vanilla
71. (Process) KAM,	72. Freezing
73. (Condition) KAH,	74. Mechanical
75.	76. Refrigeration
77. (Condition) KAH,	78. Low
79.	80. Temperature $(-20 < 0°F.)$
81. (Process) KAM,	82. Hardening
83. (Process) KAM,	84. Production
85. (Process) KAM,	86. Consumption
87. (Process) KAM,	88. Inspection
89. (Process) KAM,	90. Storage
91. (Field) KAB,	92. Review
93. (Process) KAM,	94. Historical
95.	96. Development
97. (Affected by process) KUP, (property affected) KAP,	98. Texture

Role indicator	Description
99. (Affected by process) KUP, (property affected) KAP,	100. Quality
101. (Affected by process) KUP, (property affected) KAP,	102. Palatability
103. (Affected by process) KUP, (property affected) KAP,	104. Butterfat
105.	106. Milk solid
107.	108. Bacteria
109.	110. Content
111. (Influenced by) KAL,	112. Pasteurization
113. (Influenced by) KAL,	114. Homogenization
115. (Influenced by) KAL,	116. Automatic
117.	118. Control
1·19.	120. Freezing
121.	122. Whipping
123. (Influenced by) KAL,	124. Aeration
125. (Influenced by) KAL,	126. Composition
127.	128.
129. (End of abstract)/	130.

EXHIBIT 7. "Telegraphic" abstract for article on "Ice Cream" (Exhibit 1) at a "deep" level of analysis. (Note that all "barriers" that would be included in an analysis of this depth are not shown here.)

Role indicator	Description
1. Material processed (KEJ), property given for (KOV),	2. Dairy food
3.	4. Mixture
5. Major component (KUJ), material processed (KEJ),	6. Milk
7.	8. Cream
9.	10. Emulsion (80%)
11. Major component (KUJ),	12. Milk
13. Major component (KUJ),	14. Cream
15. Minor component (KIJ),	16. Sweetener (15%)
17. Minor component (KIJ),	18. Nonfat
19.	20. Milk
21.	22. Solid (8-12%)
23. Minor component (KIJ),	24. Butterfat (8-14%)
25. Minor component (KIJ),	26. Egg

Role indicator	Description
27. Minor component (KIJ),	28. Stabilizer ($<0.5\%$)
29. Minor component (KIJ),	30. Protein
31. Minor component (KIJ),	32. Vitamin A
33. Minor component (KIJ),	34. Vitamin B
35. Minor component (KIJ),	36. Calcium
37. Minor component (KIJ),	38. Sugar
39. Property given (KWV),	40. Calorie
41.	42. Content
43. Property given (KWV),	44. Liquid
45. Process (KAM),	46. Mixing
47. Location (KIS),	48. Mixer
49. By means of (KQJ),	50. Formula
51. By means of (KQJ),	52. Recipe
53. Property given (KWV),	54. Standardized
55. Property given (KWV),	56. Balanced
57. Process (KAM),	58. Pasteurizing
59. Process (KAM),	60. Homogenization
61. Condition (KAH),	62. Fat
63.	64. Globule
65.	66. Nonfat
67.	68. Milk solid
69.	70. Blending
71. Process (KAM),	72. Whipping
73. Condition, (KAH),	74. Air
75.	76. Incorporation
77. Condition (KAH),	78. Automatic
79.	80. Control
81. Process negation (KXM),	82. Fat
83.	84. Globule
85.	86. Churning
87. Process (KAM),	88. Cooling
89. Condition (KAH),	90. Speed
91. Condition (KAH),	92. Low
93.	94. Temperature ($>40°$F.)
95. Process (KAM),	96. Freezing
97. By means of (KQJ), machine or device (KAD),	98. Continuous
99.	100. Freezer
101. By means of (KQJ), subassembly (KAG),	102. Revolving
103.	104. Blade
105.	106. Tube
107. Location (KIS),	108. Refrigerant

Role indicator	Description
109. Process (KAM),	110. Flavoring
111. By means of (KQJ),	112. Addition
113. Major component (KUJ),	114. Berry
115. Major component (KUJ),	116. Chocolate
117. Major component (KUJ),	118. Fruit
119. Major component (KUJ),	120. Nut
121. Major component (KUJ),	122. Candy
123. Major component (KUJ),	124. Vanilla
125. Property given (KWV),	126. Variety
127. Process (KAM),	128. Packaging
129. Location (KIS), property given for (KOV),	130. Container
131. Major component (KUJ),	132. Paper
133. Location (KIS), property given for (KOV),	134. Can
135. Property given (KWV),	136. Size
137. By means of (KQJ), property given for (KOV),	138. Piping
139. By means of (KQJ), property given for (KOV),	140. Automatic
141.	142. Machinery
143. Property given (KWV),	144. Sterilized
145. Process (KAM),	146. Hardening
147.	148. Low
149.	150. Temperature $(-20 < 0°F.)$
151. Location (KIS),	152. Hardening
153.	154. Room
155. Process (KAM),	156. Storage
157. Location (KIS),	158. Refrigerated
159.	160. Cabinet
161. Process (KAM),	162. Delivery
163. By means of (KQJ),	164. Refrigerated
165.	166. Truck
167. Process (KAM),	168. Inspection
169. Process (KAM),	170. Testing
171. Product (KWJ), material processed (KEJ), property given for (KOV),	172. Ice cream
173. Property given (KWV), property affected (KAP),	174. Palatability
175. Property given (KWV), property affected (KAP)	176. Consistency
177. Property given (KWV), property affected (KAP),	178. Bacteria

Role indicator	Description
179.	180. Milk solid
181.	182. Butterfat
183.	184. Content
185. Property given (KWV), property affected (KAP),	186. Texture
187.	188. Smooth
189.	190. Sandy
191. Influenced by (KAL),	192. Lactose
193.	194. Crystallization
195. Property affected (KAP), influenced by (KAL),	196. Emulsion
197.	198. Stability
199. Property given (KWV), property affected (KAP),	200. Quality
201. Influenced by (KAL),	202. Pasteurization
203. Influenced by (KAL),	204. Homogenization
205. Influenced by (KAL),	206. Automatic
207.	208. Controlled
209.	210. Whipping
211.	212. Freezing
213. Influenced by (KAL),	214. Air
215. Influenced by (KAL),	216. Composition
217. Process (KAM),	218. Comparison
219. By means of (KQJ),	220. Milk
221. Affected by process (KUP),	222. Food
223.	224. Value
225. Beginning of new telegraphic sentence (□ . . .) property given for (KOV),	226. Frozen dessert
227. Property given for (KOV),	228. Mousse
229. Major component (KUJ),	230. Cream
231.	232. Whipped
233.	234. Thin
235. Major component (KUJ),	236. Gelatin
237. Property given for (KOV),	238. Parfait
239. Major component (KUJ),	240. Cream
241.	242. Whipped
243. Major component (KUJ),	244. Cooked
245.	246. Egg
247.	248. Syrup
249.	250. Mixture
251. Property given (KWV),	252. Flavored
253. Property given (KWV),	254. Unstirred

Role indicator	Description
255. Property given (KWV),	256. Sweetened
257. Property given (KOV),	258. Fruit sherbet
259. Major component (KUJ),	260. Milk
261. Minor component (KIJ),	262. Sweetener
263. Minor component (KIJ),	264. Fruit
265.	266. Flavor
267.	268. Lemon
269.	270. Orange
271.	272. Pineapple
273.	274. Berry
275. Minor component (KIJ),	276. Fruit
277.	278. Vegetable
279.	280. Coloring
281. Property given (KWV),	282. Frozen
283. Property given for (KOV),	284. Fruit ice
285. Property given for (KOV),	286. Water ice
287. Major component (KUJ),	288. Fruit
289. Major component (KUJ),	290. Water
291. Major component (KUJ),	292. Fruit
293.	294. Juice
295. Minor component (KIJ),	296. Sweetener
297. Minor component (KIJ),	298. Fruit
299.	300. Flavor
301. Field (KAB)	302. Review
303. Material processed (KEJ),	304. Ice cream
305. Process (KAM),	306. Historical
307.	308. Development
309. Process (KAM),	310. Discovery
311. Process (KAM),	312. Milk
313.	314. Cream
315.	316. Separation
317. By means of (KQJ),	318. Centrifugal
319.	320. Cream
321.	322. Separator
323. Process (KAM),	324. Production
325. Process (KAM),	326. Freezing
327. By means of (KQJ),	328. Ice
329.	330. Salt
331.	332. Mixture
333. By means of (KQJ),	334. Mechanical
335.	336. Refrigeration

Role indicator	Description
337. Process (KAM),	338. Consumption
339. Process (KAM),	340. Manufacturing
341. Condition (KAH),	342. Health
343.	344. Legal
345.	346. Standard
347. Process (KAM),	348. Milk
349.	350. Product
351.	352. Utilization
353. Process (KAM),	354. Milk solid
355.	356. Milk
357.	358. Cream
359.	360. Concentration
361.	362. Freezing
363.	364. Storage
365.	366.
367. End of abstract (/)	368.

EXHIBIT 8. Portion of special classification system developed at an advertising agency, selected to show possibilities for classifications of article on "Ice Cream" (Exhibit 1).

      108-C Nuts, popcorn, potato chips
      108-D Juices
109. Food Beverages
      109-A General
      109-B Coffee
            109-B-1 Coffee, regular
            109-B-2 Coffee, instant and soluble
            109-B-3 Coffee containers and makers
      109-C Tea
      109-D Cocoa and chocolate
110. Confectionary and Soft Drinks
      110-A General
      110-B Candy
      110-C Chewing gum
      110-D Soft drinks (material in relation to dental caries filed here.)
     [1]*110-E Ice Cream*

---

[1] The italicized entry in this and following exhibits indicates that this is the only section under which the article is classified.

111. Household Cleansers—Scouring Powder
    111-A General
    111-B Cleaning fluids
    111-C Ammonia
    111-D Soap—bar, powder, flakes, detergents, etc.
    111-E (For future additions)
    111-F Stove polish
    111-G Metal polishers and cleaners
    111-H Starch
    111-I   Wax (household)

EXHIBIT 9. Portion of special classification system developed at a public library, selected to show possibilities for classification of article on "Ice Cream" (Exhibit 1).

TECHNOLOGY: USEFUL AND INDUSTRIAL ARTS

Summary

General works	V-VB
Metrology	VBD
Exhibitions	VC
Engineering	VD
Aeronautics	VDS
Construction and building	VE
Mechanical engineering	VF
Applied electricity	VG
Mines and mining	VH
Metallurgy and manufacture of metals	VI
Manufactures	VK
Textiles and fibres	VL
Wood, leather, rubber, etc.	VM
Other mechanical trades	VN
Chemical technology	VO
Agriculture	VP
Horticulture: gardening, fruit culture, fruit trees	VQ
Arboriculture: forestry, trees, timber, lumber	VQN
Fish and Fisheries	VR
Domestic economy	VS
Foods	VT
Military art	VW
Nautical art and science	VX
Naval history	VY

Agriculture (continued)

Dictionaries	VPB
General and systematic works, manuals	VPC
Amateur farming, personel experiences, country life	VPD
Collections, essays miscellanies, education in general	
Animal pests in general	VPE
General works on agricultural economics class here.	
Regional works, VPW-VPZ	
Fairs, exhibitions	VPF
Reports, catalogs, and bulletins of agricultural colleges and experiment stations (works on by name of institution)	VPG
Agricultural chemistry, soil, manures, fertilizers	VPH
Irrigation, drainage	VPI
Barns and other farm buildings, fences, machinery, tools	VPK
Wheat, cereals, Indian corn, potatoes, fodder, hay, silos, etc.	
Plant diseases	VPM
Per. and society publications	VPMA

EXHIBIT 10. Portion of special classification system for medical and veterinary libraries, selected to show possibilities for classification of article on "Ice Cream" (Exhibit 1).

JEZP	SEZP	CLASSIFICATION FOR MEDICAL LIBRARIES
		JEZP SEZP
		Water Pollution and Treatment—continued
JEZP	SEZP	Water treatment.
JEZQ	SEZQ	Water softening.
JEZR	SEZR	Prevention and removal of color, odor, and taste.
JEZS	SEZS	Prevention and removal of fungi and algae.
JEZT	SEZT	Iron removal.
JEZU	SEZU	Addition of iodine, flourine, etc.
		See also WIG Fluorosis of teeth
JEZV	SEZV	Industrial water supply. Alternative JQRBE, SQRBE, MAB, UDAE
JEZW	SEZW	Atomic and radioactive aspects of water supply.
		See also BS effects of high-energy radiations.
JEZX	SEZX	Corrosion
JEZY	SEZY	Public health aspects of water supply.
		Water-borne diseases. See FZT, OE.
		Effects of water on teeth. See WC.G.
JBZZ	SEZZ	Other aspects not provided for.

JF	SF	Food, Drink, Condiments, Sweetmeats, etc.
		See also note to BEW Food substances.
		and BBX Nutrition.
		FCQ, GK Food poisoning.
JFB	SFB	Home economics. Domestic science. Food studies.
		See also JQG, SQG Domestic hygiene.
JFD	SFD	Inspection, markets, etc.
JFE	SFE	Adulteration. Preservatives in food. Chemical additives.
JFF	SFF	Preservation. Storage. Refrigeration.
JFG	SFG	Milk and dairy products in general.
		See also XSP Dairy inspection.
JFGB	SFGB	Milk supply.
JFGD	SFGD	Dairy bacteriology, chemistry, etc.
		See also YL Dairying.
JFGE	SFGE	Cow's milk.
JFGF	SFGF	Pasteurization.
JFGG	SFGG	Evaporated and condensed milk.
JFGH	SFGH	Fermented milk (koumiss, yoghourt, etc.).
JFH	SFH	Special dairy products.
JFHB	SFHB	Butter.
JFHE	SFHE	Butter substitutes. Margarine.
JFHG	*SFHG*	*Cream, ice cream, etc.*
JFHK	SFHK	Cheese.
JFHP	SFHP	Goat's milk, mare's milk, etc.
JFI	SFI	Cereal foods. Bread, flour, etc. Bakehouses.
JFJ	SFJ	Vegetables, fruits.
JFK	SFK	Sugar, honey, confectionary, sweetmeats.
JFL	SFL	Eggs, poultry, game.
JFM	SFM	Meat and meat inspection. Animal foods in general.
		Meat industry.
		Slaughterhouses (abattoirs). Alternatives XSR.
		Slaughter. Alternative XWW.
		See also XSQ.

EXHIBIT 11. Portion of special classification system for industrial relations library, selected to show possibilities for classification of article on "Ice Cream" (Exhibit 1).

Synopsis

.A	Minerals and their inorganic compounds.
	Non-metallic elements.
.B	Metals and their inorganic compounds.
	Organic compounds.
.C-.E	Acyclic compounds.
.F-.I	Isocyclic compounds.
.J	Hetereocyclic compounds.

.K	Vitamins and lactones.
.L	Alkaloids and phosphatides.
.M	Carbohydrates.
	Natural mixtures.
.N	Proteins.
.O	Enzymes.
.P	Antibiotics; antisera, etc.; Nitrogen-free substances; Nitrogenous substances; Humic substances Oils, fats, waxes; Gums, resins, basalms.
.Q-.Y	Plant products.
.Z	Animal products.

Synopis

.YD	Coffee. See also .LY.	.ZC	Insects.	
.YE	Ipecacuanha. See also .LH.	.ZD	Cantharides. See also .KX.	
.YF	Valerian.	.ZE	Cochineal.	
.YG	Dicotyledons. Sympetalae 9. Cucurbitaceae.	.ZF	Fish.	
.YH	Cucumber.	.ZG	Halibut liver oil.	
.YI	Melon.	.ZH	Cod liver oil.	
.YJ	Pumpkin.	.ZI	Birds.	
.YM	Dicotyledons. Sympetalae 10. Campanulatae.	.ZJ	Poultry.	
		.ZK	Eggs.	
.YO	Lobelia. See also .L.A.	.ZL	Game.	
.YP	Brindelia.	.ZM	Mammals.	
.YQ	Jerusalem artichoke.	.ZO	Lard, lanolin, etc.	
.YR	Chamomile.	.ZP	Bile, ox gall.	
.YS	Absinth.	.ZQ	Meat (flesh foods).	
.YT	Pyrethrum.	.ZS	Dairy produce.	
.YU	Arnica.	.ZT	Milk, yoghourt, koumiss, etc.	
.YV	Artichoke.	.ZU	Butter.	
.YW	Lettuce.	.ZV	Cream.	
.Z	Animal products.	*.ZW*	*Ice cream.*	
.ZB	Shellfish, molluscs, and crustacea.	.ZX	Cheese.	

EXHIBIT 12. Portion of "universal" classification system, selected to show possibilities for classification of article on "Ice Cream" (Exhibit 1).

636.8	Katzen	Cats	Chats
636.9	Sonstige Haustiere	Other useful animals and pets	Animaux domestiques divers
.91	Meerschweinchen	Guinea pigs	Cobayes
.92	Kaninchen	Rabbits	Lapins
.93	Pelztiere	Animals bred for fur	Animaux a fourrure
.972	Schildkroten	Tortoises	Tortues
.976	Blefanten	Elephants	Elephants

.98	Tiere fur Zirkus- unternehem und zoologische Garten	Performing and ex- hibit animals (circus, zoo)	Animaux pour cirques et jardine zoologiques
637	Erzeugnisse von Haustieren	Domestic animal produce	Produits des animaux domestiques
637.1	*Milchwirtschaft im allgemeinen*	*Dairying, milk, and milk products*	*Laiterie, lait et prod- uits laitiers*
.11	Milchbetriebe, Meiereien	Milk production, dairy farms	Fermes laitieres
.12	Melken	Milking	Traite
.127	Bestandtcile der Milch	Milk composition and quality	Composition du lait
.6	Milchprufung. Milchuntersuchung	Sampling, analysis, testing	Examen et analyse du lait
.13	Milchbearbeitung	Dairy practice. Milk treatment	Traitement du lait
.131	Molkereien. Molkereiwesen	Dairies. Dairy factories	Laiteries
.132	Milchwirtchaftliche Gerate und Maschinen	Installations for handling milk in dairy: piping, etc.	Installations et ap- pareils pour laiteries
.133	Milchwirtschaftliche Verahren	Treatment. Cooling. Filtration	Procedes de conserva- tion du lait
.3/.4	Pasteruisieren. Steriliseren	Pasteurization. Sterilization	Pasteurisation. Sterilisation
.135	Milchtransport. Milchflaschen. Milchkannen. Milchwagen.	Distribution and transport: bottles, churns, cans. Milk trucks, tankers.	Transport. Bouteil- les, pots, cannes a lait. Wagons et camions laitiers
.14	Milcharten	Forms of milk. Various products	Types de lait
.141	Vollmilch. Submilch	Whole milk. Fresh milk.	Lait entier. Lait frais

EXHIBIT 13. Portion of classification of national library, selected to show possibilities for classification of article on "Ice Cream" (Exhibit 1).

Baking. Confectionary—Continued

769   Bread. Biscuits. Crackers.
770   Miscellaneous special.
            e.g., Pretzels.
771   Cake
772   Cookies.
773   Desserts, pies, and puddings. Pastry.

775 Directories of bakers, etc.
776 Bakers' trade publications.
778 Bakers' and confectioners' supplies (including catalogs).
    Confectionery
       Periodicals, see TX 761
783   General.
       Candy.
784   History of candy manufacture.
791   General works.
793   Candy makers' tools, etc.
       Desserts, see TX 773.
795   *Ice creams and ices.*
       .A1 Periodicals and societies.
799   Miscellaneous.
       e.g., Popcorn.

EXHIBIT 14. Portion of Dewey Decimal system, selected to show possibilities for classification of article on "Ice Cream" (Exhibit 1).

637.35   Varieties of cheese
   .352   Cream cheese
   .353   Soft Cheese
         Including semisoft, blue-mold, white-mold cheese
   .354   Hard cheese
   .355   Cheese from other than cow's milk
   .356   Sour milk cheese
         Including cottage cheese, pot cheese
   .358   Process cheese
         Including cheese spreads
    .4   *Ice cream industry (formerly 664.15)*
         Including sherbets, ices, frozen custards
         For ice cream making at home, see 641.86
638   Insects and other useful invertebrates for oysters and other mollusks, see 639.4
   .1   Beekeeping
         For scientific description and classification of bees, see 595.799
   .11   Management
         Including establishment of apiaries, selection of bees
         For hive management, see 638.14

EXHIBIT 15. Portion of Army Medical Library classification, selected to show possibilities for classification of article on "Ice Cream" (Exhibit 1).

SANITATION AND SANITARY CONTROL

    Food. Food supply—continued

703   Fresh foods
705   Vegetables. Fruits

707   Eggs. Fish. Meat
710   Canned foods. Preservation of foods
715   *Milk. Milk supply. Milk products*
716   Analysis
719   Pasteurization
722   Fats. Oils. Margarine
730   Drugs. Narcotics. Poisons
744   Barber shops. Beauty parlors. Cosmetics
750   Air. Air pollution. Nuisances
754   Pollution
770   Ventilating. Heating
774   Air conditioning
780   Refuse and garbage disposal
785   Sewage disposal

EXHIBIT 16. Portion of faceted classification for food technology, selected to show possibilities for classification of article on "Ice Cream" (Exhibit 1).

These schedules were planned as a development of class F, Technology, in the *Colon Classification.* Four facets are used: Products (personality), Parts, Materials (matter), and Operations (energy). The notation uses the *Colon* facet indicators and is hierarchical, using the octave device.

PRODUCTS (outline only)

F531	*Dairy products*
F5311	e.g., Milk
F53111	Malted milk
F5312	Fermented milk
F532	Sugar, confectionary, starches
F533	Cereals and cereal products
F534	Bakery products
F535	Edible oils and fats
F536	Fruit and vegetables
F538	Meats
F5391	Fish
F5395	Flavorings, spices, herbs
F5396	Additives

PARTS

F53,1	Stalk
11	Head
12	Tail
13	Leg
14	Foot
15	Wing
16	Fin

Chapter 9—Codes and Notations

Exercise 1. Redundancy

Redundancy has been defined as the amount of information transmitted in excess of the necessary minimum. Natural language is often redundant since effective communication can often take place even when some words are not available.

This exercise is designed to illustrate the extent to which a fragmentary text can be understood, as determined by the number of missing words that can be supplied from context, and as determined by how well the resulting text can be indexed.

This exercise is carried out by asking each student to spend no more than three minutes with each paragraph, first attempting to fill in all missing words (as indicated by dashes) and second providing three index entries for each paragraph. The student must progress from paragraph to paragraph, without looking ahead to the next paragraph, until the three-minute stint is over. Of course, once the student has left a paragraph and has proceeded to the next one, he may not return to an earlier paragraph.

The original text for each paragraph is identical, and is given at the end of the exercise.

The results of the exercise may be studied by observing the differences in accuracy with which missing words are filled in, as a function of the differences in context.

Paragraph 1
(Every other word missing)

[Fill in missing words wherever you see a dash (_____).]
At _____ present _____ of _____ of _____ use _____ punched _____ for _____ purposes _____ preparation _____ and _____ punched _____ system _____ more _____ an _____ than _____ science, _____ its _____ is _____ learned _____ practice. _____ chapter _____ devoted _____ a _____ of _____ methods _____ have _____ followed _____ assembling _____ on _____ cards _____ in _____ and _____ them _____ a _____ tool.

Index entries

1. _____
2. _____
3. _____

Paragraph 2
(Every third word missing)

[Fill in missing words wherever you see a dash (_____).]
At the _____ stage of _____ of the _____ of punched _____ for

scientific _____ the preparation _____ any particular _____ card system _____ more of _____ are than _____ science, and _____ procedure
is _____ learned by _____. This chapter _____ devoted to _____
demonstration of _____ methods which _____ been followed _____
assembling information _____ the cards _____ in coding _____ using
them _____ a research _____.

Index entries

    1. _____

    2. _____

    3. _____

Paragraph 3
(Every fifth word missing)

[Fill in missing words wherever you see a dash (_____).]
At the present stage _____ development of the use _____ punched cards
for scientific _____ the preparation of any _____ punched-card system
is _____ of an art than _____ science, and its procedure _____ best
learned by practice. _____ chapter is devoted to _____ demonstration
of the methods _____ have been followed in _____ information on the
cards _____ in coding and using _____ as a research tool.

Index entries

    1. _____

    2. _____

    3. _____

Paragraph 4
(Every tenth word missing)

[Fill in missing words wherever you see a dash (_____).]
At the present stage of development of the use _____ punched cards for
scientific purposes the preparation of any _____ punched-card system is
more of an art than _____ science, and its procedure is best learned by
practice. _____ chapter is devoted to a demonstration of the methods
_____ have been followed in assembling information on the cards _____
in coding and using them as research tool.

Index entries

    1. _____

    2. _____

    3. _____

Paragraph 5
(Definite and indefinite articles missing)

[Fill in missing words wherever you see a dash (_____).]
At _____ present stage of development of _____ use of punched cards for

scientific purposes _____ preparation of any particular punched-card system is more of _____ art than _____ science, and its procedure is best learned by practice. This chapter is devoted to _____ demonstration of _____ methods which have been followed in assembling information on _____ cards and in coding and using them as _____ research tool.

Index entries

1. _____
2. _____
3. _____

Paragraph 6
(Articles and adjectives missing)

[Fill in missing words wherever you see a dash (_____).]
At _____ _____ stage of development of _____ use of _____ cards for _____ purposes _____ preparation of any _____ _____ _____ system is more of _____ art than _____ science, and its procedure is best learned by practice. This chapter is devoted to _____ demonstration of _____ methods which have been followed in assembling information on _____ cards and in coding and using them as _____ _____ tool.

Index entries

1. _____
2. _____
3. _____

Paragraph 7
(All but nouns and pronouns are missing)

[Fill in missing words wherever you see a dash (_____).]
_____ _____ _____ stage _____ development _____ _____ use _____ _____ cards _____ purposes _____ preparation _____ _____ _____ _____ _____ system _____ _____ _____ _____ art _____ _____ science, _____ its procedure_____ _____ _____ _____ practice. _____ chapter _____ _____ _____ _____ demonstration _____ _____ methods _____ _____ _____ _____ _____ _____ information _____ _____ cards _____ _____ _____ _____ _____ them _____ _____ _____ tool.

Index entries

1. _____
2. _____
3. _____

Paragraph 8
(All missing except for nominative singular of nouns and pronouns,
and infinitive of verbs)

[Fill in missing words wherever you see a dash (_____).]
_____ _____ _____ stage _____ development _____ _____
use _____ (to punch) card _____ _____ purpose _____ preparation
_____ _____ _____ (to punch) card system (to be) _____ _____
_____ art _____ _____ science, _____ its procedure _____
_____ (to learn) _____ practice. _____ chapter (to be) (to devote)
_____ _____ demonstration _____ _____ method _____ (to
follow) _____ (to assemble) information _____ _____ card _____
_____ (to code) _____ (to use) _____ _____ _____ tool.

Index entries

1. _____
2. _____
3. _____

Paragraph 9
Original Text

At the present stage of development of the use of punched cards for scientific
purposes, the preparation of any particular punched-card system is more of an art
than a science, and its procedure is best learned by practice. This chapter is
devoted to a demonstration of the methods which have been followed in assembling information on the cards and in coding and using them as a research tool.

Exercise 2. Notations Versus Codes

Select any coding system which is in general use. Ask students to use two
different notations to represent the codes.

Author Index

Subject Index